Left Coast City

STUDIES IN GOVERNMENT
AND PUBLIC POLICY

Left Coast City
Progressive Politics
in San Francisco, 1975–1991

Richard Edward DeLeon

 University Press of Kansas

© 1992 by the University Press of Kansas

Photographs courtesy of Anthony Somkin, M.D.

Published by the University Press of Kansas (Lawrence, Kansas 66049), which was organized by the Kansas Board of Regents and is operated and funded by Emporia State University, Fort Hays State University, Kansas State University, Pittsburg State University, the University of Kansas, and Wichita State University

Library of Congress Cataloging-in-Publication Data

DeLeon, Richard Edward, 1942-
    Left coast city : progressive politics in San Francisco, 1975-1991
/ by Richard Edward DeLeon.
        p.   cm. — (Studies in government and public policy)
    Includes bibliographical references (p.   ) and index.
    ISBN 0-7006-0554-1 (alk. paper) — ISBN 0-7006-0555-X
(pbk. : alk. paper)
        1. San Francisco (Calif.)—Politics and government.   2. Elections—
California—San Francisco.   3. Voting—California—San Francisco.
    I. Title.   II. Series.
JS1438.D45   1992
979.4′61053—dc20   92-14119

British Library Cataloguing in Publication Data is available.

Printed in the United States of America

10 9 8 7 6 5 4 3 2 1

The paper used in this publication meets the minimum requirements of the American National Standard for Permanence of Paper for Printed Library Materials Z39.48-1984.

To
Bernice June Lyon
my mother
and
Arlene Petersen DeLeon
my wife

Contents

Illustrations

Maps

Photographs

Acknowledgments

Clarence N. Stone is first in the long line of people I must thank for their help. I had no immediate plans to write this book until the University Press of Kansas invited me to submit a proposal at Clarence's suggestion. Since he planted that seed, his correspondence with me has been thick and his criticisms of my work have been deep, sharp, and constructive. I owe him a lot.

John H. Mollenkopf gave the manuscript a very careful reading. His detailed critique forced me to rethink many points, to strengthen my evidence supporting key arguments, and to rake out chaff I had not known was there. Debra Stein gave me helpful insights into San Francisco's business community and corrected a number of factual errors. Cynthia Ingham's expert editing improved the writing immeasurably. Where the reader finds the text to be unusually clear, she probably had a hand in it. Michael Peter Smith, Dennis Judd, Sandra S. Powell, Eugene Weinstein, William Issel, Madeline Landau, Tim Ross, and Regina Sneed all generously took time to read the entire manuscript and offered numerous suggestions that helped improve it.

Several people read parts or chapters of the manuscript in earlier drafts, and I am indebted to them for their comments and suggestions: Todd Swanstrom, Rufus P. Browning, Stephen Barton, Bruce Haston, Richard LeGates, Michael Potepan, Bryan Jackson, Barbara Phillips, Peter Moylan, Victoria Randlett, Andy Nelsen, and Derek Hackett. I have talked with many community leaders and local analysts over the years about San Francisco politics. Among those who gave me the most valuable insights and ideas are Darryl Cox, Harold Yee, James Haas, Alfredo Rodriguez, Ruth Picon, David Looman, Lina Avidan, Stephanie Mischak, Louise Renne, Tim Tosta, and Richard Schlackman. I also thank Manuel Castells for his advice and encouragement.

Many of my students over the years helped to collect data for this project. The biggest contributors were Jeffrey Sutter, Lynne Laidlaw, Brent Saunders, Fran Kipnis, and Walter Maguire. Jim Stevens, my North Beach hacker pal and political junkie, zipped me piles of well-scrubbed numbers from the 1990 election. Bob Bathrick, assisted by Andy Richardson, prepared maps for the book in San Francisco State University's GIS lab. Anthony Somkin took enough fine photographs of the city to make a book by itself; five of them are shown here. Pilot Lloyd Savate deserves thanks for assisting with the aerial photography. I am also grateful to my daughters for their help. Deborah DeLeon put in hours on my bibliography. Manya DeLeon Miller took time from her nursing program to give me just the right words when I needed them. Her husband, Gary Miller—a poet and novelist—inspired me to write more the way I think: in imagery and metaphor.

I want to give special thanks to Fred M. Woodward, director of the University Press of Kansas, for his professional help and steady encouragement through all stages of writing this book. Susan McRory, UPK's senior production editor, treated my manuscript with great professional care. Susan K. Schott and other UPK staff were very helpful and a pleasure to work with.

Finally, I want to express gratitude to family and friends who kept my heart warm and my brain cool while I wrote this book. My wife, Arlene, helped me think and made me write. She lovingly forbade me to say that she suffered. That is just like her. Manya and Debby nurtured me from afar. Bernice Lyon and Ruby Petersen were supportive in ways that only mothers can be through the trial of writing this book. My sister, Sharon Moore, and her husband, Ron, always left their porch light on and helped me to write this book simply by being loving, generous, and available. Others in my big family who cheered me on were Terry, Cindy, Bob, Monique, Ron, Denise, Tina, Sherry, Judy, L. T., Janice, and Tony. My wife's sister, Diana Streblow, motivated me with her warm words and positive thinking. My niece, Alanna Streblow, also moved me along on the book by continually asking: "Are you done with the computer? Can we play now?" Friends who were friends when it counted include Anthony and Carol Somkin, Myrto Macris-Gillespie, Jamie Newton, David Tabb, Bob and Judith Shaw, Ted and Betty Klocke, Phyllis DeLeon, John Rogers, Michael Kinuchen, Joel Schwartzbart, Michelle Ruggles, Michelle Martinez, Linda Zu, and the Oxford Street gang of Barbara, Tim, Stan, Metece, Geoff, and Barbara. And over the distances that separate us, I send belated but heartfelt thanks to Ida R. Hoos, my first mentor in the world of ideas.

1

The Capital of Progressivism

Any political movement that does not embed itself in the heart of the urban process is doomed to fail in advanced capitalist society.

—David Harvey

Isn't the reason the rest of the country sees Sanctuary City as a kind of jumbo theme park of the mondo bizarro—home of the wacko, the weird, of political correctness to the exquisite degree—because, well, it is?

—Jerry Carroll

WALKWAY

Feng shui is the Chinese philosophy of harmony in the home environment. A basic principle of *feng shui* is that "good energy travels around curves and bad energy travels on a straight line."[1] A house designed on *feng shui* principles will be surrounded by shrubs to deflect bad *chi*. The walkway to the door will be curved, not straight. Inside, the house will have a curving staircase set off from the front door to prevent straight-line entry to the stairs. It will avoid sharp roof lines that create secret arrows which disrupt harmony and make the home unlucky. Once dismissed as silly superstition by hard-nosed Bay Area developers and real estate agents, *feng shui* is now taken seriously by those who wish to sell houses to a growing Chinese-American population.

San Francisco is a *feng shui* city. Visitors find it a baffling maze of hills and streets and neighborhoods. Even getting into the city is a difficult task. The Central and Embarcadero freeways were built to make access easier, but these end abruptly in knobs of concrete where neighborhood activists stopped them years ago. Nature completed their political work: The Loma Prieta earthquake weakened both structures in 1989. The Embarcadero Freeway is now rubble, and the

1

Central Freeway is deserted. People walk from A to B; they take the Bay Area Rapid Transit (BART) system, buses, streetcars, and trollies. Getting around is roundabout, and roundabout is *feng shui*.

San Francisco politics are also *feng shui*, particularly in the arena of physical development and land-use planning. Lombard Street, the "curviest street in America," is emblematic of the new political order. Developers wishing to build in the city must follow a convoluted path through a maze of restrictions to gain access to the city's urban space. City officials no longer lay out a straight red carpet of concessions to indulge investor prerogative. Handshake deals and quick bulldozing are things of the past. Instead, businesses seeking to invest in the city must follow the curved path. If they balk at this, many San Franciscans feel that is good riddance to bad *chi*, to disrupters of community. San Francisco's new political regime is an antiregime set up to deflect the straight lines and bottom lines of American capitalism. The city's residents know what they do not want. Many of them also know what they do want: a home writ large in the city where they live.

THE CAPITAL OF PROGRESSIVISM

San Francisco is an agitated city, a city of fissions and fusions, a breeder of change and new urban meanings. It is the spawning ground of social movements, policy innovations, and closely watched experiments in urban populism and local economic democracy. Congresswoman Nancy Pelosi asserts that San Francisco is "the capital of the progressive movement in this country."[2] Historian Kevin Starr concurs, declaring San Francisco to be the "temporary capital of the liberal wing of the Democratic party in the United States."[3] In an era when U.S. cities have become increasingly dependent on the private sector for leadership and resources, San Francisco has emerged as a "semisovereign city"—a city that imposes as many limits on capital as capital imposes on it.[4] Mislabeled by some detractors as socialist or radical in the Marxist tradition, San Francisco's progressivism is concerned with consumption more than production, residence more than workplace, meaning more than materialism, community empowerment more than class struggle. Its first priority is not revolution but protection—protection of the city's environment, architectural heritage, neighborhoods, diversity, and overall quality of life from the radical transformations of turbulent American capitalism. Under progressive leadership, San Francisco has asserted its local autonomy, expanded the public sphere, politicized and democratized the planning process, spurned the dictates of investor prerogative, severely restricted business use of its urban space, and inured itself to threats of private-sector disinvestment. The progrowth coalition of downtown business elites, labor unions, and city hall officials that controlled the city's economic and physical development for a quarter of a century is now in pieces, its vision for San Francisco discarded, its relentless building of high rises checked, its hegemony in land use and development erased.[5] With the destruction of the progrowth coalition, the city has begun to wriggle free of its functional role as the West Coast's Manhattan and the Pacific Rim link in the emerging global hierarchy of cities.

San Francisco's new progressive agenda emphasizes human development rather than physical development, the use value of the city's built environment rather than its exchange value, the needs of local residents and communities rather than those of developers and outside investors. Over the last few years, the city has pioneered legislation in areas as diverse as domestic partnerships, comparable worth programs, affirmative action, prohibitions on smoking in the workplace, minimum safety standards for business use of video display terminals, rent control, developer linkage fees, and annual citywide limits on high-rise construction. Known for its culture of civility and political tolerance, San Francisco has declared itself a sanctuary for gays and lesbians, conscientious objectors, political refugees, undocumented workers, HIV carriers, and all manner of nonconformists.[6]

Depending on one's perspective, San Francisco is a free space or a decadent place, a melting pot of cultures or Pandemonium itself, a sanctuary of tolerance or a Sodom deserving plagues. The city attracts and repels; it even attracts those it repels. For example, on Halloween night in 1990, Pastor Larry Lea, the Christian televangelist from Dallas, gathered thousands of his Prayer Warriors in the civic auditorium to rebuke the city for its sin and Satanism and to save its soul by reversing "the curse of a life without God, prayer and Christian values."[7] As the Prayer Warriors left the auditorium, they were met by a sculpture of a giant golden penis, Sister Sadie Sadie the Rabbi Lady, and a crowd of loud protesters chanting, among other things, "Bring back the lions." The chroniclers of this event correctly concluded, "The Prayer Warriors were no longer in Kansas."[8]

This kind of cultural combat has drawn the attention and moral scrutiny of the national media. San Francisco activists are proud of their city's nonconformist reputation and take every opportunity to show their colors, celebrate differences, and champion unpopular causes. Many see themselves and their city as the precursor of social change in this country. Symbolic gestures intended for national consumption are a staple of local politics. Hardly a week goes by without the announcement of some type of organized protest, boycott, rally, demonstration, declaration, or resolution that is almost certain to offend mainstream American public opinion. The most recent and notorious example of this occurred on 14 January 1991, when the Board of Supervisors and Mayor Art Agnos declared San Francisco to be a sanctuary for conscientious objectors to the Persian Gulf War. After hostilities began, the board unanimously passed another resolution supporting American troops. What was reported around the country, however, was the sanctuary resolution, and this against the backdrop of thousands of antiwar protesters closing down the Bay Bridge, setting bonfires, and rampaging through the downtown area. Chamber of Commerce leaders were so distressed by the image cast of San Francisco as an antiwar, unpatriotic city that they launched a bicoastal advertising campaign in the *Wall Street Journal* and *USA Today* apologizing for the demonstrations and assuring readers that most San Franciscans supported national policy in the Persian Gulf.[9] One indicator of just how stereotyped San Francisco has become as the nation's premier "Left Coast" city was Republican Congressman Newt Gingrich's dismissal of the antiwar protests as a "cheap date" —so predictable that they need not be taken seriously as expressions of outrage against the war.[10]

This is a book about San Francisco's progressivism: the conditions that gave rise to it, that sustain and undermine it, and that help and hinder its possible spread to other cities and to the national political arena. Is San Francisco so odd and exceptional that national leaders and opinion makers can afford to dismiss its politics as an aberration? Or is it truly a vanguard city, a crystal ball for seeing into the future of a new progressive era in American politics? There is no question that San Francisco is unique in many ways. It is a "post"-everything city: post-industrial, postmodern, postmaterialist, and post-Marxist. But it is also, to emphasize the obvious, a *city*—a large, densely populated, multiclass, ethnically diverse, economically complex city. In some ways it is a microcosm of national society compacted into 46.4 square miles. One might dismiss it more easily if it were a leftist college town or a small community dabbling in municipal socialism.[11] San Francisco is a progressive big city, and that alone makes it unusual, important, and worth studying. The test of whether it is a vanguard city, however, is longevity. If the progressive movement falters even under the optimal conditions found in San Francisco, there is little chance that it will survive to inspire imitation elsewhere. In this book I will argue that the key to survival is the creation of a progressive urban regime.

URBAN REGIMES, REGIME TRANSFORMATION, AND THE ANTIREGIME

The concept of "urban regime" is central to the theoretical, empirical, and polemical arguments of this study. To understand what an urban regime is and what it does, it is necessary to appreciate the problems of economic scarcity, governmental fragmentation, and political disorder that an urban regime is designed to solve. Briefly stated, city leaders operating under a federal system and in a capitalist society are *limited* in the economic resources they command, in the formal governmental powers they can exercise, and in their capacity to govern diverse populations. Two well-known analyses of these limits are found in Paul Peterson's *City Limits*[12] and in Douglas Yates's *The Ungovernable City*.[13]

Peterson argues that a city is compelled by economic necessity to compete with other cities and regions for new business and industry to expand its tax base and generate new revenues. Redistributive policies are "pernicious" and "unproductive" in the local context because they undermine a city's competitive position.[14] Developmental policies also are outside the domain of routine local politics, according to Peterson, because they seek uncontested public interest objectives and require the technical expertise of professional planners and business elites. Constrained by these limits, allocational policies involving government services and jobs are all that remain at the local level for debate, bargaining, and discretion. Yet even within that dwindled political space, Douglas Yates contends, American cities have become ungovernable because manageable pluralism has degenerated into "street-fighting pluralism," which he describes as "a political free-for-all, a pattern of unstructured, multilateral conflict in which many different combatants fight continuously with one another in a very great number of permutations and combinations."[15]

These pessimistic views of urban politics have stimulated controversy on the issue of exactly how limited and ungovernable American cities are. A number of recent studies have advanced more optimistic perspectives—e.g., John Logan and Todd Swanstrom's collection in *Beyond the City Limits*[16] and Barbara Ferman's *Governing the Ungovernable City.*[17] These authors and many others point out that nearly all local governments have at least some degree of autonomy and room to maneuver, that economic forces are mediated by political processes, and that political leadership and skill make a difference. H. V. Savitch captures this view by asking his readers to "envision national conditions as setting up the pieces on the urban chessboard, so that one player may be subject to more external pressure than another. One player may be better off than another. But the players have latitude. They can tap great amounts of wealth, they can control some of the most valuable land in the world, and most important, they can change things through political discretion."[18]

Of all the institutional devices available to city leaders to help them transcend "city limits" and to leverage the gridlock of "street-fighting pluralism," one of the most powerful is that of the urban regime. Clarence Stone defines an urban regime as "the informal arrangements by which public bodies and private interests function together in order to be able to make and carry out governing decisions."[19] This definition implicitly acknowledges that formal structures of local governmental authority are inadequate by themselves to mobilize and coordinate the resources necessary to "produce a capacity to govern and to bring about publicly significant results."[20]

Any structure that can produce a capacity to govern under seemingly ungovernable conditions has power. Power has many faces, of course, but usually it is conceptualized as some form of social control in which one group, organization, or class dominates another group, organization, or class through processes that range from crude coercion to subtle indoctrination. In this view, one part of society has "power over" another part in a conflictual relationship that is sustained and reproduced by the exercise of power itself. In contrast, urban regimes are powerful because they are empowering. They provide citizens and their government leaders with the "power to" undertake complex objectives and solve problems in a politically granulated and gridlocked world. They also produce an incentive structure of "small opportunities" in the form of jobs, housing, and other selective material benefits that attract the support of average citizens.[21] Regime power has the capacity to create some kind of whole from the parts, to unify rather than divide. Power in this model is seen as a sort of pulling force akin to gravitation.[22]

Business leaders typically play a vital role in the informal governing coalition that makes and implements public policy in an urban regime. In the normal workings of American capitalist society, businesses control the economic and organizational resources needed to achieve what Stone calls "social production" in serving public goals.[23] Once entrenched, an urban regime can maintain itself even in the face of organized political resistance. It does so through the "preemptive power" of its social production performance and its ability to plan strategically for the city as a whole—not through coercive domination or ideological hegemony.[24] As long as such a regime performs better than imagined alternatives in attaining collective goals and in providing individual opportunities, citizens and politicians will support it. And they will choose to do so lucidly and pragmatically, not because they are duped or coerced.

Stone's social production model ("power to") is superior to the social control model ("power over") in explaining regime continuity. It also explains why, once entrenched, urban regimes are hard to change. If the collective goals set for a regime remain the same, if its social production performance is adequate, and if alternative institutional means do not exist, the regime can become impervious to external threats. The archetype of such an entrenched urban regime is found in Atlanta, where a unified business elite has worked closely with local government leaders to shape that city's physical and economic development. Any city government that gives high priority to these development goals will be compelled to sustain business-centered regimes that can deliver the goods—literally. With few exceptions, progressive efforts to restructure such regimes are likely to be frustrated if they alienate business elites and lead them to withdraw their resources and coordinative capacity from the public sector. As Stephen Elkin writes, "A reputation for being antibusiness, for not listening to local businessmen's schemes for making a greater city, is an invitation to fiscal trouble that even the hardiest progressive politicians are unlikely to be anxious to accept."[25]

Progressive challenges to entrenched urban regimes face a "very large cognitive and motivational order," argues Stone, because substantial numbers of citizens must believe that (1) a new regime would be "superior *and* workable," (2) an alliance could be assembled to sustain such a regime, and (3) short-term interests are worth sacrificing to meet long-term collective goals in a new regime that does not yet exist. Exceptions to the rule, he observes, are found usually only in communities with a "resource-rich but noncorporate middle class."[26] To achieve regime transformation, it is necessary but not sufficient to dismantle the old regime. In an era of privatization and federal abandonment of cities, a new regime must be put in its place with the "power to" mobilize and coordinate resources, to push back the city's economic limits, and to buttress weak government authority in serving new social goals. Failure to establish a new empowering urban regime can lead to the chaos of what Manuel Castells calls the "wild city."

The "wild city" occurs when its inhabitants come together in a negative and reactive way to protest their economic exploitation, cultural alienation, and political oppression by social forces beyond their control.[27] Lacking political parties and other institutional means of expression, these protests form as urban social movements to block the continuing obliteration of community life and local democracy under postindustrial capitalism. Urban populism, environmentalism, consumerism, neighborhood mobilizations, and tenant revolts all spring from the same structural roots: global economic restructuring, technological change, and the rise of the corporate liberal state. Yet as movements of resistance they attack merely the localized symptoms of social decay as experienced in daily urban life: traffic congestion, pollution, high rises, unmanaged growth, sprawl, displacement, and powerlessness. They often appear atavistic, almost feudal, in their opposition to change, growth, and progress as defined by business elites. They seize and colonize bits of the city but not the city itself. Parochially defending their local enclaves of cultural identity and their parcels of privilege, they follow their own trajectories of empowerment and resist coalignment or fusion with others. There is no organization, no formation of a unified movement of movements, no emergence of transenclave consciousness, no stretching out beyond the city limits. And when there is no organization, Castells argues, "urban contradictions are expressed either in a refracted way, through other practices, or in a 'wild' way, a pure contradiction devoid of any structural horizon."[28] By digging in on their own turf, choosing depth over breadth, they forfeit the opportunity to transform society. Unable to control the world that produced the symptoms against which they react, "they simply shrink the world to the size of their community."[29] In the wild city, argues Castells, these social movements become at most "reactive Utopias" whose leaders can envision fragments of an ideal urban future but are politically incapable of working together to make it come true. They "illuminate the path they could not walk."[30]

The "wild city" is another name for the kind of chaos that San Franciscans have made for themselves and are trying to escape today. The city's progrowth regime no longer exists, but a new progressive regime has not yet emerged to replace it. Having helped to create chaos out of order, progressive leaders now face the task of creating order out of chaos. It is my contention that urban social movements in San Francisco have begun to fuse politically and are capable of establishing a new urban regime. There is evidence that elements of the old regime, particularly in the business community, are adapting themselves to serve new social goals. Thus,

San Francisco is walking, sometimes stumbling down the path dimly illuminated by its collective vision of an alternative urban future. But that path is long and uncertain. Leaders of the progressive coalition somehow must solve the problems of endemic hyperpluralism, crises of governance, internal conflicts, and mounting conservative opposition. What the city has now is, at best, an *antiregime*—a transitional political order set up defensively to block the Lazarus-like reemergence of the old progrowth regime. Such an order cannot last. Unless progressive leaders can invent a coherent ideology and a disciplined political program to harness the centrifugal forces within their electoral coalition, the loose alliance will fly apart. Unless they can find ways to reconnect city hall with downtown business, the coalition's economic base will erode. Unless they can forge links with political parties and state and national structures, the city will be isolated and its politics dismissed as an aberration.

SCOPE AND PLAN

In this book I offer a somewhat elliptical history of progressive politics in San Francisco over the period 1975–91, with emphasis on land-use and development issues, the slow-growth movement, and Mayor Art Agnos's years in office. That history is told through a series of case studies that examine critical moments in the evolution of the progressive coalition. These include the coalition's roller-coaster ride to political power with Mayor George Moscone in 1975 and then with Mayor Agnos in 1987; its battles with downtown business elites during the interregnum of Mayor Dianne Feinstein's progrowth administration (1978–87); and its continuing struggle to maintain itself and to shape the city's future in the face of internecine conflicts, recalcitrant mayors, and a resurgent downtown business community.

In its function as a work of political science, the book presents a partial but grounded theory of the political, economic, and sociocultural conditions that facilitate and obstruct the establishment of a stable progressive urban regime. I propose the antiregime model to explain San Francisco as a transitional political system that is capable of imposing limits on market processes and the private sector but is incapable of mobilizing those same resources to serve progressive goals. I also explicate the concept of progressivism itself, develop methods of measuring and observing it in political practice, and test hypotheses regarding progressivism and its correlates.

Philosophically, parts of this book serve as a polemic against progrowth ideology and business control of urban development in San Francisco and other U.S. cities. Although progressive leaders and slow-growth activists receive their full share of criticism, the reader will have no trouble discerning my sympathies and positions regarding the key issues. Yet the polemical thrust of the work is tempered by my awareness that San Francisco's business sector is not monolithic, that profit motives and progressive aspirations are not necessarily incompatible in a capitalist society, and that the city's progressive leaders do not have a monopoly on intelligence or good intentions.

Chapter 2 provides essential background for understanding the economic, social, and political conditions that gave rise to San Francisco's progressive movement. The critical focus is on the interaction of these conditions—on what Charles Ragin calls the "multiple conjunctural causation" of small-scale events and large-scale qualitative change.[31] The conditions are *multiple* in that no single factor alone can account for the city's political transformation. The list of factors is long: the city's geographical compactness and population density; its service economy and attendant middle class of professionals, managers, and petty entrepreneurs; its "place luck" as a beautiful and attractive location that ranks it high in the hierarchy of cities; its ethnic and racial diversity; its fragmented and leaderless downtown business community; its political institutions, particularly the instruments of direct democracy (the initiative, referendum, and recall); and its political culture of civility, tolerance, and leftism—the invisible broth of values and ideas in which all of the other "ingredients" are mixed. The conditions are *conjunctural* in that they interact multiplicatively (one might even say chemically) rather than merely add together to produce their effects. For example, the case will be made that it was the intersection of a large professional middle class *and* an ethnically diverse community *and* a fragmented downtown business elite *and* the institution of direct democracy (among other things) that made possible the city's pioneering growth-control efforts in the 1980s. Subtract any one of these elements and the slow-growth movement would have failed or followed a much different path with qualitatively different results. Such conjunctural conditions are only preconditions, of course, and at best they create historical opportunities which social actors may or may not exploit.[32] In San Francisco, these opportunities were seized and acted upon.

Chapter 2 also examines the concept of progressivism and the particular form it has taken in San Francisco. My argument is that the city's progressivism is a partial fusion in theory and action of three distinct leftist ideologies (perhaps the French term *tendances* is more apt), labeled here as liberalism, environmentalism, and populism. Empirical studies of voting trends and opinion data demonstrate the existence of such ideological tendencies in the city's mass electorate, each tugging in a different direction, each motivated by a different set of constituency interests and policy goals. A major part of this story is how the city's progressive leaders were able to fuse even partially these "three Lefts" in mobilizing the slow-growth coalition that helped to topple the progrowth regime. As will be discussed in later chapters, however, the challenge now facing progressive leaders is how to convert what is in fact an unstable compound of values, goals, and ideas into a coherent structure of thought that can legitimate a progressive urban regime. Although ideology probably does play a smaller role than some have argued in *maintaining* an entrenched regime, it is critical in building and legitimating a new regime after the old one has fallen. But the city's progressive leaders are in an ideological double bind. On the one hand, the more inclusive they try to be in developing an ideology that will encompass the goals of all three Lefts, the more contradictory and less coherent that ideology will be as a guide to political action and social change. On the other hand, the more these leaders try to fashion an internally consistent and coherent progressive ideology, the more exclusive they must be in order to preserve its integrity and clarity of purpose. Ultimately what is at stake is the progressive movement's "political carrying capacity"—i.e., the point at which ideological compromise begins to alienate the movement's core supporters in greater numbers than those gained by diffuse appeals.[33] One conclusion of this study is that the carrying capacity is in fact quite limited and constrains the pace and spread of progressive reforms.

Chapter 3 traces the rise and fall of the progrowth regime in San Francisco. Taking root around 1960, this urban regime dominated the city's development strategy and land-use planning for a quarter of a century. The dominant image of the city under this regime was that of a command and communications center providing advanced corporate services to Bay Area businesses and multinational firms pursuing commerce and trade with Pacific Rim nations. That became its strategic function within a developing global hierarchy of cities. A local growth machine emerged to convert strategies into plans and plans into organized action backed by government authority and popular support. Neighborhoods were leveled, populations displaced, and corporate cockpits installed in the skyscrapers that were built to give form to the function of the city as a capital machine. The "transformation of San Francisco," to use the title of Chester Hartman's excellent book,[34] was rapid and complete in the downtown financial district. Waves of development soon began hitting neighborhoods in the North Beach district, South of Market, and other areas of the city. It was around this time—the late 1970s—that the slow-growth movement emerged to do battle with the downtown business elite and its city hall allies. At the same time, the progrowth regime began crumbling. Weakened by local slow-growth opposition, it collapsed completely in 1986 under the weight of national crises in finance capital and commercial real estate markets. The city's slow-growth progressives did not cause these crises. But they did take political advantage of them by moving into the postcollapse power vacuum in 1986 and 1987 to pick up the pieces and fit them into a new image of urban function and urban form. How this was done is the subject of the next two chapters.

Chapter 4 picks up the isolated threads of early protests against high-rise development in 1971 and 1972 and documents how they were woven together over time into a more inclusive slow-growth coalition, which eventually triumphed in 1986 with the passage of Proposition M, the most restrictive growth-control legislation of any large U.S. city. Five aspects of San Francisco's slow-growth movement are then highlighted: the vital role of local political institutions, specifically the citizen ballot initiative and the judicial process, in circumventing city hall resistance to slow-growth reforms; the cumulative effects of repeated slow-growth initiative campaigns in educating public opinion and provoking preemptive growth-control measures from city hall; the essentially middle-class character of the slow-growth movement and the problems this created in mobilizing broad-based support for growth controls; the internal conflicts that arose within the slow-growth movement between controlled-growth and antigrowth factions; and the importance of leadership, technical expertise, and political skill in expanding democratic processes into the development planning arena.

The main focus of Chapter 5 is the metamorphosis of the progressive movement into an organized electoral campaign seeking political power and government authority. Compelling this transition was the need to institutionalize slow-growth reforms and to incorporate progressive leadership within the city's governing coalition and bureaucratic structures. Protest was not enough[35]—even citizen-mandated policy was not enough to insure government implementation of a new progressive agenda. The critical moment came with the election of liberal Art Agnos as mayor in December 1987. In the months that followed, the city's various boards and commissions filled up with progressive appointees. In the 1988 and 1990 elections, progressives achieved majority control of the Board of Supervisors. The progressive movement, under Mayor Agnos, became progressive government. It was then that the difference between merely illuminating the path of reform and actually walking it suddenly became clear. That path led straight into the thicket of politics, budget crises, unsolvable problems, hard choices, trade-offs, and official responsibilities. Somewhere in that tangle the progressive movement dimmed its light and began to unravel. It stopped short of building a new progressive urban regime and instead created what the city has now: an antiregime.

Chapters 6 through 8 explore the character and impact of San Francisco's antiregime. The antiregime is a defensive system of governance designed to block and filter big business power and to protect the city's environment, historical buildings, small businesses, neighborhood communities, and quality of life from unregulated market forces and grandiose progrowth schemes. It is a regime antithetical to large-scale development, high-rise construction, and strategic functioning as a corporate headquarters city. It is a regime that rejects money and materialism as the taproot of urban meaning. It is a regime, in short, that protects community from capital. That is its first priority. Its fundamental impulse is conservative; some would call it reactionary or even feudal.

Chapter 6 examines the way in which Proposition M has been used to limit high-rise office construction in the downtown financial district and to stop unwanted commercial development in the neighborhoods. Chapter 7 is a case study of how the city's progressives mobilized in 1989 to prevent construction of a new baseball park for the San Francisco Giants in the China Basin area. The defeat of the China Basin ballpark proposal almost guaranteed that the Giants will leave San Francisco after 1994, if not sooner. It also demonstrated the power of the city's slow-growth movement to thwart the combined forces of downtown business and city hall. Mayor Agnos campaigned aggressively for the China Basin ballpark, and it was during that campaign (and because of it) that Agnos's relationship with his progressive constituency began to turn sour.

Chapter 8 provides two other case studies of slow-growth power under the antiregime. The first shows how progressives stopped the Catellus Corporation's attempt in 1990 to win voter approval of an exemption from Proposition M in building a city within a city in the Mission Bay development project. The second describes the progressives' success that same year in persuading voters to impose a ban on waterfront hotels and to require greater citizen participation in planning future waterfront development. Once again, Mayor Agnos placed himself on the wrong side of his progressive constituency by making backroom deals with Catellus executives and waterfront developers in support of their large-scale projects. By the time Agnos began his reelection campaign in 1991, many of his former grass-roots supporters had come to see him as a progrowth wolf in slow-growth clothing.

Chapter 9 exposes the darker side of San Francisco's antiregime and analyzes the structural and ideological quandaries that beset leaders of the city's progressive coalition. The conservative character of the antiregime is both its strength and its weakness. It is a strength because what is being conserved is an endangered species of community, one filled with diversity, creativity, tolerance, human caring, and vibrant political life. It is a weakness because it freezes the status quo, cultivates neighborhood parochialism, and nurtures a suspicion of power. In this chapter, I explore the complex ideological, economic, and political problems that must be solved in order to create a progressive urban regime that empowers the community rather than merely protects it.

In the postscript on the 1991 mayoral election, I describe how factional conflicts ruptured the city's progressive coalition, eroded support for Mayor Agnos's reelection campaign, and opened city hall to recapture by progrowth moderates and conservatives. After beating back two major challengers from the Left in the November election, Agnos lost the December run-off election to former police chief Frank Jordan in a close race. Far from signaling a conservative turn in the city's electorate, Agnos's defeat came mainly at the hands of progressives. In the chapter's conclusion, I discuss the conflicts and contradictions within the progressive movement that made Agnos's defeat predictable and that must still be resolved if the progressives wish to establish a stable progressive regime.

2

Economic Change and Social Diversity: The Local Culture of Progressivism

The city is a fact in nature, like a cave, a run of mackerel or an ant-heap. But it is also a conscious work of art, and it holds within its communal framework many simpler and more personal forms of art. Mind *takes form in the city; and in turn, urban forms condition mind.*

—Lewis Mumford

Thirty years ago, before the invasion of massive capital and master builders, San Francisco was a city of neighborhoods with a skyline of low rises, a "Baghdad by the Bay."[1] A strong labor town, it had blue-collar workers in force, boasted a thriving port, and was the Bay Area's economic hub. Its population was predominately white. All of that has since changed. San Francisco's neighborhoods now ring a downtown mini-Manhattan bristling with skyscrapers and brimming with commuters. The city has concentrated on services, tourism, and hospitality. It is now a spoke, not a hub, in the region's economy. The port is sleepy, miles of wharves are abandoned, and most of the fishermen have gone. Office workers have replaced many of the blue-collar workers, and unionization is at low ebb. Nonwhites now outnumber whites; the immigrant population is large; gays and lesbians have formed a sizable enclave; and the neighborhoods are a patchwork of multicultural diversity.

Dennis Coyle probably has it right: Baghdad by the Bay is now the Balkans by the Bay.[2] Everything is *pluribus*, nothing is *unum*. Hyperpluralism reigns. The city has no natural majority; its majorities are made, not found. That is a key to understanding the city's political culture: Everyone is a minority. That means mutual tolerance is essential, social learning is inevitable, innovation is likely, and democracy is hard work. Economic change has produced social diversity, and social diversity is the root of the city's political culture. One of the controlling objectives of the progressive movement has been to slow the pace of economic

13

change to protect against threats to social diversity. The economic forces that helped create San Francisco's political culture could also destroy it. The first line of defense is the antiregime.

THE DEMOGRAPHICS OF CHANGE AND SOCIAL DIVERSITY

San Francisco's population has not grown, but it has changed remarkably. In 1990, the city's inhabitants numbered about 725,000, a slight drop from the total of 740,000 who lived there in 1960.[3] Its share of the rapidly growing Bay Area population (now at about 5.7 million) has declined from 29 percent in 1950 to about 13 percent today.[4] After New York City, San Francisco ranks first among large cities in population density: about 15,600 people per square mile. Given its very low residential vacancy rate (1.1 percent in 1988) and its scarcity of developable land (403 acres through the year 2005), San Francisco's scant 46.4 miles are unlikely to accommodate many more people in the decades ahead.[5]

In 1980, San Francisco was ranked as the nation's most ethnically diverse large city. Any two residents selected at random had an 83 percent chance of belonging to different ethnic groups (from a list of fourteen).[6] The city's ethnic diversity has increased since then. Patterns of foreign immigration (legal and undocumented), combined with demographic trends within the city's Anglo and African American communities, have completely transformed the city's ethnic composition.[7] In 1960, 18 percent of the people were classified as nonwhite; by 1990, that figure had grown to 53 percent, thus qualifying San Francisco for the list of "minority majority" cities.[8] In 1974, Frederick Wirt described the city's African American, Asian, and Spanish-speaking residents as "arriving ethnic groups" just then establishing themselves in a small number of neighborhoods.[9] He mentioned that Asians in particular found "their limited numbers a handicap" in political mobilization.[10] In 1990, Asians and Pacific Islanders were the city's largest single ethnic minority group (28 percent), followed by Latinos (14 percent) and African Americans (11 percent). Asians and Latinos are now the city's fastest growing ethnic groups. Between 1980 and 1990, the Asian population rose by 43 percent, the Latino population by 20 percent. The Anglo population dropped by 7 percent, the African American population by 9 percent.

Table 2.1 compares the city's four major ethnic groups on selected socioeconomic indicators drawn from 1980 census data.[11] Six general patterns can be discerned from the comparative statistics. First, Anglos occupy a much higher socioeconomic status (SES) than the other three groups. Proportionally more of them are in the upper-income strata, own income-producing assets (wealth), have formal schooling at the college level, and work in professional-managerial careers. Second, Anglos are also distinguished from the other three racial groups in their family life-style characteristics. As a group they are older, have fewer children, and are much more likely to live in nonfamily households. Third, Asians as

Table 2.1.   Comparisons of Anglos, Asians, Hispanics, and Blacks on Selected Sociodemographic Indicators: San Francisco, 1980 (5% Public-Use Microdata Sample)

Indicators	Anglos	Asians	Hispanics	Blacks	Total
% Managerial-professional	34.5	18.4	14.1	14.9	26.7
% Low-wage service occup.	6.3	14.3	15.4	10.4	9.4
% Government workers	17.5	16.6	15.8	33.4	18.8
% Some college +	59.3	47.7	34.1	35.7	51.5
Per capita income ($)	13,408	9,902	9,256	9,288	11,837
% Earning > $14,999	30.3	19.2	15.9	17.3	24.7
% Earners with income from interest, dividends, rent, or royalties	42.0	37.1	16.6	10.1	34.9
% Individuals with income below 125% of poverty line	15.3	17.1	22.1	27.8	18.0
% Earners receiving public assistance	5.7	8.0	10.0	16.7	7.8
% Home owners	39.7	49.6	38.2	39.1	41.4
% Home owners with first mortgage	52.1	77.4	67.5	80.1	62.5
% Lived in same house in 1975	48.5	47.5	45.1	53.4	48.3
% Lived in a foreign country in 1975	3.2	23.4	10.8	0.7	7.8
% Total population 15 years or younger	8.4	20.9	24.4	23.7	15.0
% Total population 60 years or older	26.5	14.4	11.8	13.7	20.3
% Individuals living in nonfamily households	49.0	14.4	21.9	27.2	36.4

Source: Bureau of the Census, Census of Population and Housing, 1980, *Public-Use Microdata Sample: San Francisco, 5% Sample* (Washington, D.C. 1983). Machine-readable data file available through Computing and Communications Resources, Chancellor's office, California State University. Unless otherwise specified, all indicators are for individuals 16 years or older.

a group are more socioeconomically advanced than Hispanics and African Americans (especially in terms of wealth and education) but are similar to them in terms of family life-style characteristics. Fourth, African Americans as a group are significantly poorer and more reliant on public assistance and local government employment than are Asians and Hispanics. Fifth, the recent growth of the Asian and Hispanic populations has been fueled by high levels of immigration. Sixth, variation in the rate of home ownership across the major racial groups is surprisingly small considering the large interracial differences in SES. This implies significant levels of low-income home ownership in all ethnic groups, a prediction confirmed by breakdowns showing home ownership rates for those earning less than $10,000: Anglos, 38.2 percent; Asians, 44.2 percent; Hispanics, 36.0 percent; African Americans, 34.8 percent.[12]

Although detailed statistics are not reported here, additional patterns are revealed in the sociodemographic characteristics of major subgroups within the Asian (Japanese, Chinese, Filipino, Other Asian) and Hispanic (Mexican, Other Hispanic) populations. First, the socioeconomic and family life-style profile of San Francisco's more assimilated Japanese is quite similar to that of Anglos and markedly different from that of the other Asian groups. Second, the Chinese and

Filipino populations share a comparable sociodemographic profile, except that the Chinese as a group display greater income inequality, own more income-producing assets, and are residentially better established. Third, those classified as Other Asians (along with Filipinos and Other Hispanics) can lay claim to the title of San Francisco's *new* "arriving ethnic groups." In the 1980 census, 46.9 percent of Other Asians sixteen years or older said they lived in a foreign country in 1975 (28.4 percent of Filipinos and 12.7 percent of Other Hispanics reported the same). Of all the ethnic subpopulations, those classified as Other Asians are the most impoverished, least settled, and youngest on average. Fourth, within the Hispanic category, Mexican Americans and those classified as Other Hispanics have virtually identical statistical profiles. Socioeconomically and demographically, these subgroups are similar on most indicators to African Americans and Other Asians.[13]

The population flows that created San Francisco's ethnic diversity were pushed and pulled there by a number of forces. Episodic wars in Southeast Asia and Central America are an obvious push factor. An important pull factor is the existence of well-established Asian and Latino neighborhood enclaves which provide security, social services, and cultural identity to arriving immigrants and refugees.[14] Another attractive force is the consequence of economic restructuring on a global scale. Recent studies of urban economic growth by Saskia Sassen-Koob and others suggest that large cities like San Francisco are emerging as regional centers in the global economy for producing advanced corporate services in management, finance, law, and communications.[15] Sassen-Koob argues that the economic growth generated by this type of regional specialization has created (1) "an increased polarization in the income and occupational structure," (2) the gradual elimination of middle-income white-collar and blue-collar jobs, and (3) a large array of "mostly low-wage or very high-income" new jobs, the former attracting an influx of semiskilled immigrants, the latter providing the "critical mass" needed for residential and commercial gentrification.[16] As will be seen, there is evidence that such occupational and income polarization is occurring in San Francisco, creating a marginal economic base supporting a growing service class of African Americans and recently arrived immigrants from Southeast Asia and Central America.

The ethnic, cultural, and life-style diversity of San Francisco's population increased even further in the late 1960s when a large gay and lesbian community emerged, residing mainly in the Castro and Polk Gulch neighborhoods of the city. This community has been estimated to range in size anywhere from 10 percent to 20 percent of the city's adult population. Their numbers have been tragically reduced during the last decade by over seven thousand deaths caused by AIDS.[17]

In sum, San Francisco's ethnic complexion and life-style variety produce a population mix that in no way resembles "mainstream" America. In their most recent *Almanac of American Politics*, Michael Barone and Grant Ujifusa estimate that in San Francisco's Fifth Congressional District (representing about 77 percent of all San Franciscans) "white non-Hispanic, non-gay, native-born Americans

Map 2.1. San Francisco's Neighborhoods

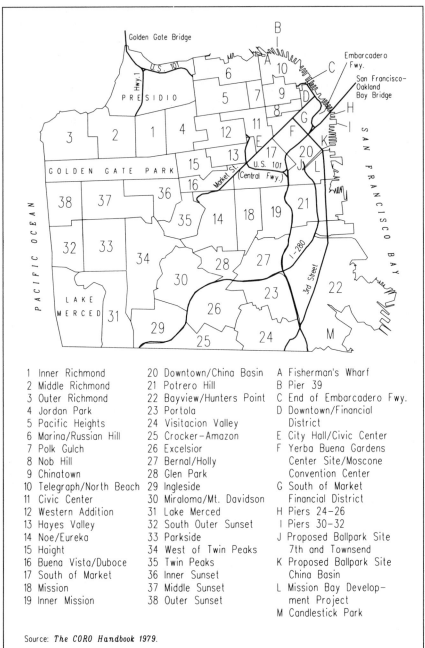

1 Inner Richmond
2 Middle Richmond
3 Outer Richmond
4 Jordan Park
5 Pacific Heights
6 Marina/Russian Hill
7 Polk Gulch
8 Nob Hill
9 Chinatown
10 Telegraph/North Beach
11 Civic Center
12 Western Addition
13 Hayes Valley
14 Noe/Eureka
15 Haight
16 Buena Vista/Duboce
17 South of Market
18 Mission
19 Inner Mission

20 Downtown/China Basin
21 Potrero Hill
22 Bayview/Hunters Point
23 Portola
24 Visitacion Valley
25 Crocker–Amazon
26 Excelsior
27 Bernal/Holly
28 Glen Park
29 Ingleside
30 Miraloma/Mt. Davidson
31 Lake Merced
32 South Outer Sunset
33 Parkside
34 West of Twin Peaks
35 Twin Peaks
36 Inner Sunset
37 Middle Sunset
38 Outer Sunset

A Fisherman's Wharf
B Pier 39
C End of Embarcadero Fwy.
D Downtown/Financial
   District
E City Hall/Civic Center
F Yerba Buena Gardens
   Center Site/Moscone
   Convention Center
G South of Market
   Financial District
H Piers 24–26
I Piers 30–32
J Proposed Ballpark Site
   7th and Townsend
K Proposed Ballpark Site
   China Basin
L Mission Bay Develop-
   ment Project
M Candlestick Park

Source: *The CORO Handbook 1979.*

Bob Bathrick / SFSU GIS Center

make up only about 25 percent of the population."[18] Many of the city's whites reside in the traditional family home-owner districts of what Castells calls "familyland" west of Twin Peaks,[19] while others live in the expensive Pacific Heights and Marina–Russian Hill areas. The other ethnic groups also have recognizable "turfs" in their spatial distribution throughout the city (see Map 2.1): Chinese in the Chinatown and the Richmond districts, with movement in recent years into the Sunset area; Southeast Asians in the Tenderloin district (near the civic center); Filipinos in the South of Market and Mission districts; Latinos in Mission and Inner Mission; and African Americans in Bayview–Hunters Point, Ingleside, and Western Addition.[20]

Relative to other large cities, San Francisco's population is well educated, affluent, and highly skilled: 28.2 percent of those twenty-five years or older in 1980 had completed sixteen years or more of school; money income per capita in 1985 was $13,575; and 19.2 percent of those employed in 1980 held professional or technical positions. John Mollenkopf writes that the "dramatic expansion in headquarters and high-level service employment" has created a "new social stratum" within San Francisco: "the middle-class professionals, typically highly educated, well paid, and increasingly drawn from the baby-boom age cohorts."[21] This new middle class of professionals and expert managers has largely supplanted an older middle class of blue-collar workers who were defined as middle class strictly in terms of income. San Francisco also has become a major urban center of small business entrepreneurs and white-collar artisans (see chapter 9), further marbling an already complicated class structure. In terms of neo-Marxian analysis, the city's occupational structure is brimming with "contradictory locations" that hold what Erik Wright describes as "contradictory interests with respect to the primary forms of class struggle in capitalist society, the struggle between labor and capital." In this analysis, for example, self-employed high-tech consultants occupy a contradictory location within class relations because they neither exploit labor nor are exploited by capital. Expert managers employed by large corporations are "like workers in being excluded from the ownership of the means of production," argues Wright, but they also have "interests opposed to workers because of their effective control of organization and skill assets." They occupy locations in the class structure that are simultaneously exploiting and exploited. According to Wright, these contradictory locations in the class structure can be combined with each other and with traditional working-class formations to create novel political alliances, progressive ones included.[22]

As a result of changes in San Francisco's social class structure, the city's population is endowed with a high level of what Ronald Inglehart calls "cognitive mobilization"—the verbal, analytical, and communication skills needed to cope with social and political complexity.[23] Cognitive mobilization is an important precondition for expanded citizen participation in shaping land-use and development policies. To exercise influence in these policy arenas, which are shrouded in protective professional planning jargon, technical terms, and legalisms, traditional political knowledge and skills usually are not enough. Cognitive mobilization is a key factor in the rise of what Ben Goddard has called "middle-class populism," a phenomenon he believes originates from the better-educated classes of the sixties generation: "The significance of the 'sixties generation' is not their raw numbers but their political skills. At a very young age, they learned how to organize—and just what they could do when they were organized. Their impact has been largely local, because their issues have been local. They are concerned about neighborhood preservation, about transportation, about controls on growth, and about pollution. Their focus is on 'quality of life issues.' "[24] The high level of political mobilization in San Francisco on these kinds of issues is a reflection of the high level of cognitive mobilization made possible by its social class structure.

THE LOCAL HOURGLASS ECONOMY

[handwritten margin note: favors big-business neighborhood munts & other clubs against this centralized]

Over the last two decades, San Francisco's economic base has become specialized in providing advanced corporate services (legal advice, accounting, insurance, financial analysis, etc.) to national and multinational firms.[25] This trend is bisecting the city's occupational structure, creating an "hourglass" image: Both the top tier of high-paying professional and managerial jobs and the bottom tier of low-paying personal services jobs (such as janitors, waitresses, and fast-food servers) are expanding, while the supply of middle-income blue-collar and white-collar jobs is shrinking. To illustrate the magnitude of change that has occurred: In 1963 about 38,000 city jobs were in the services sector; by 1982 that number had mushroomed to over 100,000. Recent studies project that the number of low-income service jobs will increase by 43 percent between 1980 and 2005, while professional/technical jobs in finance, insurance, and real estate will increase by 18 percent—these two categories alone accounting for 74 percent of the projected increase of 119,500 jobs in San Francisco over the twenty-five year period.[26] A study of Bay Area income trends reported that in San Francisco "the bottom two and the top two income classes account for the majority of change in real income between 1978 and 1987."[27] One explanation given was that the city's "economic structure is increasingly generating jobs leading to a bifurcated income structure."[28] Alarmed by these facts and projections, a widely respected local urban planning association recently warned of the "danger of becoming primarily a service-oriented economy. . . . Instead of creating jobs that sustain a growing middle class population, we could experience growth in high paying business service occupations, such as lawyers and accountants, and the kinds of low paying jobs protected by the state."[29]

[handwritten margin note: Rise of Ethnic against this]

The days have long passed since San Francisco was the economic hub of the Bay Area region. The city has not had a majority of the region's jobs since 1947, while Santa Clara County alone generated half the region's job growth over the last decade.[30] The continuing deconcentration of population and jobs throughout the region has shifted the economic spotlight to other areas—San Jose (which now matches San Francisco in population, is building its own downtown, and has much more room to grow), Oakland (with its superior port facilities), and the entire Tri-Valley area just over the East Bay hills (with its greater supply of low-cost housing). San Francisco has been reduced to the role of serving as the region's "symbolic" center and as a convenient source of cultural amenities, fine restaurants, and venture capital to fuel the region's real economic engines in San Jose and Silicon Valley. Many city leaders lament the passing of an age and long to restore San Francisco to a regional stature of at least first among equals. They particularly resent the city's gradual transformation into an urban amusement park. Approximately one in eleven city jobs is generated by nonprofit or for-profit arts organizations.[31] One in nine city jobs is in the tourism and hospitality indus-tries.[32] Fisherman's Wharf now caters to tourists with hardly a fisherman in sight.[33] These trends concern some analysts who see economic danger in such depen-dence on the kindness (and money) of strangers. The city's declining port indus-tries may yet revive through the efforts of the new port director to upgrade port facilities, to develop commercially seven miles of dilapidated waterfront, and to attract new shipping business. Similar proposals to restore the city's manufactur-ing industry sound hollow, however, given the fact that the manufacturing sector has never been a major source of jobs (27,000 employees in 1982, 26,800 in 1963) and is ill suited to the limited office space and small floorplates permitted under the city's new growth controls.

Because of these currents and patterns, developmental policy issues have dom-inated San Francisco politics over the last two decades, raising substantive ques-tions: What economic role will the city play in the rapidly growing metropolitan area? To what extent is high-rise office construction necessary to attract business-es and jobs to the local economy? How can the crisis in housing affordability be resolved before it prices even middle-class residents out of San Francisco? What should be the balance between neighborhood preservation and commercial devel-opment? Should promotion of many small businesses be preferred to the relent-less competition with other cities for a few large corporations? Should the city intensify economic development in areas where it already excels (e.g., business services, arts and design, tourism) or invest major new resources to resuscitate laggard sectors (such as manufacturing)?[34] These economic development and land-use issues are at the heart of many conflicts between the city's traditional business elites and leaders of the progressive movement.

THE "CAGE OF AUTHORITY" AND
THE "MOBILE OF GOVERNANCE"

Even after seventeen years, Frederick Wirt's metaphors have currency as descrip-tions of San Francisco's highly detailed restrictive charter and its fragmented, loosely coupled government structures.[35] In 1932, voters approved a special charter establishing a rare form of consolidated city and county government (city and county territorial boundaries being identical). A product of the Progressive Era, the 1932 charter was conceived as an instrument to safeguard local government against power grabs by corrupt politicians, especially those inclined to meddle in routine administration and licensing decisions. The charter put cages around all points of power and severely restricted discretionary authority. The original plan has grown obese from the countless voter-approved amendments advanced by special interests to change such minutiae as job classifications and salary schemes. There are frequent complaints about the entropification of the political process caused by the glut of proposed charter amendments which voters must wade through each election—twenty-five such amendments in the 1988 election alone. Despite the complaints, voters repeatedly have chosen to live with this system by rejecting every major proposal for charter reform—most recently in 1980.[36]

Through recombinant political splicing, framers of the 1932 charter created a truly novel constitutional monster. They melded elements of strong mayor, city manager, and commission systems of government into a strange hybrid that must be unique among American cities.

Executive authority is divided between an independently elected mayor and a chief administrative officer (CAO) who, although appointed by the mayor, can be removed only by a two-thirds vote of the Board of Supervisors or by recall. The mayor has appointive, budgetary, and veto powers, but administrative control is restricted to those agencies and departments outside the CAO's domain (e.g., police, fire, and land use), and even within this limited sphere the mayor's leadership is filtered through a layer of commissions and boards (such as the Police Commission, Planning Commission, and Board of Permit Appeals), whose members are appointed by the mayor and in only half the cases serve at his or her pleasure. Because the mayor lacks formal executive authority over their powers, these boards and commissions exercise considerable autonomy in making policy decisions. Mayoral appointments to certain other agencies and commissions, such as the Redevelopment Agency and the Port Commission, must be confirmed by the supervisors. The controller, like the CAO, is appointed by the mayor and operates independently of the CAO, thus dividing fiscal management functions. The offices of assessor and city attorney, typically staffed by appointment in other cities, are elective positions in San Francisco and highly prized by ambitious local politicians.

Overall, executive authority in San Francisco's city hall is divided, dispersed, and decentralized. Wirt's image of a mobile with "figures frozen in midair and interconnected in inexplicable ways by wildly zooming lines" is fairly descriptive of the city's governmental organization chart.[37] It is a structure that resists centralized authority or efforts to employ it as an instrument of social change. The human resources are there—over thirty-four thousand local government employees in 1982—but charter-ordained cages keep them in separate bureaucratic domains. To a significant degree, Wirt's earlier conclusion that what San Francisco has is "government by clerks" still applies, as does his observation that the position of mayor "is what he makes it by the force of his character and personality."[38] In his 1987 campaign for mayor, Art Agnos spelled out an ambitious agenda in his book *Getting Things Done: Visions and Goals for San Francisco.* But "getting things done" in San Francisco requires much more than a mayor's formal powers, which are modest at best, and hinges instead on his or her skills as a political entrepreneur in building coalitions, assembling resources, negotiating deals, and harnessing the energies of government clerks.

Legislative authority under the 1932 charter was placed in a Board of Supervisors whose eleven members are elected at large to staggered four-year terms. The board initiates legislation; shares authority with the mayor over the budget (at $2.3 billion in 1991, up from $238 million in 1964–65); can place proposed charter amendments on the ballot; has the power to confirm some mayoral appointees; and provides a forum for public debate during regular sessions and committee hearings. The board cannot interfere in the administrative functions of the executive branches or exercise oversight in the implementation of ordinances.

Despite the legislative responsibilities implied by a multibillion-dollar budget and a complex government apparatus, the city's voters have refused to raise supervisors' salaries above the 1990 level of $23,924 a year, making them the worst-paid county supervisors in the nine-county Bay Area. Evidently, San Franciscans continue to harbor the myth that running the city is a part-time job for public-spirited amateurs. The myth has consequences. Mayor Agnos lost one member of his liberal board majority, Nancy Walker, who resigned simply because she no longer could afford the financial sacrifice. Other members of the board must either treat their work as part-time employment, indebt themselves to financial contributors, or be independently wealthy. Nevertheless, every two years, from twenty to thirty candidates run for the board against incumbents who almost always run for reelection and are rarely dislodged. Frustrated by the sticky grip of incumbency on reelection campaigns and by the free-for-all politics that dominate board proceedings, voters in 1990 passed a citizen-initiated ballot proposition restricting incumbents to a maximum of two terms.

PARTIES, ELECTIONS, AND DIRECT DEMOCRACY

Local elections in San Francisco are officially nonpartisan. Yet the Democratic party imbues the partisan air that San Franciscans breathe, and in state and national elections the city belongs to the Democrats. In 1988, Republican registration of voters was at 18.4 percent (down from 20.6 percent in 1981), and registered Democrats outnumbered Republicans more than three to one. Until recently, the Democratic County Committee has not played a major role in city politics.

This may change, however, as a result of recent court decisions allowing political party endorsements of candidates in local races.[39] Further, the local political power vacuum created by the deaths of Congressman Phillip Burton in 1983 and of his wife and successor, Sala Burton, in 1987 has quickly filled up again with old and new Democrats working in concert to coordinate policies and anoint candidates in local races.[40] Most notable in this group are Mayor Art Agnos; Congresswoman Nancy Pelosi (who succeeded the Burtons in representing the Fifth Congressional District); Congresswoman Barbara Boxer (Sixth Congressional District); Assemblyman (and Assembly Speaker) Willie Brown; Assemblyman John Burton (Phillip Burton's brother); and Supervisor Carole Migden, chair of the county committee.

During the period 1977–80, the city's voters flip-flopped through several elections in deciding between district versus at-large election of the city's supervisors.[41] In 1980, following a brief but consequential experiment with district elections, the voters restored at-large elections and have stuck with them ever since. One reason citizens have resisted a return to district elections is that the board, under at-large elections, has become more demographically representative of the city's population: five women, six men; three gay or lesbian persons; two African Americans, one Chinese American, and one Latino. Moreover, for the first time in memory, the board now has at least a six to five progressive majority to push for social change from inside city hall. Therefore, the pragmatic attitude of "if it ain't broke, don't fix it" now prevails in discussions of the city's electoral laws. Following passage of the two-term limit, however, an initiative for district elections might once again succeed. It is still an item on the progressive agenda.

The city's brief experiment with district elections was significant because, among other things, a crowd of new candidates ran for the Board of Supervisors. Many of them lacked the financial backing or name recognition usually required to win an at-large election. One who succeeded was Harvey Milk, who won in his district as the city's first openly gay elected official; another was Dan White, who won in his district on a wave of antigay sentiment and conservative resentment toward the new liberal mayor, George Moscone. The eventual tragic outcome of this conjuncture is now well known. On 27 November 1978, Dan White shot and killed both Harvey Milk and George Moscone. As discussed in chapter 3, this sad episode in San Francisco's political history almost certainly delayed the opportunity to fulfill Mayor Moscone's progressive agenda through the nine years of centrist Mayor Dianne Feinstein's administration, until Art Agnos won election as mayor in 1987.

As in most western cities, San Francisco's voters are endowed with the instruments of direct democracy: the initiative, referendum, and recall. These electoral tools, particularly the citizen initiative, have allowed progressive leaders to circumvent recalcitrant elected officials, to shape the city's political agenda, and to legislate policy directly.[42] The slow-growth movement was organized almost entirely around initiative campaigns, and it is hard to imagine how that movement could have succeeded without them. The citizen ballot initiative is especially well suited to the city's growing population of highly educated middle-class professionals, who are inclined to be "elite directing" rather than "elite directed" even in the arcane policy spheres of land use and physical development.[43] The frequent adoption of the citizen ballot initiative as a land-use planning tool is disturbing to many professional planners and business elites. Planning lawyers Daniel Curtin and M. Thomas Jacobsen, for example, contend that "the hallmarks of good land-use planning are that decisions are well-informed, that the planning process is flexible and responsive to changing circumstances and values, and that decisions reflect a comprehensive planning process and are accommodations of competing public interests. Arguably, each of these land-use goals is thwarted when land-use planning is done via the ballot box."[44] Richard Morton, a former San Francisco Chamber of Commerce official, concurs with such criticisms, adding: "The city's lengthy battle over planning initiatives has contributed to political instability and a feeling of uncertainty among business people who need to plan for the long term."[45]

The city's conservative groups also know how to employ the instruments of direct democracy. In 1989, for example, the Board of Supervisors unanimously passed and the mayor signed a "domestic partners" ordinance allowing city-employed unmarried couples who live together (including gay men and lesbians) to register their relationship at city hall. City workers who signed up under the law would receive many of the same rights, such as hospital visitation leaves, accorded to married couples. A week before the new measure was to take effect, a petition-gathering campaign organized by religious leaders and conservative groups succeeded in stopping implementation of the new law until it was put to the voters as a referendum on the November 1989 ballot. This citizen-initiated referendum measure, Proposition S, was fiercely contested and eventually lost by a slim margin. The pioneering ordinance was rendered null and void. A year later the progressives came back to the voters with an *initiative*, Proposition K, which was a slightly watered-down version of the *referendum*, Proposition S. Proposition K won by a significant margin, and the proposed domestic partners ordinance finally became law.

Recall elections are rare in San Francisco, but one held in 1983 illustrates the vagaries of direct democracy. Infuriated by Mayor Feinstein's support of a hand-gun control ordinance, a maverick leftist group oriented to self-defense and known as the White Panthers organized a successful petition drive that subjected the mayor to a special recall election. But the maneuver backfired. Not only did Feinstein receive 82 percent of the vote, her landside victory discouraged other candidates from opposing her in the general election. The result solidified her control for another four years.[46]

HYPERPLURALISM REVISITED:
CHALLENGE AND OPPORTUNITY

An attempt to identify "the" power structure in San Francisco politics is as futile today as it was in 1971, when Frederick Wirt aptly described the city's highly granulated interest-group politics and decentralized governmental system as "hyperpluralistic."[47] If "government by clerks" captures the essence of what goes on inside city hall, then "politics by clubs" describes fairly well what goes on outside. "Clubs" is used here as a rubric to cover not only the city's 27 clubs chartered with the Democratic County Committee but also another 750 politically active clubs, caucuses, committees, associations, organizations, groups, councils, unions, societies, forums, task forces, collectives, projects, campaigns, and mobilizations. The term also includes a second tier of 30 coalitions, 21 alliances, 14 leagues, 10 networks, and 5 federations that coordinate the activities of first-tier groups. Tony Kilroy's 1990 *Directory of San Francisco's Politically Active Groups* classifies 216 of these 772 groups as being politically active "always."[48] As a rough indicator of turnover, 342 of the 772 groups listed in 1990 were not in Kilroy's 1985 directory, and 148 of the groups listed in 1985 did not reappear in 1990. The constituencies represented by these groups are not all politically equal, of course, and they range from sliver-sized and specialized (Gay American Indians, Give Peace a Dance, Blue Collar Asian Women) to sizable organizations with multiple-issue agendas and substantial clout (Service Employees International Union [SEIU] Local 790, San Francisco Tomorrow, San Francisco Chamber of Commerce). In election years, the frenzied competition among candidates for group endorsements often has the quality of an elaborate political scavenger hunt. Club membership enrollments typically expand just before endorsement votes, then shrink again after the election amid charges that this or that candidate stacked the vote. It is a venal form of corruption and lucrative for some clubs. To generalize, there are few major arteries in the city through which political influence can flow, so capillaries hold the juice. Because they are so necessary, the political arts of building coalitions and forging alliances are highly advanced in San Francisco.

Over the last twenty years, several trends have intensified the city's hyperpluralism, including (1) the coming to power of the neighborhood movement, (2) the crumbling of the downtown business-dominated progrowth coalition, (3) the shrinking size and political quiescence of labor unions, and (4) the political awakening of ethnic and gay minorities. The first two are major themes of this book, but the third and fourth are discussed here briefly.

The Fall (and Possible Rise) of Organized Labor

National economic restructuring is a prime cause of local crises in organized labor. Although the nationwide decline in union membership certainly affects organized labor in many communities,[49] economic restructuring, as labor scholar Gordon Clark points out, is itself "an intensely local phenomenon"[50] that is "highly structured by *community* culture, institutions, and technological advantage."[51] In San Francisco, overall unionization rates have dropped because of changes in the local economy, the loss of blue-collar jobs, and the rapid growth of a new class of service workers. In 1987, only 34.5 percent of San Francisco's work force was unionized, which is much higher than the Bay Area average of 19.9 percent but much lower than in the days when the city was known as a strong labor town.[52] Local union leaders could do more to soften the impacts of restructuring on the communities in which they reside. But the union "as an institution," Clark explains, "is caught between representing and adjudicating workers' interests at the local level and simultaneously brokering deals which would protect the future of its [national and multinational] corporate partners."[53] Clark concludes that "the crisis of organized labor is more than the loss of membership; it is deeper and perhaps more fundamental: the welfare of unions is no longer consistent with the welfare of communities."[54] San Francisco's organized labor community is no exception to this generalization, although there are recent signs of change.

At the turn of the century, according to William Issel and Robert Cherny, San Francisco's politics "exhibited sharply etched polarities" between labor and capital.[55] A "highly unified business community stood at one pole, arrayed against a unified labor force at the other."[56] And "among both business and labor, feelings of class unity submerged ethnic differences."[57] This historical perspective suggests just how far the city's labor community has fallen from collective mobilization into collective contractualism, from being a unified, politicized force for social change into a fragmented, depoliticized aggregate of unions, each minding its own interests. The principal historical factors explaining this political decline, argue Issel and Cherny, were the federal protections of collective bargaining provided by New Deal legislation and the acceptance of this labor-relations structure by leading employers "so long as labor limited itself to collective bargaining over wages, hours, and working conditions."[58] As a consequence of their domestication and self-preoccupation, San Francisco's labor unions became "less active than before in city politics, as some unions came to consider their previous defensive politics as unnecessary and others came to view politics solely in terms of their own jobs."[59] San Francisco's unions have only very recently begun to mobilize and organize the city's single largest class of workers in the rapidly growing service sector. As one local union president admitted, "We have not done very well in the service sector."[60] The city's electrical workers and building trades unions opposed public ownership of electrical utilities on the grounds that "federal protection of bargaining rights was preferable to that available to city employees."[61] These and other unions, along with the city's AFL-CIO Labor Council, have opposed progressive slow-growth initiatives because of the anticipated negative short-term impact of growth controls on job opportunities for union members. In doing so they have clashed repeatedly with other unions, particularly the large SEIU Local 790, which represents many city employees.

There are indications that San Francisco's new progressive political culture is nurturing a revitalized labor movement that could have a marked impact on city politics in the years ahead. Consider the following examples. (1) Walter Johnson, leader of the Labor Council, recently declared, "We're back in the agitation stage. The big thing that has to happen in the labor movement is to define new boundaries. We can't stay on our own turf and expect to change anything."[62] (2) The Hotel and Restaurant Employees and Bartenders Union Local 2 recently scored a major victory in forcing the city's new Marriott Hotel to adopt hiring practices favorable to union members, ethnic minorities, and local residents.[63] (3) Local 250 of the Hospital and Health Care Workers' Union is leading an aggressive campaign to organize all nonunion hospitals in San Francisco. Sal Rosselli, president of Local 250, declared that his workers "are on the cutting edge of a renaissance in labor organizing in San Francisco hospitals."[64] (4) Working closely with Supervisor Nancy Walker, Supervisor Angela Alioto, and various progressive groups, labor union leaders played a vital role in the passage of San Francisco's pioneering legislation establishing minimum safety standards in city businesses that use video display terminals.[65] (5) In late summer of 1991, the United Food and Commercial Workers rallied outside BankAmerica's downtown headquarters to protest that company's alleged antilabor tactics in the United States and abroad.[66] (6) David Arian, a self-described radical, recently succeeded James Herman as president of the San Francisco-based International Longshoremen's and Warehousemen's Union (ILWU). Promising to revive the ILWU's militancy and leftist traditions, Arian defeated Herman's protégé, Randy Vekich, in a close election.[67] (7) Finally, and perhaps symbolic of the shifting labor tides in San Francisco, the Industrial Workers of the World ("Wobblies") recently moved its international headquarters to the city from Chicago.[68]

If these kinds of activities expand into a full-blown labor *movement* in San Francisco, and if the city's unions succeed in mobilizing class solidarity (vis-à-vis the competing solidarities of race or turf) among the city's service workers, the new structure of labor relations that emerges could support a progressive urban regime.

The Political Mobilization of Ethnic Minorities

Another trend that has contributed to San Francisco's hyperpluralism is the political mobilization of the city's ethnic minority groups. Fueled by immigration and rapid ethnic diversification over the last thirty years, growing numbers of African Americans, Latinos, and Asians have achieved greater political clout and representation at city hall. Factors to consider in gauging the relative political power of the city's ethnic minority groups include population size, voter registration and turnout rate, and degree of consensus in voting on candidates and issues. Additional indicators of political power are a strong and unified leadership, efficient organization, control of resources, and formal representation in government.

African Americans. African Americans are now the smallest of the three major ethnic minority groups in terms of population size, but they have mustered the highest rates of voter mobilization, consensus on issues, and representation in government. Supported by political organization and leadership at the state and national levels, the city's African American leaders have converted limited numbers and economic resources into a power bloc to be reckoned with in local politics. "Since at least the mid-1970's," writes political journalist Tim Redmond, "blacks have been a significant political force in San Francisco, wielding influence far greater than that enjoyed by other ethnic groups—Asians and Hispanics, for example." Redmond contrasts the political success of the black population with that of the Asian community, which is more than three times its size in terms of sheer numbers. "Black representation in top policy-making posts dwarfs that of Asians," he points out, citing a long list of African American supervisors, agency heads, board members, and commissioners under the Feinstein administration compared with a very short one of Asians.[69]

Despite the current political ascendancy of African Americans among San Francisco's ethnic minority groups, there are signs that the African American power base is eroding, mainly because of demographic attrition and developing schisms within African American leadership groups over issues such as growth controls. Redmond quotes a local political analyst's view that African American leaders are aware of the decline and feel threatened by the political emergence of other ethnic groups. "They see a Hispanic threat, and they see an Asian threat. . . . And that's logical, since the black population of the city is declining, while other minority groups are growing."[70] African American supervisor Willie Kennedy recently remarked that "for years we were considered *the* minority. Then everyone else become a minority, and we started to get pushed back." In her opinion, African Americans "ought to be further advanced than these other groups, because we got here first.[71]

Latinos. San Francisco's growing Latino population has only recently begun to translate its demographic potential into political power. Grant Din cites studies that show very low rates of voter mobilization within San Francisco's Latino community, which has a very high proportion of noncitizens and formidable language barriers.[72] Louis Freedberg writes that although the Latino community has been divided on some issues (e.g., aid to the Contras, the death penalty), education "is the great unifier on which virtually all Latinos agree."[73] In San Francisco, Latinos have made their greatest political inroads in that field, particularly in the appointment of Ramon Cortines as school superintendent and the election of Latinos to the Community College District Board and to the San Francisco School District Board of Education. With Mayor Feinstein's appointments of Latinos to the Health Commission and to the Board of Supervisors, and with Mayor Agnos's appointments of Latinos to the Police and Planning commissions, the Latino community now has representation in broader areas of public policy. The Latino Democratic Club has become one of the city's more influential political organizations and is working with other groups and committees to register voters and fund election campaigns. Recently considered to be on the "periphery of San Francisco's dominant coalition,"[74] Latinos are quickly closing the gap with African Americans in the exercise of political power.

Asians. Long considered to be the forgotten minority in studies of urban ethnic politics, Asian Americans in San Francisco have begun to mobilize as a political force. Although the city's Asian population has become too large for politicians to ignore, the Asian community still has a long way to go in converting its growing numbers into votes. Grant Din's careful study of eligible voters in Chinatown, Richmond, and the Sunset, for example, revealed extremely low voter registration rates among Chinese Americans.[75]

San Francisco's Asian community continues to be underrepresented on the Board of Supervisors, with Chinese American Tom Hsieh (pronounced "shay") the only Asian member. In other areas of the city's political life, Asian leaders have had notable success. Three won posts on the Community College District Board, and two on the city's Board of Education. Following Agnos's election as mayor in 1987, hundreds of Asian Americans applied for jobs in the city's bureaucracy—"a vast increase over previous years," according to Frank Viviano.[76] Mayor Agnos's appointments of Asians to key commissions and administrative positions boosted their representation at the top levels of government.

It is important to note that most of these political accomplishments were those of Chinese Americans, who compose about half of the city's total Asian population. Although some segments of the "other" Asian community, particularly Filipinos, have achieved greater visibility and political clout in San Francisco, for the most part they exist at the fringes of city politics. It is doubtful that even the most committed pan-Asianists within the Chinese American political elite can adequately represent the concerns and aspirations of all segments of San Francisco's large and diverse Asian community. Henry Der, a prominent leader in the city's Chinese American community, observes that "in the last two decades people have come to this community from all over the place, from every part of China, Hong Kong and Taiwan, Vietnam, Laos, Cambodia, Thailand, Burma and Malaysia. The diversity of origins, opinions and belief systems is staggering. There's no way that any single organization can claim to represent 'Chinese San Francisco.' "[77]

If this summary may be used as a guide to the future of ethnic politics in San Francisco, the prospects appear somewhat discouraging for African Americans, encouraging for Latinos, and very encouraging but more problematic for Asians. The city's African American leaders will have to work even harder just to preserve their existing power base. They must cope with demographic erosion, leadership schisms, limited resources, and competition from other ethnic groups. Latino leaders must continue to politicize immigrants, accommodate their housing and employment needs to stabilize residency, and mobilize voters. Asian leaders must do the same, but they face a greater problem of creating political forms of racial-ethnic solidarity in a community riven by cultural and language differences, competing elites, and social class disparities.

The Rise of Gay and Lesbian Power

Of all the groups in San Francisco's diverse population, gays and lesbians can claim the highest level of electoral mobilization, representation, and political assimilation in the city's political system. One indicator of how established gays and lesbians have become within the city's political culture is the turnout for the 1991 San Francisco Lesbian/Gay Freedom Day Parade, conservatively estimated at 250,000—the largest crowd ever in the parade's twenty-two-year history.[78] Gays and lesbians probably constitute about 16 percent of the city's adult population,[79] and they tend to register and vote at very high rates.[80] Their political clubs are extremely active and highly respected. As a group, their position on most social policy issues is consistently progressive, and they have achieved significant representation and incorporation in the city's elective political structures. A columnist for a local gay newspaper writes, "We've got power here because we're great voters. Politicians can be destroyed by the gay vote. As long as we keep our vote, they're going to kiss our ass for a long time."[81]

In 1990, a banner year for San Francisco's gay and lesbian community, Donna Hitchens became California's highest-ranking open lesbian by defeating an incumbent in a race for superior court. Two avowed lesbians, Carole Migden and Roberta Achtenberg, won seats on the Board of Supervisors. An openly gay candidate, Tom Ammiano, won his race for a seat on the Board of Education. The Domestic Partners Initiative, Proposition K, won handily. In every instance, the gay and lesbian candidates who succeeded did so mainly by declaring their bona fides as progressives and by dint of hard political work in nongay communities. Donna Hitchens's campaign is a case in point. Commenting on her victory, Richard Sevilla, a Latino Democratic Club vice president, noted, "Donna's victory is a victory for Latinos, African Americans and Asians as well as the gay community. She won by reaching out to us."[82]

San Francisco's gay and lesbian voters are aware of their political clout in the local government arena. For example, in a 1989 sample survey of registered voters, respondents were asked, "How much influence do you think people like you can have over local government decisions—a lot, a moderate amount, a little, or none at all?" Seventy percent of the gay or lesbian respondents answered "a lot" or "a moderate amount" of influence as compared with only 48 percent of heterosexuals. Another question asked, "If you had some complaint about a local government activity and took that complaint to the San Francisco Board of Supervisors, would you expect the Board to pay a lot of attention, some attention, very little attention, or none at all?" Sixty-seven percent of the gay or lesbian respondents answered "a lot" or "some" attention as compared with only 49 percent of heterosexuals. These percentage differences are substantively and statistically significant (especially so since the survey was taken the year *before* the electoral successes of 1990), and they hold even when controlling for race, gender, age, income, housing tenure, and other factors.[83]

Interestingly, at the very time an older generation of gay and lesbian leaders has arrived to power in the realm of conventional city politics, many younger gays and lesbians have split into separate political groups, such as ACT UP, Queer Nation, and Bad Cop, No Donut, all of which practice a confrontational, direct-action style of politics. These fissions within the younger stratum of the gay and lesbian community appear to have emerged at least in part as a reaction to the increasingly more diffuse social agendas being pursued by the city's more established gays and lesbians.

As a consequence of these and other trends, San Francisco's hyperpluralism is even greater now than it was thirty years ago. It remains to be seen whether the city's new progressive leaders can chart a course for the city amid all this social turbulence and political disarray. Yet with the challenge come opportunities. Citizens, politicians, and business leaders are redefining their roles and relating to each other in new ways. New political alignments, coalitions, and ideologies are forming, signaling the deeper restructuring associated with regime transformation. The general drift of all this change is toward a progressive urban regime. But what is progressivism?

PROGRESSIVISM AND THE THREE LEFTS IN SAN FRANCISCO POLITICS

Clarence Stone argues that "urban regimes and civic cooperation are shaped less by ideology than by the ability to allocate small opportunities."[84] In other words, ideologies alone cannot attain social goals. They can inspire, but they cannot pay the bills or provide shelter or get people to work on time. If a regime performs well enough in serving individual needs and social goals, a critical mass of political support will form around it.[85] In their social orbits around the regime, radical critics will appear romantic or quixotic in calling for fundamental change. They might as well rally political support to repeal Newton's laws. In this view, urban regimes are neither maintained by ideologies nor toppled by them.

Stone's theory is useful in explaining regime continuity—that is, how established regimes survive politically and sustain themselves over time. The theory is less useful, however, in explaining regime building in a city like San Francisco that lacks an established regime and is in the transitional process of creating a new political order. Political ideology is the closest thing to a blueprint in giving leaders an overall perspective on how to proceed. In his study of progressive cities, Pierre Clavel emphasizes the importance of the transformative "structure of thought" that emerges from political mobilizations and electoral struggles. This structure of thought combines "principles of public participation with substantive visions and models of possible reconstructions of the local economy and social structure."[86] It gives progressive leaders a theoretical rationale for social change, a reform agenda, and a rhetoric for public argument. It also provides a manifesto for mobilizing mass political support in building a progressive regime. In San Francisco, progressive leaders have attempted to distill such a structure of thought—a progressive ideology—from their political practice and their thinking about social change. Success in building a new progressive urban regime depends in part on the capacity of progressive ideology to inspire a common vision, legitimate new power structures, give coherence and direction to policy, and embrace diverse and sometimes divergent constituency interests. San Francisco's brand of progressivism has evolved in novel and fruitful ways to serve these regime-building functions.

Defining Progressivism

In his cross-national study of political cultures and ideologies, Inglehart contends that the Left-Right dimension has worn well through the years in "providing an overall orientation toward a potentially limitless number of issues, political parties, and social groups."[87] Further, the Left-Right dimension is "absorptive" of new political values and ideologies that emerge as a result of social and cultural change.[88] This process of absorption entails recalibration of the Left-Right vocabulary so that it continues to reduce complexity and yet convey new meanings. In American politics, the "liberal-conservative" dichotomy is preferred to the Left-Right terminology in discussions of political beliefs and ideologies. In San Francisco, a city most observers would describe as both "liberal" and "leftist," neither term can absorb the flux of new values and ideas arising from the city's various social movements and political campaigns. San Franciscans themselves tend to use the words *progressive* and *progressivism* to describe a wide range of social reforms and to simplify conceptualization of the transformations taking place. As a consequence, *progressive* as a term of local political discourse has become saturated with multiple and sometimes contradictory meanings. It is often used as a synonym for "leftist," "liberal," "libertarian," "antistatist," "populist," "environmentalist," "community activist," and even "Progressive" in the old-fashioned Hiram Johnson sense. A richer and more precise vocabulary is needed to capture the multidimensionality and ideological complexity of San Francisco's political universe—but not so rich and precise as to defeat the purposes of simplifying analysis and identifying general patterns and trends.

As used in this book, *progressive* embraces all of the meanings of "Left," "liberal," and "progressive" discussed above, but no one of these meanings embraces it. Progressives are liberals, for example, but liberals are not necessarily progressive. To be more specific, San Francisco's progressivism is a composite of three distinct Left subcultures and ideological tendencies found in the city's political culture: liberalism, environmentalism, and populism. Although there is much overlap and flux, each of these political subcultures (hereafter referred to as the "three Lefts") has its own identifiable tradition, social base, political organization, agenda for change, and style of participating in San Francisco politics.

San Francisco's liberals support government redistributive programs and active intervention in the economy to promote social equality and individual opportunity. Liberals also champion the protection and expansion of individual liberties and civil rights. They give highest priority to the goal of equal economic opportunity for poor people and ethnic-racial minorities, particularly in the areas of jobs, housing, and education. The Left-Right cleavages that form around these kinds of issues have a materialist basis arising from class and racial conflicts and are aligned with established state and national partisan divisions.

San Francisco's environmentalists seek to enhance the quality of life through government regulation of the private sector and limits on economic growth. They are motivated by concerns for the ecological balance, social harmony, and aesthetic quality of urban life, particularly in the areas of environmental protection, land use, transportation, commercial development, and historical preservation. Inglehart uses the term *postmaterialism* to describe the Left-Right cleavages that form around these kinds of issues.[89] Such cleavages are value-based rather than class-based, and they crosscut established partisan divisions.

San Francisco's populists are neighborhood activists and preservationists who seek to protect turf-based communal traditions, property-use values, and cultural identities from incursions by corporate businesses and government bureaucracies. Although some populists frame their agenda in explicitly ideological terms—community empowerment, free spaces, cultural revolution from below, the capillary spread of local democracy, and so on—most do not. They are characterized as populist because of their grass-roots style of direct democracy, their communitarian ethos, and their antistatist hostility toward bigness in both the private and public sectors.[90] Left-Right cleavages do not arise from exclusively materialist or postmaterialist concerns but from conflicts about the control of urban space. The populist Left is territorially based in residential neighborhood communities and is not aligned with established partisan divisions.

San Francisco's progressives are "leftist" in all three dimensions: liberal, environmentalist, *and* populist. Progressives subscribe to all three agendas and perceive no ideological contradiction in doing so. Still in its formative stage, progressive ideology in San Francisco can be summarized as a system of values, beliefs, and ideas that encourages an expanded role for local government in achieving distributive justice, limits on growth, neighborhood preservation, and ethnic-cultural diversity under conditions of public accountability and direct citizen participation. Progressivism so defined attacks all structures of social domination, imposes conditions on business elites for access to the city's space,[91] gives priority to community-use values over market-exchange values in land-use and development planning, and seeks to empower neighborhoods and groups historically excluded from public leadership roles.

A factor analysis of precinct voting data on thirty-four ballot propositions during 1979–90 reveals three distinct patterns of electoral cleavage (labeled "liberalism," "environmentalism," and "populism") that correspond to the three Left-Right axes just discussed. (See appendix B for statistical results and methodological details.) Precinct scores were computed (and standardized on a zero to one hundred scale) measuring each precinct's propensity to vote Left on each of the separate isms. An overall progressivism score was calculated as an average of the other three. Using these scores, it is possible to examine the social base and spatial distribution of each of the three Lefts and to draw some empirical conclusions about the social structural conditions that support progressivism in San Francisco.

Social Bases of Progressivism and the Three Lefts

Table 2.2 shows the patterns of correlation (positive and negative) between various social indicators and progressive voting tendencies in San Francisco precincts. With one qualification to be made about the effects of social class, these correlation results suggest the following. First, liberal voting is positively linked to low socioeconomic status (SES), renter status, gay sexual orientation, African American race, and Hispanic race. Liberal voting is negatively correlated with Asian race. Second, environmentalist voting is positively linked to high SES,

Table 2.2.   Social Bases of Progressivism and the Three Lefts (Liberalism, Environmentalism, and Populism) in San Francisco, 1979–90: Correlations of Voting Patterns in 710 Precincts on Ballot Propositions with Selected Social Indicators[a]

Social Indicators[b]	Factor Score Indexes Measuring Left-Voting Tendencies[c]			
	Progressivism	Liberalism	Environmentalism	Populism
Socioeconomic status (SES)	−.34	−.54	.30	−.41
Percentage of renters	.42	.53	.45	−.16
"Gay" classification (0,1)	.33	.28	.26	.14
Percentage black	.04	.45	−.54	.09
Percentage Hispanic	.37	.27	.06	.45
Percentage Asian	−.19	−.20	−.06	−.12

[a]Entries are Pearson zero-order correlation coefficients. See appendix C for results of multiple regression analysis using all social indicators combined as predictors.

[b]Constructed from 1980 census tract data (n = 105) and mapped onto 710 precincts for analysis. See appendix A for data sources and details on index construction.

[c]Factor scores derived from principal factor analysis of precinct voting data on 34 ballot propositions. Index scores are standardized to a 0–100 scale. See appendixes A and B for data sources and methodological details.

renter status, and gay sexual orientation; it is negatively correlated with African American race and has little or no correlation with Hispanic or Asian race. Third, populist voting is positively linked to low SES, home-owner status, gay sexual orientation, and Hispanic race, but it is negatively correlated with Asian race and has little or no correlation with African American race. Fourth, overall progressive voting is positively linked to low SES, renter status, gay sexual orientation, and Hispanic race. Progressive voting is negatively related to Asian race and has little or no correlation with African American race.

With one exception, these patterns in the social bases of support for Left voting in San Francisco hold even under multivariate statistical controls. (See appendix C.) The qualification is that the relationship between Left voting and social class (SES) is nonlinear—specifically, it is parabolic. This means that Left voting tends to be highest in middle-class precincts, not in working-class precincts, everything else remaining the same. This finding holds for overall progressive voting, liberalism, populism, and especially environmentalism. If Left-voting tendencies (as measured here) were in fact a working-class phenomenon, we would expect to see Left voting at a maximum when SES equals zero on the SES index. Instead, the maxima occur when SES is at 47, 51, 73, and 47, respectively, for progressivism, liberalism, environmentalism, and populism.[92] The working-class conservatism implied by this analysis is offset considerably by nonclass factors such as race and housing status—although, in the case of African Americans voting on environmental issues, such putative working-class conservatism is reinforced rather than dampened by race.[93]

Spatial Distribution of Progressivism and the Three Lefts

Table 2.3 reports average precinct scores on liberalism, environmentalism, populism, and overall progressivism for thirty-eight San Francisco neighborhoods.[94] Map 2.2 shows maps indicating the ten neighborhoods scoring highest on each of these four indexes. The first important result to consider in Table 2.3 is that the Haight-Ashbury district ranks high on all three indices of Left voting and first on the index of progressivism. At the other extreme, the West of Peaks district ranks low on all three indexes and last on the index of progressivism. This is worth noting because any other highest and lowest ranking would undermine the intuitive validity of these measures of leftism and progressivism in San Francisco. All politically informed local observers "know" that the Haight is the neighborhood headquarters for the city's progressive movement, just as they "know" that West of Peaks is the neighborhood headquarters for the city's conservative opposition. The factor scores are fancy and precise—but most knowledgeable San Franciscans would challenge their validity as measures of political culture if they had failed to register these most obvious facts about San Francisco's political life.

A second observation about the results in Table 2.3 is that a neighborhood's

Table 2.3. Liberalism, Environmentalism, Populism, and Overall Progressivism in Thirty-eight San Francisco Neighborhoods

Neighborhood	Liberalism		Environ-mentalism		Populism		Overall Progressivism	
Haight	91.60	1	84.09	1	68.65	3	81.11	1
Hayes Valley	88.51	2	61.56	15	61.96	8	70.34	7
South of Market	82.97	3	68.36	11	68.35	5	72.89	5
Buena Vista/Duboce	81.17	4	83.69	2	60.23	12	74.70	4
Inner Mission	81.08	5	66.70	13	71.79	2	72.86	6
Mission	81.05	6	78.56	3	68.53	4	75.71	3
Western Addition	80.96	7	38.77	33	35.30	33	51.34	21
Bayview/Hunters Point	78.71	8	8.25	38	52.68	20	46.21	30
Potrero Hill	76.88	9	74.07	6	84.42	1	78.12	2
Bernal/Holly	76.52	10	69.58	8	65.76	6	70.29	8
Noe/Eureka	70.18	11	76.96	4	57.58	15	67.91	9
Ingleside	69.91	12	25.39	37	49.34	24	47.88	28
Civic Center	67.83	13	59.60	21	51.52	23	59.32	12
Inner Sunset	63.30	14	74.64	5	56.57	16	64.50	10
Polk Gulch	62.76	15	70.61	7	42.43	30	58.27	13
Visitacion Valley	62.64	16	29.43	36	61.47	10	50.85	22
Downtown/China Basin	60.44	17	50.91	29	45.58	27	51.98	18
Glen Park	58.99	18	69.18	9	53.40	19	60.19	11
Nob Hill	56.88	19	60.01	19	39.27	32	51.72	19
Inner Richmond	56.79	20	66.75	12	40.99	31	54.51	14
Telegraph/North Beach	54.83	21	68.73	10	35.03	34	52.53	16
Chinatown	52.76	22	56.69	23	27.78	36	45.41	31
Middle Richmond	47.57	23	63.68	14	43.82	28	51.36	20
Portola	45.78	24	37.42	34	64.27	7	48.82	26
Crocker-Amazon	45.67	25	37.00	35	52.11	22	44.59	32
Twin Peaks	45.11	26	59.64	20	46.07	26	49.94	23
Outer Richmond	45.04	27	60.33	18	52.18	21	52.19	17
Outer Sunset	43.03	28	56.62	24	61.68	9	53.44	15
Excelsior	43.01	29	42.62	32	60.63	11	48.42	27
Jordan Park	42.19	30	61.22	17	21.84	37	41.42	34
Pacific Heights	39.16	31	61.49	16	16.67	38	38.78	37
Middle Sunset	37.20	32	57.20	22	53.56	18	48.99	25
Miraloma/Mt.Davidson	36.89	33	55.64	26	55.99	17	49.17	24
Marina/Russian Hill	35.05	34	55.86	25	29.08	35	39.67	36
South Outer Sunset	32.28	35	48.19	31	59.61	13	46.36	29
Lake Merced	25.84	36	51.12	28	46.56	25	40.84	35
Parkside	24.48	37	50.63	30	58.87	14	44.33	33
West of Peaks	18.73	38	53.31	27	42.46	29	37.83	38

Entries are neighborhood average precinct scores on three principal factors (scaled to 0–100) and overall index of progressivism (left) and rank (right). Neighborhood boundaries are defined in *Coro Handbook, 1979.* See appendices A, B, and C.

Map 2.2. Progressivism, Liberalism, Environmentalism, and Populism in San Francisco's Neighborhoods

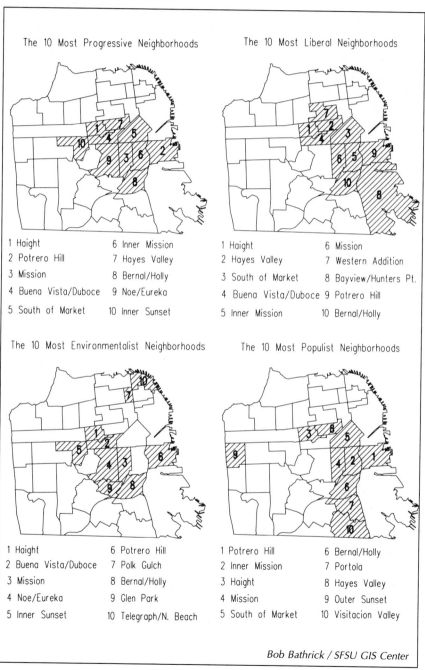

The 10 Most Progressive Neighborhoods

1 Haight
2 Potrero Hill
3 Mission
4 Buena Vista/Duboce
5 South of Market
6 Inner Mission
7 Hayes Valley
8 Bernal/Holly
9 Noe/Eureka
10 Inner Sunset

The 10 Most Liberal Neighborhoods

1 Haight
2 Hayes Valley
3 South of Market
4 Buena Vista/Duboce
5 Inner Mission
6 Mission
7 Western Addition
8 Bayview/Hunters Pt.
9 Potrero Hill
10 Bernal/Holly

The 10 Most Environmentalist Neighborhoods

1 Haight
2 Buena Vista/Duboce
3 Mission
4 Noe/Eureka
5 Inner Sunset
6 Potrero Hill
7 Polk Gulch
8 Bernal/Holly
9 Glen Park
10 Telegraph/N. Beach

The 10 Most Populist Neighborhoods

1 Potrero Hill
2 Inner Mission
3 Haight
4 Mission
5 South of Market
6 Bernal/Holly
7 Portola
8 Hayes Valley
9 Outer Sunset
10 Visitacion Valley

Bob Bathrick / SFSU GIS Center

San Francisco's famous Haight-Ashbury neighborhood, scene of the counterculture hippie community in the 1960s and current political headquarters of the city's progressive movement (top). A residential neighborhood in San Francisco's politically conservative West of Peaks area (bottom).

score and ranking on any one index are of limited value in predicting scores and rankings on the others. Dramatic examples are the Western Addition, which ranks 7th in liberalism, 33d in environmentalism, and 33d in populism, and Visitacion Valley, which ranks 16th in liberalism, 36th in environmentalism, and 10th in populism. Even a locally well-known conservative district like Pacific Heights ranks 16th in environmentalism, placing it in the "high" group of neighborhoods on that index.

A third point is that certain liberal neighborhoods (e.g., Bayview–Hunters Point) are politically miles apart from other liberal neighborhoods (e.g., Haight-Ashbury) on environmental issues. Progressive Haight residents usually vote Left on such questions, while liberal Bayview–Hunters Point residents tend to vote Right. Both neighborhoods are *liberal*, but only one of them is *progressive*: the Haight.

Political Implications

The three Lefts typology is a theoretically plausible and empirically grounded conceptual tool that simplifies analysis of San Francisco's political culture without doing excessive violence to its incredible richness and complexity. If that claim is accepted, the analysis just conducted poses a problem of ideology, which the city's new progressive leaders must solve. The progressive agenda is very ambitious and embraces all of the goals pursued by each of the three Lefts. But liberal, environmentalist, and populist leaders do not necessarily return the favor. Each Left has its own constituency, turf, and political interests to defend, as well as a political perspective that is mainly one-dimensional. Progressive leaders have ideological commitments that compel *strategic* efforts to build alliances and coalitions with elements of the three Lefts. In exchange, leaders of each Left can promise only *tactical* support of the more comprehensive and transformative progressive program. A major political challenge facing progressive leaders is how to translate ideology into strategy in such a way that their visions and principles are not compromised and yet are of sufficiently wide appeal to attract mass citizen support. Progressive leaders must ask themselves: Are the aspirations of the progressive movement internally consistent or self-contradictory? Are there limits to the movement's political carrying capacity in mobilizing mass support? Can the city's progressivism evolve in both theory and practice to the point that it can sustain the allegiance of a diverse citizenry while pursuing common goals that transcend group interests?

3

The Invention and Collapse
of the Progrowth Regime

This is a straight business proposition. . . . I think I'm going to make a lot of money out of it, or I wouldn't be spending all this time on it.

—Benjamin Swig

Power suffers, as in Shakespearian tragedy; the more it consolidates, the more afraid it is. It occupies space, but space trembles beneath it.

—Henri Lefebvre

Crumbling is not an instant's Act.

—Emily Dickinson

Dreams are important in the making and remaking of cities—especially if such dreams have profit in them. An old dream made San Francisco what it is today. A new dream views its predecessor as a nightmare and is shaping the San Francisco of tomorrow.

From the early 1960s to the mid-1980s, San Francisco's political universe had a gravitational center, a progrowth urban regime that brought order out of hyperpluralistic chaos. The city's top business and political leaders invented the progrowth regime to transform San Francisco into a growth machine.[1] The city's function would be to provide the physical and social means of capitalist production and accumulation within a global division of labor. The progrowth regime became the author of the city's vision, architect of its plans, and source of its power to get things done. Most of the city's far-flung influentials were drawn into orbits around it: mayors, planners, union bosses, civic leaders, real estate moguls, corporate executives, newspaper owners, and a majority of voters. The regime's definition of the city as a growth machine imposed a new urban meaning on the life of San Francisco, one that would have implications for the city's function and form.[2]

The progrowth regime accomplished much, for better and for worse. It changed

40

the face of San Francisco. In doing so, however, it fostered resistance among those the regime threatened or whose own dreams for the city were ignored. In dialectical fashion, the progrowth regime created the conditions that gave rise to its nemesis, the slow-growth movement. At the same time, the national economy provided the conditions that caused the progrowth regime to crumble from within. Caught between hammer and anvil, the progrowth regime collapsed in 1986 with passage of Proposition M, the Accountable Planning Initiative, which enacted the most stringent growth-control legislation of any large U.S. city. The architects of Proposition M rejected the growth machine image of the city. They saw the city as a place and not as a space, as a community and not as a commodity, as a democratic polity and not as a unit of corporate rule. What haunts them today is the ghost of the progrowth regime.

INVENTING THE PROGROWTH REGIME

Those who conceptualized the progrowth regime envisaged downtown San Francisco as the Bay Area's commercial, financial, and administrative headquarters linking the United States to an emerging transpacific urban community that included Singapore, Seoul, Hong Kong, Tokyo, and other cities of the Far East. This ambition to make San Francisco a "world class" city and a gateway to the Pacific Rim dates back to wartime planning studies in the early 1940s. John Mollenkopf quotes the city's first study on urban renewal in 1945: "San Francisco is to the Bay Region what the Island of Manhattan is to the New York Region."[3] Even then the development and land-use implications of this vision for the city were apparent: clearance of blighted areas near the downtown business district, particularly the Western Addition; removal of undesirable populations; improvements in regional transportation; and construction of high-rise office buildings. But this vision of the city's future remained dormant for more than a decade because an urban regime did not exist to plan strategy, mobilize resources, and coordinate efforts. From 1930 to 1958, for example, only one major office building was constructed in San Francisco.[4] The only "power to" evident in San Francisco's weak, decentralized political system was the power of ad hoc neighborhood groups and merchant associations to obstruct any citywide development projects that encroached on their turf—the Embarcadero and Central freeway projects, for instance, which opponents stopped literally in their tracks in the early 1950s.[5] San Franciscans had the power to stop great projects but not the power to build them. An effective regime structure had to be *invented* and put in place to convert the progrowth dream into reality.

Wirt, Mollenkopf, and Hartman all provide excellent accounts of how a progrowth coalition arose in San Francisco and organized an urban regime that supplied the strategic leadership, resource mobilization, and coordination required to guide and empower the city's dramatic transformation.[6] The Bay Area

Council (BAC), a regional planning body set up by the Bay Area's top corporations in 1946, developed a regional growth strategy and was instrumental in creating the BART system and the Metropolitan Transportation Commission (MTC). Industrialist James Zellerbach and stockbroker Charles Blyth founded the Blyth-Zellerbach (B-Z) Committee to catalyze renewal efforts in San Francisco itself. Committee membership overlapped considerably with the BAC and included the city's most powerful business leaders. The B-Z Committee established the San Francisco Planning and Urban Renewal Association (SPUR) to translate strategic visions into detailed plans and proposals for downtown renewal. Another SPUR objective was to mobilize government, business, and citizen support for redevelopment. To complete this structure, the mayor and other pivotal players at city hall were invited into the cockpit of the emerging new regime. In 1959, Mayor George Christopher appointed M. Justin Herman as executive director of the then-moribund San Francisco Redevelopment Agency (SFRA). Given free rein by Christopher to run his own shop, Herman rapidly expanded his staff of planners and consultants, brought in tens of millions of dollars in federal renewal subsidies, and worked closely with the mayor's office, SPUR, and his own business-dominated SFRA commission on eight substantial renewal projects. Under

Aerial view of San Francisco's "Manhattanized" downtown financial district looking south. The Mission Bay development project is shown in the upper left. The now-dismantled Embarcadero Freeway and parts of the waterfront near the Ferry Building are shown in the lower left and foreground.

Herman's leadership, the SFRA "became a powerful and aggressive army out to capture as much downtown land as it could: not only the Golden Gateway and the South of Market, but Chinatown, the Tenderloin, and the Port. Under the rubric of 'slum clearance' and 'blight removal,' the Agency turned to systematically sweeping out the poor, with the full backing of the city's power elite."[7]

The BAC, the B-Z Committee, SPUR, the mayor's office, and SFRA composed the institutional leadership core of a broader "progrowth coalition" of labor unions, newspaper owners, business associations, municipal authorities, and citizen groups that together formed a critical mass of political support.[8] In a socially fragmented, politically decentralized city, the progrowth coalition exercised preemptive power over the city's land-use and development policy. It cleared away whole sections of the city to make room for such major renewal projects as the Golden Gateway (a five-block office-hotel complex that includes the Embarcadero Center) and the still-unfinished Yerba Buena Center. It also opened the floodgates to downtown high-rise office construction. From 1965 to 1985, San Francisco's supply of downtown office space swelled from 26 million square feet to more than 60 million square feet, an annual growth rate of more than 1.4 million square feet per year.[9] Unquestionably, the progrowth coalition had organized an urban regime with a formidable capacity to get the job done. It paved a smooth road that led to a new San Francisco.

But was this vision of a new San Francisco one that most San Franciscans shared? In the early 1970s, the answer was yes. Based on his case studies of growth politics during that period, Frederick Wirt concluded that "most citizens by the bay put their money, votes, labor, and skills into another urban dream, in which not cable cars but gleaming new towers 'reach halfway to the stars.' These are the politics of income, in which the shared values of acquisition fuse most social strata into a coalition of mutual interest."[10] Residing safe in the avenues far from the scenes of destruction and renewal downtown, most San Franciscans bought into the dream of transforming the city into a West Coast Manhattan, a gleaming global gateway to the Pacific Rim. In that ambition were jobs, profits, and glory. Most of the people loved it and voted accordingly. And the politicians were eager to please.

SLOW GROWTH: FIRST STIRRINGS

At the time of Wirt's assessment in 1974, slow-growth opposition to the progrowth regime was still embryonic. Most organized protests were ad hoc, uncoordinated, and ineffectual. Even when there were victories, the alliances that achieved them quickly fell apart. That is exactly what happened, for example, after neighborhood groups successfully mobilized against freeway construction under the 1951 trafficways plan. Alarmed by threats to local communities and property values, neighborhood organizations and merchant associations combined to pressure the Board of Supervisors into junking the plan and halting construction where it stood. This alliance included such groups as the West Portal Home Owners' Association, the Marina Civic Improvement and Property Owners' Association, the Telegraph Hill Dwellers Association, the Council of District Merchants Associations, and the Central Council of Civic Clubs. After the board gave in to their demands in 1959, "neighborhood organizations fell into inactivity and the Central Council of Civic Clubs ceased to exist."[11]

From the beginning, there were some progressive activists and observers who saw the deeper economic forces and latent common interests linking these isolated attacks on the progrowth regime. The *Bay Guardian*'s polemic in their compilation of essays, *The Ultimate Highrise*, for example, warned of the wide-ranging threats to all aspects of urban life posed by unrestricted downtown development and high-rise construction.[12] Such synoptic critiques would later prove valuable to slow-growth leaders in fusing opposition to the progrowth regime. During this early period, however, the three Lefts traversed separate orbits around the progrowth regime—the environmentalists farthest out, the liberals closest in.

Environmentalists cared most about the broader threats of downtown growth to the quality of life, the environment, and the city's architectural heritage. These concerns were articulated colorfully by the city's leading columnist, Herb Caen, who railed against the high rises and questioned the "pellmell helter-skelter willingness to trade the God-given beauties of San Francisco for a mess of blottage."[13] Neighborhood populists reacted mainly against specific threats to local turf, community life, and property values, as the neighborhood revolt against the freeway plan illustrates. Liberals were more attracted to the progrowth regime than repelled by it because they saw it as a source of jobs for residents and new tax revenues. When the bulldozers began removing cheap housing and light industry to make room for office buildings and middle-class commuters, however, their support for the progrowth regime waned.

Low-rise Politics

Local businessman Alvin Duskin was one of the first slow-growth activists to dramatize the high-rise controversy as a citywide issue. Duskin and his followers put Proposition T on the ballot in 1971 to set a six-story limit on all future private and public construction in San Francisco. The voters overwhelmingly rejected this "low-rise" initiative 62 percent to 38 percent.[14] Duskin and supporters offered a watered-down version of the same initiative in 1972, this time proposing height limits of 160 feet on downtown construction, 40 feet elsewhere. The voters also rejected this measure, 57 percent to 43 percent.[15] Given these opportunities to clamp down on the process of "Manhattanization," only a minority of voters chose to do so. But the failed initiative campaigns did convey two important political messages: The minority in question was large and could easily become the majority; and citizen initiative campaigns were an effective instrument for mobilizing broad-based citizen protest against downtown development.

The Pseudo-Victory over U.S. Steel

Wirt's incisive case study of the anti-high-rise "victory" in 1971 over the U.S. Steel Corporation shows how weak and disorganized the slow-growth movement was at that time. It also provides further evidence that *citywide* debates on growth control issues during this period were cast almost entirely in environmentalist and conservationist terms. The nub of the case is that U.S. Steel lost its bid for approval of a 550-foot height limit that would have allowed construction of a twenty-five-story hotel and a forty-story office building over the water south of the Ferry Building. Slow-growth won, progrowth lost. But as Wirt points out, the U.S. Steel proposal was not defeated by "outraged public opinion" or by the actions of "ad hoc conservation groups" and architectural preservationists, who objected to it mainly on aesthetic grounds.[16] Public opinion generally supported the proposal, and the conservationist groups, as one opposition leader admitted, "were just too disorganized, too petty and too poor to really stop those projects."[17] What really thwarted the U.S. Steel proposal was the "miracle" intervention and rejection by the Bay Conservation and Development Commission (BCDC), a state-established regulatory agency with jurisdiction over development projects close to the Bay shore.

Proletarian Flurry in the Western Addition

In the redevelopment arena during this period, prolonged and bitter confrontations took place between SFRA and residents of the Western Addition and Yerba Buena project sites. At stake in these struggles were community preservation, not architectural or historical preservation, and the material means of life (particularly housing and jobs), not the aesthetic quality of life.

In the mid-1960s, SFRA began implementing redevelopment plans on two sites (A-1 and A-2) in the Western Addition, an area located near city hall and only minutes away from the central business district. SFRA planners had targeted the Western Addition for redevelopment years before, describing it as blighted, substandard, and rife with social pathologies. The Western Addition did have its problems, but it was also a thriving urban village with an ethnically diverse population and a strong sense of community identity. Its residents were predominately African American, poor, and the beneficiaries of cheap housing. Encountering little organized resistance, the A-1 project displaced four thousand households to build a Japanese trade center, luxury residences, and a major expressway through the area.[18] The larger A-2 project that followed, however, ran into stiff opposition from residents, who demanded a halt to construction of a new housing complex until an acceptable program was instituted for relocating displaced residents to decent and affordable housing in the neighborhood.

The Western Addition Community Organization (WACO) was formed to lead the battle against SFRA and the A-2 project. WACO and its supporters employed a variety of tactics, including organized protests and demonstrations. An injunction was also filed by the San Francisco Neighborhood Legal Assistance Foundation on WACO's behalf against relocation, demolition, and federal funding pending an acceptable relocation plan.[19] Although the legal action failed and although SFRA's Herman firmly dismissed WACO as a "passing flurry of proletarianism,"[20] this organized neighborhood revolt did force the creation of an agency to monitor displacement and stimulated an increase in subsidized housing construction.[21] Mayor Joseph Alioto, in an effort to mobilize community support and to buy some peace in the project area, appointed many African Americans to SFRA, making it a more representative body in its dealings with neighborhood groups.[22]

Yerba Buena Center: The Endless Journey

The Yerba Buena project was conceived in 1954 by Ben Swig, real estate magnate, philanthropist, and community leader. The original plans called for a convention center, sports stadium, high-rise office building, and large parking garage to be constructed in the South of Market area. This neighborhood was directly in the path of projected expansion of the downtown financial district. After many stalls and long delays, the SFRA under Justin Herman received more than $20 million in federal grants and began demolition and population displacement in 1966. Labor unions, businesses, and South of Market residents immediately organized to oppose the project. The labor unions protested the loss of blue-collar jobs that would result from remaking the area into a financial and service center. Residents wanted decent and affordable replacement housing within the project boundaries. Mayor Joseph Alioto, elected in 1967 with strong organized labor support, eventually persuaded leaders of the Labor Council, Building Construction and Trades Council, ILWU, and other unions to endorse the project—starting a pattern of labor union support for progrowth proposals that would persist into the 1980s. The area's residents continued to resist, however, and coalesced with local merchants to form the Tenants and Owners in Opposition to Redevelopment (TOOR), fighting the project mainly through legal channels. Herman and SFRA rejected TOOR's proposal for two thousand units of new and rehab housing within the project area, primarily because, in Barbara Ferman's words, they "wanted to change the demographics of the area."[23] SFRA also thwarted Mayor Alioto's efforts to negotiate a settlement with TOOR out of court.

After Herman died in 1971, Alioto and his attorneys had a freer hand in bargaining with TOOR, and a deal was struck in 1973 giving residents around two thousand replacement housing units in or near the area in return for TOOR's dropping its legal suit against the city.[24] Five years of complicated legal battles, protests, and bureaucratic in-fighting then gave way to another five years of the same, this time around issues involving project design, financing schemes, and environmental impacts. In 1978, after scaling down the project, securing voter approval, and settling remaining lawsuits, the city received a green light to begin construction. In 1980, the city contracted with a Canadian development firm, Olympia and York, in partnership with Marriott Hotels, to build the project. After another decade of delays, voter amendments, financing hurdles, and developer foot-dragging, *final* approvals were obtained, and on 2 July 1990, Olympia and York delivered a check for $4.4 million to Mayor Art Agnos as an installment on amenities for the $1.5-billion project.[25] To date, the only part of the project that has been completed is the Moscone Convention Center, which opened in 1981. After more than twenty-five years of progrowth–slow-growth thrusting and parrying, Ben Swig's dream is still mainly a hole in the ground.

THE FIRST PROGRESSIVE WAVE: THE MOSCONE YEARS

The slow-growth coalition was a political wheel that had to be reinvented again and again until 1975, when the outlines of a more permanent and powerful alliance began to appear. Before George Moscone's mayoral campaign, liberals, environmentalists, and populists had mounted separate offensives in diverse arenas against different negative aspects of redevelopment and high-rise construction. Now, for the first time, elements of the three Lefts came together for a combined assault on the city hall pillar of the progrowth regime.

The year 1975 was thus a turning point in San Francisco politics. The tides of demographic and economic change were at maximum flow. New populations that were streaming into the city, settling into enclaves, and beginning to assert themselves politically included gays and lesbians, Latinos from Central America, ethnic Chinese from Southeast Asia, and middle-class professionals in search of an urban quality of life. Growing numbers of high rises were jutting from the downtown central business district, and the Manhattanization of San Francisco was in full swing. The social and aesthetic consequences of unmanaged growth had ceased to be merely irritating and were beginning to assault San Franciscans where they lived in the Western Addition, South of Market, the North Beach district, Clement Street, Potrero Hill, and other neighborhoods.[26] Meanwhile, neighborhood activists were organizing to move from the defense to offense in preparing to battle city hall and the downtown business establishment. During this moment of transition a window of political opportunity opened. Joseph Alioto was stepping down as mayor, restricted by law from running for a third term. City hall and all its power beckoned to the ambitious, and one of them was George Moscone.

The three principal candidates in the 1975 mayoral campaign covered the ideological gamut from Left to Right. On the Right was Supervisor John Barbagelata, a conservative populist advocate of the city's older white home-owner districts. In the center was Board President Dianne Feinstein, a self-described progrowth moderate who had run unsuccessfully against Alioto in 1971. And on the Left was State Senator George Moscone, a liberal Democrat, former supervisor, and member of Congressman Phillip Burton's inner circle (the vaunted "Burton Machine," which at the time also included Phillip's brother John and Assemblyman Willie Brown).

Moscone's campaign was a dramatic departure from San Francisco's political traditions. In building his grass-roots electoral coalition, he reached out for the support of neighborhood activists, high-rise opponents, African Americans, Latinos, Asians, gays and lesbians, and other community groups previously neglected by establishment politicians. He attacked the progrowth policies of the Alioto administration and promised to end the Manhattanization of San Francisco. Unimpressed by progrowth trickle-down theories, he promised unemployed workers and low-income renters that he would give a high priority to creating jobs and affordable housing for residents. A strong gay rights advocate and civil rights liberal, Moscone committed his administration to eliminating homophobia and racial prejudice in the city's departments and agencies. He also promised to use his appointments to expand representation of ethnic minority groups and gays and lesbians on the city's boards and commissions. He directed few appeals for support to downtown business elites, and he worked around rather than through the Democratic party. He gave his campaign an unmistakable populist twist by refusing to accept donations of over one hundred dollars. In 1975, all of this seemed very new—a political breakthrough that inspired many citizens and threatened others.[27]

On election day, Moscone received 45 percent of the vote, while Barbagelata edged Feinstein 28 percent to 27 percent for the second spot in a run-off election. In that contest, after a hard-fought campaign, Moscone beat Barbagelata by the paper-thin margin of four thousand votes, becoming the next mayor of San Francisco. His supporters were euphoric and expectations were high. As the new mayor would discover, however, gaining power was much easier than exercising it. Confronting him were the obstacles posed by the city's bureaucracy and the Board of Supervisors.

Mayor Moscone quickly delivered on his promise of empowerment by appointing a transition commission to recruit people from the gay and minority communities and from the neighborhoods for slots on the city's boards and agencies. His appointments of slow-growth leaders to the Planning Commission and the Redevelopment Agency pleased the environmentalists and neighborhood activists. Although neither of these government bodies actually did much under Moscone to dispel their progrowth reputation, the Planning Commission was still tagged as "anti-growth" by downtown business leaders.[28] From the slow-growth perspective, there were some tangible successes. For example, Moscone's Planning Commission helped to design the city's innovative downtown linkage fees, and his Redevelopment Agency began to consult more with the community and to bulldoze less.

Some of Moscone's appointments later proved embarrassing or bred deep resentments in the agencies affected. He installed Jim Jones, a leftist preacher and superb political organizer, as head of the city's Housing Authority Commission. Two years later the Reverend Jim Jones led hundreds of his People's Temple followers into Guyana and mass murder-suicide. Moscone appointed Charles Gain as police chief with a mandate to liberalize the Police Department and halt police harassment of gays and racial minorities. Chief Gain's efforts were resisted by rank-and-file cops and their conservative allies, many of whom were incensed by Gain's decision to paint police cars a kinder, gentler baby blue. Moscone also named gay activist Harvey Milk to the Board of Permit Appeals but then quickly fired him when Milk announced his decision to run for the assembly against Art Agnos, a member of the Burton Machine.

During Moscone's short tenure as mayor, the Board of Supervisors repeatedly thwarted his legislative agenda and his efforts to control the bureaucracy. At that time (and now) the eleven board members were elected at large to staggered four-year terms. Incumbency advantage almost guaranteed reelection; strong challengers were hard to find and to fund. Ideologically, the board as a whole was right of center, and conservatives John Barbagelata and Quentin Kopp were effective in persuading the moderates to vote against the mayor's programs. (Kopp, in particular, was a formidable rival who was positioning himself to run against Moscone in the 1979 mayoral election.) The board had sufficient votes to block Moscone's nomination of Rudy Nothenberg as CAO, partly on grounds that Nothenberg lacked business experience and would be too politically aligned with the mayor.[29] The compromise choice for CAO was Roger Boas, an auto dealer and former supervisor. The board also humbled the pro-union mayor by denying wage increases to city craftworkers and then refusing to negotiate when they struck. The board's anti-union stance was popular with voters, and Moscone could do little more than offer striking workers his symbolic support.[30]

Long before Moscone's election in 1975, community activists had viewed the Board of Supervisors as a conservative bulwark against progressive leadership and reforms. Many of them blamed the at-large system of electing supervisors, arguing that it favored candidates who were unresponsive to neighborhood concerns and were obliged to downtown businesses for the campaign contributions needed to win in citywide elections. In 1970, these activists organized themselves as Citizens for Representative Government (CRG), aiming to replace the at-large system with district-based elections. The specific district plan developed by CRG divided the city into eleven election districts and required that candidates be residents of the district they sought to represent. This plan and a variant were rejected by the voters in 1972 and 1973, but the margins of defeat revealed widespread dissatisfaction with the at-large system. This encouraged CRG and other progressive groups in 1975 to form the Community Congress, an umbrella organization that conducted a series of meetings throughout the city to educate voters about the advantages of district elections in responding to neighborhood concerns. At a later citywide convention, nearly one thousand participants adopted "A Community Program for Change in San Francisco," a progressive manifesto that featured district elections as the centerpiece of proposed structural reforms. Moscone supported these efforts and also the formation of San Franciscans for District Elections, a broad coalition of neighborhood and citywide groups that placed an eleven-district initiative on the November 1976 election ballot as Proposition T. Facing only token opposition from overconfident downtown business leaders, Proposition T won, 52 percent to 48 percent. After the voters rejected two separate repeal measures at a special election in August 1977, the first district-based election was held in November of that year.[31]

A total of 113 candidates ran in the eleven districts, about four times the typical number in at-large elections. Six board incumbents (including Dianne Feinstein, John Molinari, and Quentin Kopp) campaigned in separate districts, and all were reelected. Five incumbents (including John Barbagelata) chose not to run, thus guaranteeing turnover no matter what the outcome. The five new supervisors included gay activist Harvey Milk of District 5, representing the gay/progressive Haight-Ashbury, Castro, and Noe Valley neighborhoods, and Dan White of District 8, representing the predominately white, Catholic, working-class households in Visitacion Valley, Crocker Amazon, Portola, and Excelsior. Harvey Milk personified the progressive hope, and Dan White the conservative fear, that would fatally collide in city hall on 27 November 1978.

Harvey Milk had moved to San Francisco from Manhattan in 1972 and had quickly established himself as a skillful politician with progressive ideas. After consolidating a power base as "the Mayor of Castro Street," he inspired an emerging national gay movement by running for supervisor as an openly gay candidate and winning. Dan White was a native San Franciscan, Vietnam veteran, former police officer, and firefighter. He represented a declining constituency that resented the growing gay and minority populations and also the new liberal mayor who seemed so eager to cater to them. An excerpt from White's campaign literature conveys the animosity expressed by many in these "forgotten" parts of the city: "I am not going to be forced out of San Francisco by splinter groups of radicals, social deviates and incorrigibles. You must realize there are thousands upon thousands of frustrated angry people such as yourselves waiting to unleash a fury that can and will eradicate the malignancies which blight our beautiful city."[32]

White resigned his seat eleven months after taking office, citing family finances as the main reason. After supporters implored him to change his mind, he asked for his seat back a few days later. Initially sympathetic, Moscone gave in several weeks later to pressures from his own backers to deny White's request and to appoint liberal Don Horanzy to White's vacated seat. In response to these and other frustrations, White sneaked into City Hall on 27 November and shot and killed George Moscone and Harvey Milk. The trial that followed bitterly divided the city. White was seen as a hero by many San Franciscans, including the police and firefighters who raised over $100,000 for White's defense fund. Many in the gay and progressive community felt that the jury was stacked in White's favor and that the prosecution was deliberately inept. The jury found Dan White guilty of voluntary manslaughter for firing four bullets into George Moscone, reloading, then discharging five more into Harvey Milk. White was sentenced to seven years and eight months in jail for his crime. (He was paroled in 1984; he later committed suicide.) The night of the sentencing, gays and others exploded in outrage, battled with police, and burned seven police cars. This violent episode became known as the White Night riot.[33] San Francisco's progressive movement had collapsed in tears and anger.

Some analysts have described George Moscone as a "weak" mayor and have compared him invidiously with "strong" mayors like Joseph Alioto.[34] Such judgments might be warranted if the focus is restricted to the exercise of power and political skill. As a pure politician, Moscone made mistakes—and he was given no time to learn from them. But Moscone also aspired to be the city's first progressive mayor, not merely a liberal mayor in the mold of Alioto. He widened the doors of City Hall to let more people in—perhaps too many for his own political good. His appointments pierced established bureaucracies and transfused new blood and progressive ideas into city government.[35] Within his limited powers and against great obstacles, he challenged the conservative establishment and the downtown business elite. At the very least he made progressive government thinkable. If he was weak, it might be only because he decided to swim upstream rather than downstream in the treacherous currents of San Francisco politics.

THE FEINSTEIN INTERREGNUM

The Moscone-Milk assassinations shattered the emerging progressive movement by eliminating two key leaders, traumatizing the citizenry, and installing Board of Supervisors President Dianne Feinstein in the mayor's office as Moscone's successor under the city charter. Mayor Feinstein's centrist inclinations were reinforced by the tragic violence that brought her to power. "The City is best run from the center of the political spectrum," she said, "rather than from either extreme."[36] The path of social change that had moved sharply leftward under Mayor Moscone, albeit against stiff resistance, now veered just as sharply back toward the status quo ante under Mayor Feinstein.

Soon after assuming office, Mayor Feinstein fired Police Chief Gain and directed that all police cars be repainted black and white. In 1980, with her support, voters dismantled the district election system, restoring the at-large system. With her encouragement, developers built high rises at "breakneck speed," erecting the equivalent of thirty-seven Transamerica Pyramids between 1979 and 1985.[37] Against the resistance of an increasingly progressive Board of Supervisors, she vetoed domestic partners legislation, provoking an infuriated gay and lesbian community into supporting an unsuccessful recall election in 1983. She boosted the home-porting of the USS *Missouri*, using the trickle-down argument that such an arrangement with the U.S. Navy would generate a net increase in blue-collar jobs. She defended the progrowth regime from attacks long after downtown business leaders themselves had abandoned their own defense.

If the Feinstein administration is judged by the policy checklist of the progressive agenda, one would have to conclude it was a retrograde failure on nearly every point. On the other hand, Feinstein's centrist political instincts may have been well adapted to the requirements of governance during this period of turmoil. Sheldon Wolin writes that the "order of problems with which political judgment has to deal is concerned with the achievement of tentative stabilities within a situation of conflict."[38] He also argues that "one of the continuing tasks of statecraft is to discover at what points disagreement, conflict, and variety may be tolerated without their endangering the supporting framework that makes waywardness possible."[39] By these standards, one might plausibly describe Feinstein's performance as mayor as a success. Her centrist policies helped to secure the supporting framework that made progressive "waywardness" possible years later under Mayor Art Agnos. At the time she assumed office, however, San Francisco was not yet ripe for progressive government. Her opponent Calvin Welch would later characterize her administration as an "interregnum" and a "historical anomaly."[40] But it was a politically necessary hiatus—one that achieved system stability at the price of policy backsliding.

SLOW-GROWTH LESSONS

Most of the early slow-growth revolts were directed not against the progrowth regime itself but against isolated development *projects* in specific places that threatened the values of distinct constituencies. In Castells's terms, San Francisco during this period was still a "wild city."[41] The grass-roots alliance that elected George Moscone as mayor had raised hopes that a new political order was in the making. When the assassinations abruptly dashed those hopes, it became clear that leaders were tragically mortal and laws highly perishable in the polarized society that San Francisco had become. With four or more years of a centrist progrowth administration ahead under Mayor Feinstein, slow-growth leaders realized that it was necessary to circumvent city hall and to change policy directly. To mobilize an effective attack on the progrowth *regime* would require: a broad-based coalition that embraced all three Lefts and responded effectively to the constituency demands of each; a long-term campaign of slow-growth opposition through multiple institutional channels (the courts, ballot initiatives, planning bureaucracies, and public opinion); a high degree of technical knowledge and skill in the intricacies of land-use and development planning; a structural understanding of the underlying causes and broader impacts of unrestricted growth; and an alternative, positive vision for the future of San Francisco—a new urban meaning, a new dream—that would inspire citizens to sacrifice and fight. But even before slow-growth leaders had translated these lessons into the victory of Proposition M, the progrowth regime had already begun to fall apart.

CRUMBLINGS

Why did the progrowth regime that had run the city and charted its future for a quarter of a century come tumbling down in the mid-1980s? Briefly, it collapsed from the inside and was crushed from the outside. The internal collapse partly resulted from the dissolution of the entrepreneurial core of *local* business leaders (the Swigs, Zellerbachs, and Blyths). J. D. Zellerbach died in 1963, and Charles Blyth moved to New York. At the same time, corporate takeovers and mergers brought in management-oriented executives with fewer ties to San Francisco.[42] This created a leadership vacuum in a city whose own business leaders have been characterized as "too slow, too nice, and too clubby to meet the threat of a changing economy."[43] That threat was all too real and took many forms: the continued globalization of production made possible by improvements in information technology; the local impact of massive corporate restructuring; increasingly formidable competition from other cities in the region; the corruption and breakdown of national financial institutions; federal government cutbacks in development subsidies and urban assistance; federal tax reforms that made it less profitable to lose money; the chaos brewing in commercial real estate markets; the emergence of growth-control movements aimed at imprisoning capital in urban built environments; and declining public confidence—a "legitimation crisis"—in capitalism itself. These forces were positioning San Francisco on the brink of hard times, but aggressive business leadership loyal to the city had vanished.

Corporate restructuring (i.e., takeovers and mergers) took its toll on the progrowth regime. The whole point had been to remake San Francisco into the Bay Area's headquarters city, the administrative and financial heart of the region. Yet corporate restructuring between 1979 and 1986 made San Francisco a "net loser" of *Fortune* 500 companies, while the Silicon Valley cities in the South Bay (Santa Clara and San Mateo counties) were net gainers at San Francisco's expense.[44] A Bay Area Council study concluded, "As a historical hub in the Bay Area region, San Francisco does seem to have suffered from its recent history of corporate restructuring." Further, the "recent economic shifts toward concentration in high technology" in the South Bay "have imperceptibly shifted the economic center of gravity away from San Francisco."[45] Although some of San Francisco's business leaders later would blame Proposition M and the city's "hostile business climate" for these reversals of fortune, BAC, the business community's own leading think tank, was aware that the workings of capitalism itself were to blame.

In addition to the effects of leadership failure and corporate restructuring, the progrowth regime also collapsed from financial earthquakes whose epicenters were located in Washington, D.C. The first temblor was caused by the 1981 Economic Recovery Tax Act and the 1982 Garn–St. Germain Depository Act (savings and loan deregulation bill). The first act shortened the period for depreciation write-offs on real estate investments, thus increasing the tax-shelter benefits of owning real property in syndicated partnerships. These incentives spawned the tax syndication industry, which amassed billions of dollars ($12.7 billion in 1985 alone[46]) for speculative investments in commercial real estate, particularly office buildings. The second act put a large amount of capital into the inexperienced (and in some cases corrupt) hands of savings and loan lenders, who in turn poured more billions of dollars into commercial real estate. Hearing the invitation to build and enrich themselves in San Francisco, developers rushed in with no worries about leasing tenants beforehand or financing their projects. Investors stood to profit even if the buildings were vacant. In 1986, after a gush of high-rise construction, San Francisco's commercial office vacancy rate peaked at 18 percent for Class A space.[47] The city's progrowth regime feasted on surplus capital.

It is worth pausing here to make what only appears to be a digression about political economy and system legitimation. What can describe these movements of capital and their impact on local polities? The word *irrational* leaps to mind as a term an average citizen might use in trying to make sense of turbulent economic processes. The word adds nothing to an understanding of those processes, but it does convey a feeling of perplexity and irritation toward capitalist society. When the "law" of supply and demand appears to behave in mysterious and unpredictable ways, public confidence in the private sector begins to fade and the legitimacy of unregulated markets becomes suspect. A leftist scholar writing in the Marxian tradition might use *accumulation crisis* to characterize these processes and their outcomes. Surplus capital accumulates (in syndicates, banks, and pension funds), seeks outlets through the secondary circuit of capital (speculative investments in land, high rises, hotels, and ownership of things that do not yet exist), drives up prices (and other market indicators that presumably signal what things are really worth), yields short-term profits (in the form of rents, interest payments, and dividends), but eventually must be devalued (in the form of write-downs, write-offs, plant closings, and disinvestment), thus causing crises that are geographically uneven in their effects on regions and cities.[48]

In context, the term *accumulation crisis* does illuminate the apparently irrational workings of American capitalism. Since many may dismiss it as disagreeably Marxist in origin, the description by Randall K. Rowe, who calls these same processes a "capital orgy," may be a palatable substitute. Rowe, executive vice-president of Equity Financial and Management Company of Chicago, made this analysis in the *National Real Estate Investor* trade journal: "Instead of funding our federal budget deficit with domestic sourced capital, we borrowed offshore capital so that we could build empty buildings. Instead of investing more capital in our factories so we could be more competitive in the world markets, we built empty buildings. Instead of investing capital in programs that would have increased the human capital of this country (education, job training, etc.), we built empty buildings."[49] This capitalist, addressing other capitalists, was saying that capitalism had gone haywire, had become irrational to the point of undermining public confidence in the market system itself. In San Francisco and other large U.S. cities, fissures were appearing in what Jürgen Habermas calls "the legitimation system" that supports capitalist society: "With the appearance of functional weaknesses in the market and dysfunctional side effects of the steering mechanism, the basic bourgeois ideology of fair exchange collapses. Re-coupling the economic system to the political—which in a way repoliticizes the relations of production—creates an increased need for legitimation."[50] The un-couplings and re-couplings of economy and polity have occurred many times before. The legitimation crises that followed were somehow always resolved, usually at the national level. In the Reagan era, however, cities were compelled to perform the re-coupling and legitimation on their own. In San Francisco, these adaptive processes took place (and are still taking place) in a culture of progressivism.

In the middle of the "capital orgy" came more financial earthquakes. Congress passed the Tax Reform Act of 1986, greatly reducing the tax-shelter benefits of real estate investments. Speculative mobile capital from that source dried up almost immediately as a result (e.g., the tax syndication industry raised only $3.5 billion in 1989[51]). Meanwhile, near the end of the decade, federal regulators began to crack down on the out-of-control savings and loans and even the commercial banks. Compelled to be prudent and rational, lenders began tightening credit and imposing harsh terms on developers—such as demanding pre-leasing of buildings, equity partnerships, and so on. These events in the *national* financial and commercial real estate markets trickled down to San Francisco, one result being that many city-approved high-rise projects now exist only on blueprints because they do not have the financing to be built. Feast turned into famine.

Just as an airplane will develop cracks in its hull from changes in pressure after too many flights, San Francisco's progrowth regime began to crack from oscillating pressures in the secondary circuit of capital. These stresses were nonlocal in origin and had little to do with the city's business climate or the vagaries of slow-growth politics. The most important fracture that appeared in the progrowth regime was the growing conflict of interests between landlords and investors, who already owned commercial property and/or had permits to build, and the developers, architects, and others who wished to build but lacked the capital or permits to do so. With commercial office vacancy rates high, construction of new buildings would simply lower the rents that might be charged to existing tenants. Commercial landlords such as Walter Shorenstein, who owns or manages over twelve million square feet of properties in the city, had less incentive under these conditions to support any policy that would increase supply.[52] These kinds of fissures in the city's downtown business community were caused internally or from afar and were not the effects of local slow-growth mobilizations or policies. Instead, they undermined the progrowth regime and made it more vulnerable to political attack and final collapse.

The progrowth regime's economic development strategies fostered the growth of a professional middle class and a postindustrial petty bourgeoisie. These new San Franciscans had the knowledge and skill required to cope with social and political complexity, and their postmaterialist sensibilities were affronted by the overbuilt and congested environment in which they worked and lived. They formed the nucleus of a slow-growth coalition that expanded to include neighborhood activists, tenant union leaders, small business owners, and disillusioned ethnic minorities. As discussed in the next chapter, this coalition eventually achieved a critical mass that crushed the weakened progrowth regime on its downward trajectory.

A plausible case can be made that the progrowth regime over a long period of time created the instrument of its own destruction. By overbuilding office space, it produced a surplus that divided the interests of the business community. By inducing formation of a service economy, it encouraged a new middle class of slow-growth postmaterialists while displacing blue-collar workers who supported progrowth materialist goals. By Manhattanizing the downtown financial district, menacing nearby neighborhoods, obliterating sunlight, accelerating housing costs, burdening the infrastructure, and snarling traffic, the progrowth coalition assaulted the environmentalist sensibilities and communal identities of the new populations it had brought forth. By displacing the poor, creating high-end jobs for commuters, and building housing for the rich, the progrowth promises of "small opportunities" for low-income minorities and resident workers could not be kept. In effect, the progrowth regime's social production performance significantly altered the physical and social environment that had originally given rise to the progrowth regime. The collective goals first set for the progrowth regime had begun to change dramatically. To many residents, that regime had become vestigial and even dysfunctional. A fundamental shift took place in the struggle over urban meaning—a struggle that took concrete form in the battle over Proposition M.

4

The Birth of the Slow-Growth
Movement and the Battle
for Proposition M

Capitalist production, government investment, private consumption, and public house-keeping all find their nexus in land use. Land use is, in fact, a cool, technocratic euphemism for the organization and production of our entire existence.

—Sidney Plotkin

Cities are human resource complexes and built environments that contain a significant fraction of capital's fixed investment in the social and physical means of production.[1] Even taking into account the globalization of production and improved information technologies that foster "placeless power" and "powerless places,"[2] capital at some point in its circulation must take concrete form in places and things, factories and buildings, which are, in Marx's words, "welded fast to the surface of the earth."[3] Much of that welding of capital has occurred in cities and is therefore potentially hostage to local governmental jurisdictions and political processes. As David Harvey writes, "The circulation of capital is increasingly imprisoned within immobile physical and social infrastructures which are crafted to support certain kinds of production, certain kinds of labor processes, distributional arrangements, consumption patterns, and so on."[4] The confinement of capital in urban built environments is the consequence of what Harvey calls the "second nature" of capitalism—the production of an increasingly urbanized space, which he believes has allowed capitalism to survive into the twentieth century.[5]

Within the city's legal limits, the powers of local citizens are not trivial in regard to the use of land and space. M. Gottdiener observes that "building codes, zoning regulations, historical preservation, variances, and so on, are some of the forms that State control of land and space can take. Among all the powers ascribed to the local State by other levels of government, in fact, this ability is most central."[6] Capitalists have little to fear from cities as long as local residents stay

57

dutifully within their Petersonian "city limits" and delegate land-use and develop-ment policy-making to business leaders and professional planners. Once the gates to this policy arena are opened to wider citizen participation, however, capitalists have good reason to worry about the disposition of their investments in urban land and property. Those gates have been opened in San Francisco.

On 4 November 1986, San Francisco voters passed Proposition M, the Ac-countable Planning Initiative, thus enacting the most restrictive growth-control measure of any large U.S. city. Passage of Proposition M hastened the crumbling of the progrowth regime. It allowed expanded citizen participation in the city's development policy arena. It set new rules for the land-use game and altered the terms of the city's public-private partnership with business. It imposed order and discipline on the local commercial real estate market. Most important, it laid the foundations for building a new urban regime.

BACKGROUND

To recapitulate the state of affairs circa 1970, the progrowth coalition had com-plete command of San Francisco's physical and economic development. The dream of remaking San Francisco into a West Coast Manhattan was rapidly taking solid form as skyscrapers went up, BART tracks were laid, and lands were cleared for redevelopment. It was a dream that captivated most San Franciscans, who conceded control over development policy to the strategic leadership of down-town business elites and their city hall allies. The city's development politics during this period could be described as consensual, despite sporadic, uncoordi-nated resistance from neighborhood activists, displaced low-income residents, and middle-class conservationists.

San Francisco Bay Guardian journalists and other progressives had begun sounding alarms in the late 1960s about the long-term social and environmental consequences of downtown high-rise development. Alvin Duskin's anti-high-rise initiative campaigns in 1971 and 1972 triggered broader public concern about growth as a citywide issue. But an organized slow-growth *movement* did not begin to take shape until 1975, when a number of neighborhood associations, environ-mentalists, small businesses, political clubs, ethnic minority groups, gay and lesbian organizations, tenant groups, and labor unions came together in a grass-roots coalition to elect progressive George Moscone as mayor. Moscone had promised his supporters that, if elected, he would not allow another high rise to be built during his administration. That was a promise he was unable to keep. Any lingering hopes that Mayor Moscone might fulfill his pledges of growth control ended abruptly with his assassination in 1978. By that time, however, the slow-growth movement was walking on its own legs.

The city's leading environmental organizations (particularly San Franciscans for Reasonable Growth and San Francisco Tomorrow) formed a loose but stable alliance with various Democratic political clubs, tenant unions, small business associations, neighborhood preservationists, and community activists in Haight-Ashbury, Duboce Triangle, Potrero Hill, and other areas. This alliance became the organizational core of the slow-growth wing of the broader progressive movement that would build up political steam over the nine years of Mayor Feinstein's administration.

Against this background, there are three general observations to be made about the development of the slow-growth movement over the period studied here. First, the slow-growth movement expanded, in fits and starts, to include constituencies typically excluded from similar movements elsewhere, particularly working-class home owners, low-income renters, and ethnic minorities. This evolution broadened the movement's social base, but it also produced internal contradictions that taxed the slow-growth coalition's political carrying capacity and its ability to govern in the post–Proposition M era.

Second, the slow-growth movement's success was cumulative over a series of initiative campaigns, most of which failed electorally. That long-term success was achieved in part through a dialectical process of threatening substantial reforms that frightened progrowth leaders into making unilateral minor reforms and concessions aimed at preempting voter support for more drastic measures. Incrementally, these minor reforms added up to a major transformation of how development policy was made. They slowly eroded the ideological foundations of the progrowth regime, and they made each successive slow-growth initiative appear less drastic and therefore less threatening than the ones that preceded it.

Third, the slow-growth movement eventually broke through with Proposition M not so much because the movement had gained strength as because the progrowth opposition had weakened after 1983, collapsing completely in 1986. Mayor Feinstein's political armory almost recaptured the field, but eventually the fragmented downtown business community was defeated at the ballot box by slow-growth forces. The victory of Proposition M was not only a great triumph for the city's progressive movement but also a surrender of business elites to their own worst enemy: themselves.

THE LONG ROAD TO PROPOSITION M

In 1979, progressive leaders saw no prospect of slow-growth reforms coming from city hall. Even during Mayor Moscone's administration, the rate of high-rise construction had changed little from that of the previous five years. With Moscone now gone, there was no hope at all that Dianne Feinstein, a moderate, progrowth mayor, would respond to the concerns of environmentalists and neighborhood activists. Slow-growth leaders had little choice but to wage a guerilla war against the planning bureaucracy, to block progrowth policies in the courts, and to appeal directly to the voters through the initiative process.

Proposition O: Battle Alarms

San Franciscans for Reasonable Growth (SFRG) placed Proposition O on the November 1979 ballot, intending to reduce the height and bulk limits on new downtown construction. The initiative also called for a revised bonus system that would allow developers to exceed the new limits in return for public transit improvements, energy conservation designs, additional affordable housing, and other measures mitigating the impact of growth on the city's infrastructure and quality of life. Leading the fight against Proposition O was San Francisco Forward (SFF), a coalition of downtown business interests and labor unions. During the campaign, SFF leaders spent half a million dollars to convince voters that Proposition O would discourage business, eliminate jobs and tax revenues, and promote urban sprawl. Outspent by a ratio of more than ten to one and committed to a measure widely perceived as antigrowth and narrowly aesthetic in its goals, Proposition O supporters had good reason to brace for a lopsided defeat.

To the surprise of many, Proposition O received 46 percent of the vote—an impressive result that encouraged the slow-growthers and rang some alarms in the downtown business community. The campaign itself politicized debate about growth issues, exposed the conflict in public opinion regarding development goals, and began the painstaking process of educating voters about the negative effects of unrestricted growth. The closeness of the vote signaled the burgeoning power of the anti-high-rise movement and its potential to wreak democratic havoc in the development arena. The last thing leaders of the progrowth regime wanted was ad hoc reactive planning by citizen initiative. To deter future initiative campaigns, the Planning Commission was forced to respond—modestly and haltingly—to slow-growth arguments and demands.

Developer Linkage Fees: Tickets to Ride

As early as the summer of 1979, the Planning Commission began imposing transit mitigation requirements on building permit applications. In 1981, the mayor and the Board of Supervisors instituted a one-time development fee of five dollars per square foot on new downtown office buildings to pay for increased public transportation services. Initial city hall support for a special transit assessment district (which would have required not only new buildings but also existing ones to pay an annual fee per square foot) disintegrated under attacks led by real estate magnate Walter Shorenstein and the Chamber of Commerce. To address housing concerns, the city established the Office Housing Production Program (OHPP), which exacted formula-based fees from developers to subsidize construction of at least some new or rehabilitated housing to meet the needs of workers employed in downtown office buildings. Such fees had been imposed for years on a project-by-project basis under the mandates of the California Environmental Quality Act, which defined growth-induced problems in the housing market as environmental impacts requiring relief. The OHPP codified mitigation rules in a rather slippery formula that allowed developers to fulfill housing commitments by accumulating variable "credits" for different kinds of housing. Clever developers exploited this formulaic flexibility in several ways, with the consequence that much less housing was produced under OHPP than was needed.[7] The system produced *some* affordable housing, however, and it showed how private-sector resources could be linked to public-sector needs.

In practice if not in principle, most of the city's downtown business leaders came to accept the city's linkage policies and one-time development fees. The amounts of money involved were relatively modest as a fraction of total development costs, so they were not a large factor in business investment or location decisions.[8] Further, the development fees could be viewed as side payments compensating the victims of growth. As such, they helped keep the peace, cultivated an image of social responsibility, and portrayed developers in a favorable light. "In the process," writes Chester Hartman, "the developers and large corporations create an image for themselves as socially conscious public benefactors, whose officials are featured in the newspapers and on television handing over checks to the mayor and planning director."[9] Perhaps most important, a formula-based system of one-time development fees clarified the rules of the game, reduced uncertainty, and insulated developers from political pressures for additional concessions linked to any *future* impact of growth. As Michael Peter Smith observes, "Once developers pay a legally required 'mitigation fee' they are in the position to use the payment as a way to escape future taxation. If oppositional groups mobilize to demand further impact assessments or new taxes to pay for the actual social costs of development, developers can argue that they already have paid a linked development impact fee. Used in this way 'linkage' could amount to a license to externalize the social costs of development."[10] For these same reasons, the city's slow-growth leaders came to view mitigation fees as an inadequate solution to the problem of growth, one that rationalized and depoliticized the development process while failing to regulate the amount, type, or location of allowable growth.

The Downtown EIR

One consequence of the Proposition O campaign was that it motivated members of the Planning Commission to negotiate a truce between high-rise foes and the Chamber of Commerce. In early 1980, slow-growth advocates agreed to refrain from putting further initiatives on the ballot. In exchange, the Chamber of Commerce, SPUR, and other business interests raised $500,000 to pay City Planning Department consultants for an in-depth environmental impact report (EIR) analyzing the effects of various downtown growth-control scenarios on the city's job opportunities, housing stock, transportation systems, and physical environment. After two-and-a-half years of study, Planning Director Dean Macris redefined the downtown EIR as merely a consultant's report to be used in developing a "downtown plan." By changing the scope of the project in this way, Macris insured that the EIR would have no legal standing, require no public hearings, and attract minimum media coverage. Some critics charged that the EIR process had been used as a stalling tactic and as an excuse for inaction. Others later claimed that Macris had wanted to downplay public exposure of EIR findings because they painted a grim portrait of what San Francisco would look like in the year 2000 under the proposed Downtown Plan.[11] The downtown office district would continue to expand; the number of commuters would increase markedly; income classes would continue to polarize into the very rich and the very poor; and high rises built in the South of Market area would rival those of midtown Manhattan. The EIR projections undermined justification for the Downtown Plan and provided evidence strengthening the slow-growth position. The *Bay Guardian*'s evaluation of the EIR described it as "probably the most important planning document to reach the San Francisco public in more than a decade." However, noting that the EIR was a thick, highly technical document, the *Guardian* concluded that "perhaps the best ally of city officials is the likelihood that most of the city's residents will never read [it]."[12]

Proposition M 1983: The San Francisco Plan Initiative

Impatient with the delays in producing the EIR and disturbed by its findings, slow-growth leaders gathered once again in early 1983 to place another growth-control initiative on the November ballot. This measure, the San Francisco Plan Initiative (also known as Proposition M—not to be confused with the 1986 Proposition M, the Accountable Planning Initiative), did not specify any height or bulk limits on downtown buildings. Such restrictions had tagged Proposition O as an antigrowth measure in the eyes of labor union leaders, particularly those in buildings and trades, and had aroused their opposition. The San Francisco Plan Initiative required the Planning Commission and the Board of Supervisors to revise the city's Master Plan to achieve internal consistency among the various plan elements (housing, transportation, etc.) and to assign highest priority to the goals of neighborhood preservation, economic diversity, protection of small businesses, job opportunities for residents, cultural and ethnic diversity, conservation of affordable housing, and improved public transit. The initiative also mandated that the city's zoning ordinances be changed to conform with the revised Master Plan, that new ordinances be passed requiring new office developers to provide affordable housing and additional public transit for office workers, and that the Redevelopment Agency (normally exempt from Planning Commission controls) certify fulfillment of housing and transit obligations before approving any projects. In sum, the San Francisco Plan Initiative demanded nothing less than a complete overhaul of the Master Plan and extensive rewriting of the city's land-use and development policies.

The heart of the San Francisco Plan Initiative was the statement of development goals and priorities. Seemingly innocuous, this statement pointed to a future San Francisco much different from the one projected under the Downtown Plan. By assigning precedence to the preservation and protection of neighborhoods, small businesses, and ethnic and cultural diversity, the initiative sent a clear message to planners, developers, and speculators that the city was much more than a growth machine to be used by investors in accumulating capital.[13] Proposition M was in fact a radical plan that threatened to imprison fixed capital investment within a protected built environment and to reduce new inflows of capital to a disciplined, measly trickle.

The Plan Initiative came very close to winning, earning 49.4 percent of the vote in the November election. This was a remarkable achievement considering that the Chamber of Commerce and other downtown business interests had raised $608,000 in campaign funds to kill the measure against only $87,000 raised by initiative supporters.[14] A key factor undermining potential support for the Plan Initiative was the decision by Dean Macris to unveil his much more moderate Downtown Plan in August 1983, just three months before the election. Backed by Mayor Dianne Feinstein and heartily endorsed by editors of the city's two leading daily newspapers, the Downtown Plan gave many voters the impression that city hall was taking positive action to deal comprehensively with the problems of growth. Once again, as Chester Hartman notes, "the City was trying to head off a popular revolt by proposing or enacting something in the direction of change demanded but far less stringent."[15] Leaders of the city's progrowth regime had dodged another slow-growth bullet, but only at the price of agreeing to live with a new piece of growth-management machinery: the Downtown Plan.

The Downtown Plan

The initial emphasis of the Downtown Plan was on urban design, public amenities, and architectural preservation. The plan virtually banned "refrigerator box" high rises in favor of slimmer, shorter, and more delicate buildings with sculptured rather than flat rooftops. It permanently protected 251 historically or architecturally significant buildings from demolition or further development. But in doing so it granted building owners "transfer of development rights" (TDRs), which could be used or sold for the purpose of erecting very tall skyscrapers on other sites, particularly in the South of Market area. Among other provisions, the Downtown Plan also required developers to spend 1 percent of building costs on public art, to provide one dollar per square foot (or equivalent services) for childcare, and to set aside one square foot of open space for every fifty square feet of building. Linkage fees for transit and housing would continue as before.[16]

The most important feature of the Downtown Plan was added in response to pressure from community activists. The Board of Supervisors insisted on a growth cap as a condition of approval. Thus, the Downtown Plan also included an annual limit of 950,000 square feet on construction of downtown office buildings 50,000 square feet or larger. Buildings in the "pipeline" (i.e., those approved but not yet constructed) would not be affected by the cap, which would expire in three years. The local dailies hailed the Downtown Plan as "undoubtedly the most famous urban design document in this nation right now."[17] News of the plan's unveiling made the front pages of the *New York Times.* Admiring the Downtown Plan from afar, New York City Councilwoman Ruth Messinger declared that "a lot of us are interested in the 'San Francisco-ization' of Manhattan."[18] Boston Mayor Raymond Flynn was actually present in chambers when the San Francisco Board of Supervisors gave final approval to the Downtown Plan in 1985, after two years of bitter debate. He was there to pick up pointers for a growth-control measure his city was considering at the time.[19]

Despite all this national praise and local chest-thumping, the Downtown Plan was sharply criticized by the city's slow-growth advocates. SFRG's Sue Hestor, for example, declared that the Downtown Plan "created an illusion of dealing seriously with the problem. It's not growth control at all." She announced SFRG's intention to place another growth-control initiative on the ballot in 1986.[20] Sue Bierman, the Planning Commission's only slow-growth member, complained that the Downtown Plan had been rammed through the commission by its president, Toby Rosenblatt, without due process or adequate public hearings. "It's very hard," she said, "to be an outsider in this city, trying to fight against the odds."[21] Allan Temko, the *Chronicle*'s architecture critic, worried openly about the plan's provision for TDRs, which he viewed as a "faustian pact between preservationists and real estate promoters."[22] Three of the five supervisors who voted against the Downtown Plan said that they did so because it was not stringent enough.[23]

Most business leaders grudgingly accepted the Downtown Plan. They could tolerate the temporary growth limits during a period of glut in the supply of office space. Besides, the pipeline was packed and would continue to disgorge new office buildings without restriction. The exemption of smaller buildings (under fifty thousand square feet) from controls, the availability of TDRs, and the wide open spaces outside the downtown office district all gave developers considerable flexibility. And the new one-time development fees provided a way to pacify social activists without causing too much financial damage. All in all, considering this was San Francisco, the Downtown Plan was not a bad deal.

What business leaders liked most about the Downtown Plan were precisely those features that slow-growth critics hated. The growth limits were only temporary, and so-called small buildings of less than fifty thousand square feet were exempted. The plan applied mainly to downtown and placed few if any restrictions on development elsewhere in the city, including the massive Mission Bay project. The pipeline pumped out buildings that would not count against the 950,000-square-feet limit. TDRs could be bought and sold to build skyscrapers on top of skyscrapers. No provision was made to enforce consistency among Master Plan elements or to formulate development planning priorities. For all these reasons, slow-growth opponents viewed the Downtown Plan as a very bad deal.

Slow-Growth Jabs before the Haymaker

Slow-growth advocates were not discouraged by the defeat of the Plan Initiative nor pacified by the nationally acclaimed Downtown Plan. Over the 1983–85 period, they continued to maintain steady political pressure on the progrowth regime. Mayor Feinstein's success in cordoning off city hall only intensified agitation in other parts of the government system or redirected it into alternate channels of reform. Lawsuits against developers applied one kind of pressure; precisely targeted ballot initiatives exerted another.

Suing developers was Sue Hestor's specialty. Hestor, an SFRG attorney, was described as "indefatigable" in challenging "virtually every building and environmental impact report that came before the Planning Commission" in 1981 and 1982.[24] Development projects might chug through city hall, but at the end of the line was Sue Hestor waiting to exact a social tithe. By 1985, as high-rise construction reached its peak, Hestor's lawsuits were entangling developers in a web of legal obstruction and costly delays. Many developers found it necessary to settle out of court in order to speed approval of their projects before tax laws changed, markets crashed, and permanent growth caps were imposed. These settlements, which exacted developer concessions and payments to SFRG and other citizen groups, reimbursed SFRG's legal costs and financed educational programs, impact studies, and mitigation measures.[25] Developers and their city hall allies were not amused.

Planning Commission President Toby Rosenblatt, who just months before had been accused of stifling public debate on the Downtown Plan, called these private settlements "regrettable" and "not in the long-term best interests of the city" because they took planning "out of the public sector, out of the public realm."[26] Community activists agreed with Rosenblatt in principle but argued that citizen objections to development projects had fallen on deaf ears and that city planners were unresponsive to neighborhood needs and concerns. Edwin Lee, an attorney representing Chinatown residents in one lawsuit, said, "Toby is right. We don't like it, either. But the question is, is the process adequate enough?"[27] According to business reporter Kirstin Downey, many developers perceived the settlements "as part of a power struggle between the city and San Franciscans for Reasonable Growth, with developers caught in the middle." Further, "many developers think they have little choice but to deal with SFRG because the city's waffling policy guidelines have left them all exposed to lengthy court battles."[28]

In the absence of a comprehensive growth-control policy, lawsuits were one effective means of monitoring downtown development in a semiclosed political system and of pressuring developers to pay for mitigation. Another approach to policy change was to legislate by initiative, piece by piece, targeting specific growth controls for voter approval. An example of this was Proposition K, a ballot measure aimed solely at shadows.

In June 1984, voters overwhelmingly approved Proposition K, which mandated year-round, all-day sunlight for the approximately seventy parks and open spaces under the city's jurisdiction. Studies had shown that the rapid pace of high-rise construction threatened to reduce "visible sky to slivers of light" and could create a "partial-eclipse-like darkness along sidewalks."[29] Known as the "sunlight law," Proposition K prohibited new buildings over forty feet tall from casting any shadows on these city-owned parcels of land. The law also required shadow measurements within a one-foot accuracy range for every parcel and for nearly every daylight hour. The city had to appropriate $200,000 just to assemble the shadow data needed to implement this one provision. In 1985, the shadow ban was put to its first test. Walter Shorenstein, one of the city's leading developers, had to abandon plans for a twenty-four-story office tower because studies indicated that any building exceeding six stories on the proposed site would cast shadows on St. Mary's Square in Chinatown.[30] Proposition K, a relatively minor ordinance tucked by initiative into the rapidly accreting growth-control machinery, imposed yet another layer of restrictions on the city's downtown development.

As these examples illustrate, the Downtown Plan was not working either as a political compromise or as a disciplined process of development planning. Slow-growth leaders continued to jab at developers and to press relentlessly for more radical change. Meanwhile, city hall was failing in its attempt to buffer downtown business from slow-growth demands. The bane of business rationality is uncertainty, and uncertainty was leaking through everywhere. The capacity of local government to balance community and accumulation was being called into question. The fulcrum of that balance, the Downtown Plan, was collapsing, and with it went the progrowth regime.

Proposition F: No Growth versus Slow Growth

In 1985, as downtown business leaders caught their breath after skirmishes over the Downtown Plan and the San Francisco Plan Initiative and as slow-growth leaders sketched strategy for the next initiative campaign, a maverick group of neighborhood activists led by Joel Ventresca lunged onto the political scene with Proposition F. This ballot initiative proposed a three-year ban on construction of hotels and office buildings exceeding fifty thousand square feet. The sudden appearance of Proposition F surprised nearly everybody, including most organizers of past slow-growth campaigns. Ventresca and his followers had grown impatient with SFRG's tactic of legal challenges aimed at forcing developers to make concessions to avoid lawsuits. They also felt bridled by the slow pace of efforts to broaden the base of the slow-growth coalition. Calling themselves San Franciscans for a High-rise Moratorium, they demanded an immediate and total suspension of high-rise construction projects. Their ballot measure, Proposition F, temporarily split the slow-growth movement into antigrowth and controlled-growth factions.

Many of the city's more prominent slow-growth organizations, including SFRG and San Francisco Tomorrow, refused to endorse Proposition F, thus remaining officially neutral. But some individual leaders, such as Calvin Welch and Sue Hestor, publicly attacked the initiative and urged its defeat in ballot arguments that were published in the official voter handbook. They resented Ventresca for his failure to consult with them in drafting Proposition F and especially for his refusal to withdraw the initiative from the ballot when asked to do so in the interest of coalitional harmony. They viewed the measure as a sham because it would not halt construction of the fourteen million square feet of office space already approved by the city. They also worried that the Proposition F campaign would ruin chances of passing a more effective growth-control measure in 1986. Welch argued that "the very presence of this measure on the ballot is damaging to the future of more effective controls on downtown development."[31] Others feared the loss of political momentum. "We don't want to be associated with a loser," said high-rise opponent Dale Carlson.[32] Even the progressive *Bay Guardian* editorialists came out against the proposition, acknowledging that they did so despite feeling "deeply uncomfortable with the idea of opposing a measure that would have even a symbolic impact on controlling downtown development."[33]

Meanwhile, downtown business leaders seemed more bemused than alarmed by this spectacle of internecine struggle within the growth-control movement. In public statements, the Chamber of Commerce condemned Proposition F, and Mayor Feinstein attacked it while defending the Downtown Plan. The *San Francisco Chronicle* dismissed Proposition F as a "crude, meat-ax approach" to growth control.[34] Even so, Don Solem, manager of the "No on F" campaign, was unable to arouse enough business concern to raise funds to fight the measure. "People don't perceive it as a real problem for some reason," he said.[35] John Jacobs, executive director of the Chamber of Commerce, gave one reason for the downtown business community's reluctance to support more than a token opposition campaign: "We pass the hat again and again. People are tired of us walking down the street with our tin cups."[36] Although a note of collective battle fatigue could be heard in Jacobs's remarks, it is perhaps more to the point that downtown business elites had little to fear from Proposition F. Commercial vacancy rates were high, the pipeline was full, developer interest was low, and the slow-growthers were divided. It would be no great loss even if Proposition F won. In fact, two years earlier, the Chamber of Commerce itself had proposed a three-year moratorium in exchange for a Downtown Plan without an annual growth limit.[37] Under these conditions, as many downtown business leaders saw it, a victory for Proposition F would do more good than harm, especially if it took the steam out of the slow-growth movement.

Proposition F lost in the November election, gaining only 41 percent of the vote. Analysis of the precinct election returns shows that the vote for Proposition

F roughly matched the pattern of the vote for the San Francisco Plan Initiative in 1983.[38] But voter support for Proposition F fell short of levels achieved in the vote for Proposition M in 1983, especially in the Haight-Ashbury precincts, where the drop-off averaged 20 percent. The Haight-Ashbury district is political headquarters for both Joel Ventresca and Calvin Welch. If Proposition F was a contest for leadership control, there can be no doubt who won. The defeat of Proposition F made it clear that the movement's goals were slow growth, not no growth. It also demonstrated the movement's capacity to exercise discipline within its own ranks, and it affirmed the principle of collective leadership. The slow-growth movement was not going to be sidetracked or split in two by wildcat populists going their own way. Following Ventresca's visit to the electoral woodshed, the slow-growth coalition began to form its critical mass and to plan serious strategy for the coming year.

PROPOSITION M:
THE ACCOUNTABLE PLANNING INITIATIVE

In January 1986, leaders of the slow-growth coalition formed the Interim Organizing Committee (IOC) to develop battle plans for yet another initiative campaign.[39] With Calvin Welch serving as chair, the IOC's first active membership roster of thirty-one names listed seven representatives from San Francisco Tomorrow (including Dick Grosboll, Regina Sneed, and the slow-growth movement's éminence grise, Jack Morrison), four from San Franciscans for Reasonable Growth (including Sue Hestor and John Elberling), two from the Sierra Club, one from the Greenbelt Congress, and at least nine from various neighborhood associations. The IOC also included a sprinkling of leaders representing some of the city's more progressive Democratic clubs (such as the gay and lesbian Harvey Milk and Alice B. Toklas clubs), neighborhood merchant associations, tenant groups, and public employee unions. Thus, about two-thirds of the IOC's initial core membership consisted of essentially the same group of white middle-class environmentalists, conservationists, and neighborhood preservationists who had worked together on previous slow-growth initiative campaigns. The IOC had few if any participants from the African American and Latino communities, white working-class homeowner districts, or private-sector labor unions. Also missing from the IOC were Joel Ventresca, the Victorian Alliance, and other no-growth neighborhood preservationists who refused to participate—partly on ideological grounds, partly out of lingering resentment toward slow-growth leaders who had deliberately sabotaged the Proposition F campaign. (Later, after some delicate fence-mending, leaders of the no-growth wing were coaxed back into the broader coalition.)

At this earliest stage of the 1986 growth-control initiative campaign, therefore, two of the city's three Lefts—the environmentalists and the neighborhood populists—were braided loosely together in a formative but still incomplete progressive slow-growth alliance. The IOC organized for battle and, after extended debate, chose the name Campaign for Accountable Planning (CAP) as its nom de guerre. It formed committees for fund-raising, community outreach, public relations, and drafting the initiative. It hired David Looman, a professional political consultant, to run the campaign; he would be joined later by political consultant Clinton Reilly, who became honorary chair.

The Text of Proposition M

The IOC's draft initiative committee followed Calvin Welch's advice to "keep it simple" and to emphasize continuity with the city's Master Plan and Downtown Plan. The final legal text of the initiative was unusually lucid and short (two pages in the voter handbook). Yet it also was carefully researched to insure that the new legislation would be legally bulletproof and would fit properly within the city's existing planning machinery. Indeed, the point is worth emphasizing that a high degree of cognitive mobilization and technical expertise was required to translate slow-growth goals and rhetoric into a legally enforceable urban planning document. A major internal criticism of Ventresca's high-rise moratorium initiative had been that it was crude and poorly written. If urban populists wished to move into the development policy area, the voice of the people would need tutoring in the arcane language of FARs and TDRs, floorplates and absorption rates.[40]

The final text of the initiative, later entered on the ballot as Proposition M, contained the following provisions.

Growth limits: Proposition M imposed a permanent citywide limit on new office construction of 950,000 square feet per year. (This is roughly the equivalent of two Transamerica Pyramids or three twenty-story office towers.) The limit applied to any construction, modification, or conversion producing 25,000 square feet or more of additional office space. To encourage smaller-scale buildings, 75,000 square feet of the total quota was reserved each year for buildings with an area between 25,000 and 49,999 square feet. To empty the pipeline of high-rise projects already approved, Proposition M allowed no more than 475,000 square feet per year in new permits until the backlog disappeared. (No limit was imposed on how much of this backlog could be constructed each year.) This provision effectively limited *new* approvals to the equivalent of one thirty-story office building annually until 2002, when the pipeline was expected to be clear.

These proposed growth caps plugged the most important loopholes in the Downtown Plan. The caps would be permanent, apply citywide, include smaller buildings, and reach back into the pipeline.

Citizen participation: Proposition M stipulated that voters at a regularly scheduled election had to approve an exemption for any proposed office development exceeding the stated limits. This provision gave citizens the last word in deciding the fate of any large-scale development projects within the city's jurisdiction—such as Mission Bay.

Priority policies: Proposition M instructed the Planning Commission to conduct public testimony for the purpose of amending the city's Master Plan in accordance with eight "priority policies." For the most part, these planning priorities were carried over from the defeated San Francisco Plan Initiative. The city could issue no permit for any demolition, conversion, change of use, or project requiring environmental assessment unless such proposals were consistent with the priority policies and the revised Master Plan. As written in the official text, the eight policies specified:

1. That existing neighborhood-serving retail uses be preserved and enhanced and future opportunities for resident employment in and ownership of such businesses enhanced;
2. That existing housing and neighborhood character be conserved and protected in order to preserve the cultural and economic diversity of our neighborhoods;
3. That the City's supply of affordable housing be preserved and enhanced;
4. That commuter traffic not impede Muni transit service or overburden our streets or neighborhood parking;
5. That a diverse economic base be maintained by protecting our industrial and service sectors from displacement due to commercial office development, and that future opportunities for resident employment and ownership in these sectors be enhanced;
6. That the City achieve the greatest possible preparedness to protect against injury and loss of life in an earthquake;
7. That landmarks and historic buildings be preserved; and,
8. That our parks and open space and their access to sunlight and vistas be protected from development.[41]

Job training for residents: Finally, Proposition M mandated creation of a coordinated training program for city residents in new jobs opened up by economic growth. Along with the priorities specified for affordable housing, the emphasis on jobs for residents responded to the primary needs and concerns of the city's ethnic minorities, workers, and low-income renters.

Considered as a whole, the CAP initiative was a well-crafted piece of legislation that welded three distinct Left agendas (environmental protection, neighborhood preservation, and jobs and housing) to form a single *progressive* reform package.

By late July, CAP volunteers had collected the voter signatures needed to place the initiative on the 4 November ballot. At this point, however, the Registrar of Voters stopped the campaign in its tracks by refusing to certify the signatures on grounds that the petitions were improperly drafted. Fortunately for the CAP organizers, city election rules allow any four members of the Board of Supervisors to place measures of this sort on the ballot. The four who came to the rescue were supervisors Harry Britt, Richard Hongisto, Willie Kennedy, and Nancy Walker.[42] They took the necessary steps to convert the CAP initiative into Proposition M. If they had not done so, the initiative almost certainly would have died in the Registrar's Office. That would have delayed the campaign at least a year or two, enough time to allow the Downtown Plan to become entrenched and the progrowth coalition to regroup. Technical details matter; one small technical error almost unraveled the slow-growth coalition and put Proposition M on ice.

The Setting for Battle

The CAP organizers had every reason to believe that 1986 would be the breakthrough year for passing tough growth-control legislation. Conditions were optimal. Of particular significance was the slow-growth movement's political momentum. Not counting the wildcat Proposition F campaign, each succeeding slow-growth initiative had come closer to winning than the previous one. Since the San Francisco Plan Initiative lost by a hair in 1983, simple extrapolation made the Accountable Planning Initiative a winner in 1986. Moreover, the relentless pressure of these campaigns and the threat of more to come had provoked city hall into making preemptive policy reforms: mitigation fees, neighborhood downzoning (prescribing less intensive land uses), the Downtown Plan. This accretion of slow-growth policy smoothed the way for still further reforms, such as those advanced by Proposition M.

These earlier campaigns had also educated citizens about the social and environmental costs of unregulated growth. Cumulatively, they made public opinion more receptive to the kinds of growth restrictions proposed by Proposition M. For example, a poll conducted in May 1985 found that 66 percent of the city's registered voters supported an annual limit on construction of new office space, while 59 percent disagreed with the progrowth argument that building new office space was necessary for a strong economy.[43] The poll also found that slow-growth support had become broad-based. Table 4.1 reveals that voter majorities in nearly all social groups approved an annual growth limit: whites and nonwhites, owners and renters, labor union members and nonmembers, Democrats and Republicans, and most income groups. (Note the recurring parabolic pattern of support by income level: strongest support for growth limits in the middle-income groups, weakest in the poorer and richer income groups.) As shown in Table 4.1, voter majorities in most of these same groups also questioned the validity of a claimed connection between high-rise office construction and a healthy economy. These poll results reflected the emergence of a more sophisticated public understanding of the negative effects of growth, particularly among ethnic minorities, labor union members, and low-income renters and home owners.

Many residents in the African American community had become disenchanted with progrowth ideology and were beginning to repudiate what Adolph Reed, Jr., has called the "growth/jobs, trickle-down mystification" dispensed by downtown

Table 4.1. Sample Survey Results Showing Voter Support for Growth Controls in May 1985 (%)

	Total Sample	White	Non-White	Own	Rent	<$10K	10-20K	21-30K	31-50K	50K+	Union	Non-Union	Republican	Democrat
Question: "Some people in San Francisco are proposing to limit the amount of new office space that can be built in the City each year. Others oppose such an annual limit. How about you? Do you strongly support, moderately support, moderately oppose, or strongly oppose this proposal?"														
Strongly support	35	35	33	29	40	27	37	39	37	30	36	34	31	38
Moderately support	31	32	29	36	28	18	35	33	31	30	27	33	26	33
Moderately oppose	19	19	20	18	19	24	15	18	21	22	14	21	24	18
Strongly oppose	15	14	18	16	13	30	13	10	12	19	23	12	19	11
Total	100	100	100	99	100	99	100	100	101	101	100	100	100	100
(n)	(376)	(265)	(100)	(152)	(206)	(33)	(75)	(79)	(95)	(54)	(78)	(290)	(88)	(237)
Question: "It is necessary to continue building new office space in order to keep the City's economy strong. Do you strongly agree, somewhat agree, somewhat disagree, or strongly disagree?"														
Strongly agree	14	12	21	20	11	11	20	16	8	19	16	15	18	15
Somewhat agree	27	28	23	25	27	20	22	34	26	32	17	29	31	24
Somewhat disagree	27	26	30	31	25	29	27	21	36	23	29	27	26	27
Strongly disagree	32	34	25	24	37	40	31	29	31	26	39	29	26	33
Total	100	100	99	100	100	100	100	100	101	100	101	100	101	99
(n)	(387)	(274)	(103)	(158)	(211)	(35)	(74)	(76)	(101)	(57)	(83)	(297)	(90)	(244)

Telephone sample survey of 407 San Francisco registered voters conducted during the period 4–12 May 1985, by the Public Research Institute, San Francisco State University. (Note: total percentages may not add to 100% due to rounding.)

business elites to legitimate their development plans.[44] As Darryl Cox, a local African American political consultant and slow-growth activist, remarked, "Leaving aside the question of whether we own a high rise, a window in a high rise, or even a faucet in the bathroom, we certainly know there has been no increase in jobs. We certainly have no equity interest in any high rise, despite our support in the past. Even those blacks who have tried to get into the development game have been thwarted. Banks and developers have not been willing to help blacks."[45]

It had also become clear to many low-income renters that growth-induced escalations in house prices were making the city affordable only for the rich. In 1988, for example, the average price for a house in San Francisco was $300,000, more than three times the national average. Even in the least expensive neighborhoods, the average price of a small two-bedroom unit was $180,000, requiring for purchase a household income of close to $60,000. Only 5 percent of the city's households could afford single-family home ownership at those prices.[46] Operating through actuarial and market processes, these trends were rapidly changing the ethnic composition, social class structure, and overall character of working-class neighborhoods. Under these market conditions, for example, elderly low-income homeowners were enticed to sell their houses to affluent buyers. The wind-fall capital gains allowed them to retire comfortably outside the Bay Area. In their place, those with higher social status put down stakes. The more recent slow-growth campaigns had begun to illuminate the subtle causal linkages between downtown development and such neighborhood-level outcomes.[47]

The May 1985 poll results also indicated that most rank-and-file union workers supported growth limitations and rejected progrowth arguments. One interpretation is that worker consciousness was shaped more by residence than by workplace on these types of issues. Union *leaders* were a different story. With the important exception of public employee unions, most of the city's labor union leaders supported downtown development or were officially silent on the issue. Yet even some of the city's most powerful union chiefs had begun to reevaluate their traditional alliance with downtown business elites on growth-control matters. In a 1984 interview, for example, Jack Crowley, head of the AFL-CIO's San Francisco Labor Council, observed that union power waned with each new office building. Steady union jobs in light industry were being replaced with union-resistant white-collar office workers. "The blue collar jobs move out, never to return again," he said. "We don't have the main thrust of downtown anymore. It's a bitter pill to swallow." Leaders of the building trades unions were likely to continue supporting downtown growth, Crowley acknowledged, but the writing was on the wall. In the future, he said, "the only blue-collar services available will be in the automotive industry."[48]

Another point in Proposition M's favor was the widespread perception that the city's quality of life was getting worse, not better, as high rises continued to be built. Housing prices were accelerating, gridlock was becoming more frequent on bridges and freeways, and even the downtown EIR showed increasing traffic congestion at ten key downtown locations, with total gridlock projected in four of them by the year 2000. Most important, voters were beginning to view these problems as the direct consequence of high-rise construction. For example, the May 1985 poll found that 60 percent of voters agreed (28 percent strongly) with the slow-growth argument that "overcrowding on buses and the high costs of housing are a direct result of all the new building in downtown over the past 10 years." The slow-growthers had made their case. The issue now was whether the claimed benefits of growth outweighed the obvious and well-documented costs. The CAP organizers were to argue no, at least for San Franciscans.

Also improving voter reception of the proposition was the fact that public confidence in market processes and the downtown business community was at a low point. Voters did not require Marxist lectures on the evils of capitalism to see that supply and demand were marching to different drummers in downtown San Francisco. Somehow the growing demand for affordable housing had signaled the market to supply a glut of empty skyscrapers. Even as commercial office vacancy rates soared to 18 percent and office rents plunged to new depths, buildings continued to shoot up into the skyline at an unprecedented rate. Many business leaders themselves were becoming skeptical that the long-awaited market correction was just around the corner. Something was very wrong with the economy. Residents needed only to open their eyes and see the cement being poured downtown, the BART trains unloading commuters, and the homeless throwing down sleeping bags in civic center plaza. Capitalism gone haywire meant votes for Proposition M.

One last condition suggesting victory for Proposition M was the disunity and collapse of leadership in the downtown business community. Local place entrepreneurs who owned existing commercial property or had permits to build saw that they would profit from Proposition M's restrictions on supply. Those less fortunate, particularly developers, architects, and construction firms, stood to lose under the proposed new rules. Richard Deringer, a developer, put it bluntly: "The developers who already have permits to build, or who own downtown property, favor Prop. M because it would make their properties more valuable. They own it, they're finished, and they don't want competitive development."[49] Faced with all this internal conflict, and battered to the point of exhaustion by previous slow-growth initiative campaigns, the Chamber of Commerce was only too glad to relinquish its traditional leadership role to someone, anyone else.

All in all, the prospects for Proposition M in mid-1986 looked very promising indeed. Few disagreed when CAP manager David Looman declared, "I'm sure that this is the year."[50]

The Campaign

Slow-growth leaders had used previous initiative drives to educate voters about the detrimental effects of downtown office growth. In this campaign CAP organizers attacked the validity of progrowth claims that such development generated net benefits for the city in terms of jobs and revenues. Further, they emphasized the continuity of Proposition M with the Downtown Plan, arguing that Proposition M was needed to do the job right—i.e., to clarify and enforce policy priorities that voters already had approved. Anticipating the opposition's defense of the Downtown Plan, they prepared critiques of the plan and of the way it was implemented.

CAP organizers also decided to broaden the social base of the slow-growth coalition by investing most of their limited funds (about $80,000) in targeting African American residents, working-class home owners, labor union members, and other traditional liberal voters who had been neglected in previous campaigns. Although these groups were especially hooked on progrowth claims that downtown expansion created jobs and economic opportunities, they also were the ones most susceptible to conversion from a progrowth to a slow-growth position. The time was ripe for enfolding all three Lefts—environmentalists, populists, and liberals—into a single progressive slow-growth coalition.

The "No on M" forces offered little resistance during the early stages of the election campaign. Their fund-raising efforts yielded little more than half the money raised in the 1983 Proposition M campaign ($361,000 versus $608,000). One frustrated opposition leader, Mark Buell, stated, "In the past, we had developers ready to throw money at the issue. Now, because of overbuilding, we don't have downtown [interests] jumping in with all that money."[51] The Chamber of Commerce had been instrumental in organizing previous opposition campaigns, but it chose to sit this one out. Chamber official Dick Morton said, "We will oppose the measure, but it is not our intention to lead if there are no followers."[52] He asked, "What if we beat this thing? How do you know we won't get it right back again next year?"[53] Expressing the fatalism of many other downtown business leaders, Morton added, "There is substantial sentiment that maybe the city should suffer and feel economic pain."[54] Echoing that gloom, one developer said he was inclined to "let the voters go out and hang themselves."[55] This was not exactly throwing in the towel, but it came close.

The prospects of defeating Proposition M looked even worse after *Examiner* reporters Gerald Adams and John Jacobs published a four-part series of investigative articles entitled "Inner Circles," documenting hidden sweetheart deals and mutual back-scratching among city hall politicians, planning bureaucrats, and favored developers seeking privileged access and exemptions for their projects.[56] The *Bay Guardian* had been raking this muck and reporting it for years. But since the exposé appeared in one of the more conservative major dailies, it created a ripple of moral revulsion and a large public-relations problem for progrowth apologists. Not surprisingly, polls conducted between June and September consistently showed Proposition M winning by a two-to-one vote. If Mayor Feinstein had not intervened at this point to take charge of the opposition campaign, it is likely that Proposition M would have waltzed into the history books with scarcely a harsh word exchanged.

Feinstein viewed the Proposition M vote as a referendum on the Downtown Plan, which she considered to be one of her primary accomplishments as mayor. She also was nearing the end of her second and last term. With aspirations for higher office, she did not want to exit city hall as a loser. After forming her own campaign steering committee in late August, Feinstein dismissed Don Solem as campaign manager and appointed Jack Davis instead. With two months remaining before the election, she and Davis devised an unusual strategy. The chamber's well-worn style of campaign leadership had been to get the big business wagons into a circle, raise lots of money, and hire a consultant to crank out tons of progrowth mail. Breaking from that tradition, Feinstein and Davis decided to reach out to the community to mobilize workers, small business owners, and ethnic minorities in defense of the progrowth regime.

Mayor Feinstein talked with dozens of city officials and community leaders, urging them to speak out and sign ballot arguments attacking Proposition M as racist and elitist. Many who heard the mayor's pitch refused to cooperate because they did not like the tone or the script. Supervisor Willie Kennedy, for example, reported that Feinstein and her aides "wanted us to make a public statement that people who want jobs for blacks should oppose Proposition M. They were trying to make it a racial deal—to say that a few white people were trying to cut off opportunities for blacks."[57] But other community leaders promised to support the mayor in carrying out a desperate but clever campaign strategy. That strategy had two main parts.

First, the campaign would back off from its defense of the Downtown Plan, which carried little weight with most voters, and would soft-pedal arguments touting the benefits of growth. Such claims were becoming harder to substantiate, and CAP supporters had been sharpening their pencils on those issues for years.[58]

Second, the "No on M" people would go on the attack using what CAP consultant Clint Reilly called the "fatal flaw" technique of focusing criticism on parts of an initiative while faintly praising the whole for its good intentions.[59] The two fatal flaws to be spotlighted in Proposition M were the permanent *citywide* annual cap on any construction, modification, or conversion producing twenty-five thousand square feet or more of additional office space; and the priority policy calling for *preservation* of existing neighborhoods and businesses. These provisions would be used as rhetorical levers to pry ethnic minorities, small businesses, and labor unions away from Proposition M. Target groups would hear the familiar assertion that growth caps eliminate job opportunities for workers and minorities. In addition, the campaign would make the novel and ingenious argument that citywide growth caps, combined with neighborhood preservation, condemned many low-income and minority residents throughout the city to an impoverished status quo by prohibiting neighborhood revitalization. In other words, poor people in the neighborhoods were the innocent victims of well-intended efforts to control downtown development. As characterized by the progrowth strategists, this flaw was the worm in the apple pie of Proposition M.

The "fatal flaw" arguments in particular were greeted with denigrating hoots from Proposition M supporters. Responding to one "No on M" broadside of this sort, Sue Hestor exclaimed, "It's such a crock, I can't believe it."[60] As instruments of strategy, however, such claims almost worked to stop Proposition M, simply because they put proponents of Proposition M on the defensive. Ironically, the same rhetoric used for years by neighborhood activists in calling for growth controls was now spouted by those who defended the progrowth regime. The effect was to reactivate a latent cleavage within the progressive coalition (working-class and minority liberals versus white middle-class environmentalists) and thereby deflect public debate from the deeper conflicts between community and capital that Proposition M exposed. It was a brilliant tactic, and no one was more gifted at executing it than the Reverend Cecil Williams of Glide Memorial Methodist Church.

Williams, a prominent African American leader and a staunch defender of the city's homeless and poor, kicked off the mayor's campaign on 27 August by delivering a speech to thirty African American ministers at a church in the Western Addition. In a prepared statement released after the speech, he attacked "so-called conservationists who seem to conveniently forget and openly exclude the survival of poor people in our city. . . . They seem to take a self-righteous position on keeping the environment clean but ignore the pollution of conditions in our poor communities."[61] Later he added more harsh words about growth-control advocates: "I have sat with them in meetings. They never talk about poor people and there's a self-righteousness in these groups that really bugs me."[62] To illustrate the evils of Proposition M, he pointed out that the initiative would prevent final approval of Executive Park, a proposed office-hotel-housing-shopping complex occupying nearly two million square feet, to be located near Bayview–Hunters Point. Hunters Point was a predominately African American neighborhood whose residents would presumably benefit from the project. Williams also worried that Proposition M would undermine the city's ability to wring concessions from developers. "I want to be able to go to developers and say, 'Here are things we must have . . . jobs, food and to make sure that people can stay in the city.' "[63]

The minister's attacks "clearly distressed" the Proposition M advocates, according to reporter Gerald Adams.[64] Proposition M was on trial—and so were the motives of those who proposed it. Dick Grosboll and other CAP leaders defended the measure's goals of providing affordable housing and job training for minorities. They also promised that if Proposition M passed, they would support legislation exempting Executive Park from the new growth restrictions. (They kept their promise, and the project was approved.) Sue Hestor, who is not famous for sugar-coating her opinions, preferred to counterattack, calling Williams a "pretty good shakedown artist" who opposed Proposition M only to get a "piece of the action" from developers.[65] Beneath the bombast, the important kernel of political truth illuminated by this exchange is that San Francisco's liberals and progressives are at best asymmetrically aligned. Progressives tend to support most liberal policies aimed at helping the poor and minorities, but liberals are inclined to support progressive growth-control efforts only in part and mainly on tactical grounds.

The rest of the campaign played out these themes. The "No on M" people sent out one piece of mail featuring a green worm poking out of a piece of apple pie, and another showing a large cockroach that symbolized the bleak conditions of neighborhoods neglected by Proposition M. For their part, the CAP people plastered the city with "Don't Buy the Developers' Bull" house signs, issued "Bull-Fact" statements rebutting claims about the benefits of growth, and sent out mail with the slogan "They always lie, don't believe them." As election day approached, final polls showed that momentum had shifted to the "No on M" campaign and that the likely outcome was too close to call. On 4 November, ballots were cast and counted. Proposition M won—just barely—by 5,311 votes.

ANALYZING AND INTERPRETING
THE PROPOSITION M VOTE

Election victories tend to be highly perishable in San Francisco. Reformers who live by the initiative often die by it as well—as happened between 1977 and 1980, for example, with the roller-coaster campaign for district elections. Such are the hazards of direct democracy in a hyperpluralistic system. Was the close Proposition M vote merely a conjunctural accident of local history, an electoral flash in the pan? Or did it signal a deeper, structural shift in the city's politics, one that might endure?

San Francisco's social diversity and political hyperpluralism are made to order for the political entrepreneur "who manipulates natural social cleavages, who makes certain of those cleavages *politically salient*, who exploits, uses, and suppresses conflict."[66] Growth-control issues in particular have the capacity to activate multiple social cleavages in different combinations to produce varying and sometimes unpredictable outcomes. (See the discussion in appendix B.) In the hands of political experts, growth-control issues can furnish versatile tools for sculpting constituencies. Under these conditions, statistical analyses of election results might "find" structural causes of the vote that were in fact "made" by designing politicians.

In the absence of postelection survey data, regression analysis of precinct voting results and 1980 census tract data can be used to cast at least some statistical light on the social base of the slow-growth vote. Table 4.2 reports the findings of such an analysis for both the Proposition M vote and the vote on the San Francisco Plan Initiative in 1983. (Analysis of voting on the 1983 initiative provides a benchmark for gauging changes in the slow-growth social base over the three-year period.) As predictors of a precinct electorate's percentage "yes" vote on the two initiatives, four types of social cleavage are considered in the

Table 4.2. Multiple Regression Analyses of the Precinct Vote for the San Francisco Plan Initiative (1983) and the Accountable Planning Initiative (1986) as a Function of Social Class, Housing Tenure, Sexual Orientation, and Race

	San Francisco Plan Initiative	Accountable Planning Initiative
SES Index	.799[a]	.607[a]
SES^2	−.008[a]	−.006[a]
Percentage of Renters	.321[a]	.227[a]
Gay (dummy)	7.255[a]	6.240[a]
Percentage of Black	.100[a]	.126[a]
Percentage of Asian	−.009	−.032
Percentage of Hispanic	.360[a]	.254[a]
Constant	6.708	18.714[a]
Standard error of estimate	9.591	7.245
Adjusted R^2	.51	.50
(without SES^2)	(.44)	(.43)
Number of Precincts	682	682

Source: See appendix A.
[a]p < .01

analysis: social class (precinct SES), housing tenure (percentage renters), sexual orientation (precinct is scored one if classified as gay, zero if not), and ethnicity (percentage black, Asian, and Hispanic). The regression analysis estimates the independent effect of each social cleavage on the vote while statistically controlling for the effects of the others. The following interpretation of the Proposition M vote is based on these regression results.

A comparison of regression estimates for 1983 and 1986 suggests that the social bases of voter support for the two initiatives were broadly congruent.[67] In both elections, the precincts most likely to vote *for* growth controls were those with a high percentage of renters, middle-level SES, and large gay, Hispanic, and/ or African American populations. The precincts most likely to vote *against* growth controls were those with a high percentage of home owners, high *or* low SES, and predominately Anglo and/or Asian nongay populations. These similarities in voting patterns for the two initiatives are important to note because they reflect the overall stability of the slow-growth coalition's electoral social base over the three-year period.[68] Moreover, this social base is quite distinct from that observed in slow-growth movements in other cities. In Los Angeles, for example, Mike Davis writes that "the taproot of slow growth" is a "local history of middle-class interest formation in homeownership" and a "vision of eternally rising property values in secure bastions of white privilege."[69] In San Francisco, while the taproot of slow growth also is the middle class, renters and nonwhites form a major part of the slow-growth constituency.

Important shifts did occur in the slow-growth coalition's social base between 1983 and 1986. These changes were consistent with the targeting strategies pur sued by both sides during the 1986 campaign. The CAP organizers made a special effort to win votes from African Americans and home owners, for example, and the regression results in Table 4.2 indicate they were successful. Neighborhood-level tracking studies corroborate the regression findings. In the predominately African American Bayview–Hunters Point and Ingleside neighborhoods, for instance, the average precinct slow-growth vote increased by nine percentage points and six percentage points, respectively, over 1983 levels. This surge of support occurred despite the fact that the Reverend Cecil Williams, one of the African American community's most respected leaders, had urged voters and particularly African Americans to reject Proposition M. Backing for growth controls also increased in the working-class home-owner districts of Visitacion Valley (nine points), Crocker Amazon (five points), and Excelsior (five points).

The CAP emphasis on low-income residents and workers also appears to have widened the beachheads of slow-growth support among these traditionally pro-growth voters. Evidence for this is hard to see in Table 4.2 because the social class variable has two parts, SES and SES^2, that must be evaluated together to make sense of the findings. Table 4.3 clarifies matters by showing the predicted slow-growth vote in 1983 and 1986 for different combinations of SES and housing tenure status, with all other variables in the model held constant at their means. Comparing equivalent cells in the subtables for 1983 and 1986, we can see that the predicted "yes" vote for low-SES precincts increased from 12 percent to 23 percent in home-owner districts (Renters = 0 percent), from 28 percent to 34 percent in mixed owner/renter districts (Renters = 50 percent), and from 44 percent to 46 percent in renter districts (Renters = 100 percent). Clearly, the predicted gains in slow-growth support were greatest in home-owner districts (+11 percent) and least in renter districts (+2 percent)—a pattern consistent with the CAP targeting plan.

Table 4.3 also shows that the city's social class and housing tenure cleavages were less salient as determinants of the 1986 vote than they were in 1983. The (parabolic) inverted U relationship between slow-growth voting and SES is found in both election years, but the tails at both ends are pulled up and the curve as a whole is flatter in 1986. (The flatter the curve, the less salient that cleavage is as a determinant of the vote.) In Table 4.3, for example, compare the support for growth controls in home-owner districts (zero percent renters) in 1983 and 1986. The percentage "yes" vote in 1983 rises steeply from 12 percent in the low-SES precincts to 34 percent in the middle-SES precincts (a difference of twenty-two percentage points), then drops seventeen points to 17 percent in the high-SES precincts. The percentage "yes" vote in 1986 increases from 23 percent in the low-SES precincts to 39 percent in the middle-SES precincts (only a sixteen-point difference), then drops only twelve points to 27 percent in the high-SES precincts. All home-owner precincts in 1986 increased their support for growth controls over 1983 levels, but that increase was greatest in low-SES and high-SES precincts—producing the picked-up tails of the inverted U and the flatter curve.

Another way to put this is that social class differences had less effect in shaping the growth-control vote in 1986 than they did in 1983. Comparing equivalent columns in the subtables of Table 4.3, we see the same flattening effect for the owner-renter cleavage.

This overall reduction in the political salience of social class and housing tenure cleavages was produced not only by CAP's success in mobilizing slow-growth support among normally progrowth working-class home owners, but also by the opposition's success in mobilizing progrowth support among traditionally slow-growth voters. Precincts in Haight-Ashbury, for example, dropped an average of seven percentage points in slow-growth support from 1983 levels, and precincts in the Potrero Hill district dropped an average of eleven points. Further, contrary to local conventional wisdom that links high-turnout elections with surges in progressive voting, increased voter turnout over 1983 levels was negatively correlated with increases in precinct slow-growth support.[70] Evidently, at the same time the CAP organizers were concentrating most of their limited resources on the goal of conquering new territories, the "No on M" forces were making considerable inroads on the neglected and exposed flanks of the slow-growth coalition's home base.

In executing their respective campaign strategies, the two contending parties poached on each other's core constituencies. By doing so, in effect, they traded places on the slow-growth–progrowth seesaw: One pushed up on the traditional progrowth end, the other pushed down on the traditional slow-growth end. The net result was that the seesaw movement was flatter (the salience of social cleavages was reduced) and the outcome of the election was much closer than it would have been in the absence of a vigorous opposition campaign.

A generalization to be drawn from this analysis is that the overall cumulative effect of repeated slow-growth initiative campaigns has been to depolarize and deactivate important social cleavages as sources of political conflict on development issues. Voter support for (and opposition to) slow-growth policies has become less and less confined to specific neighborhoods, classes, housing groups, or

Table 4.3. Expected Values of the Precinct Vote for the San Francisco Plan Initiative (1983) and Accountable Planning Initiative (1986) for Different Combinations of SES and Owner/Renter Status

	San Francisco Plan Initiative				Accountable Planning Initiative		
	SES Score				SES Score		
	0	50	100		0	50	100
Percentage Renters	0	12	34	17	Percentage Renters	0	23	39	27
	50	28	50	33		50	34	50	38
	100	44	66	49		100	46	62	49

Entries are expected values of voting support for growth controls computed from regression equations reported in Table 4.2, with all other variables held constant at their means.

races. (The May 1985 poll results reported earlier in Table 4.1 tell the same story.) The slow-growth coalition's social base has broadened considerably in recent years, and this is at least partly the result of a deliberately inclusive strategy pursued by slow-growth leadership. If the movement were to continue to develop a truly multiclass, multiracial, multicultural social base, at some point its leaders could claim that the San Francisco *community*, in whole and in part, supports a slow-growth regime. As will be shown in later chapters, however, this vision of the city's political future remains only speculative.

THE SIGNIFICANCE OF PROPOSITION M: IMPACTS AND REVERBERATIONS

On top of existing developer linkage fees, bulk limitations, commercial zoning regulations, and shadow bans, Proposition M's growth caps and priority policies would eventually close the vise on the weakening progrowth regime. Proposition M represented not merely a change *in* the system but a change *of* the system. Even during the campaign, friend and foe alike recognized the historic nature of the Proposition M vote. No longer would land-use and development policy-making be the exclusive preserve of downtown business elites and local government planning experts. Under Proposition M, community groups, neighborhoods, and ordinary citizens would have greater voice in decisions affecting the built environment. Investors, architects, developers, and builders would be constrained to serve new social goals and to play by new rules in the land-use game. H. V. Savitch has argued that "national conditions" do no more than set up pieces on the local "urban chessboard," allowing players considerable discretion to make important moves.[71] Pursuing that analogy, one could say that Proposition M blocked access to certain squares, restricted the moves of major pieces, required that the game be played in public, and redefined "winning" as the protection and promotion of pawns. Master builders might balk at their diminished role, but most citizens would applaud the idea of giving pawns more power and guarding their squares against grandiose development schemes.

Proposition M also showed how a city could take steps to buffer itself against the wild oscillations of capital investment in the built environment. In his study of postindustrial cities, Savitch argues that the local state's "autonomous path" is "not always free from the winds of capitalism, but it has been insulated against its most forceful gusts. The upshot is that politicians and technocrats, rather than capitalists, have a strong hand on the tiller of urban development."[72] The case of Proposition M demonstrates Savitch's point, except that in San Francisco the reluctant hands of politicians and technocrats had to be lashed to the tiller by a strong citizen initiative. With its stringent annual caps on growth, Proposition M has acted as a kind of local surge protector to regulate and stabilize the cyclical flows of capital investment in the city's built environment. Although many of the city's business leaders still view Proposition M as a deterrent to outside investors and needed mobile capital, others—particularly those representing foreign investors—appreciate Proposition M's stabilizing effects in creating a disciplined growth environment.

The Proposition M victory also inspired progressive leaders in other U.S. cities to press for similar reforms. In 1989, for example, Seattle's voters passed Initiative 31, which limited construction in downtown Seattle to five hundred thousand square feet per year for five years and one million square feet per year after that. The measure also prohibited construction of buildings taller than 450 feet. Although considerably less restrictive than San Francisco's Proposition M, Seattle's Initiative 31 is a strong piece of growth-control legislation. It won 62 percent of the vote in a special election despite the fact that downtown businesses outspent community activists ten to one in their efforts to defeat the measure.[73] Even Los Angeles, notwithstanding its progrowth image, adopted a citizen-initiated growth-control measure in 1986 which severely curtailed commercial construction in most parts of the city outside the downtown area. Bernard Frieden and Lynne Sagalyn write that "California often leads the way in political fashions, as it did with the environmental movement and the taxpayer revolt of the 1970s. When both San Francisco and Los Angeles have second thoughts about city development at the same time, trend watchers are bound to take notice."[74] These examples suggest that progressive leaders in other large U.S. cities have been inspired by San Francisco's slow-growth reforms. But none of these larger cities has been willing or able to pull (some might say "yank") as hard on the development reins as San Francisco has.

The passage of Proposition M, then, was another major turning point in San Francisco's political history, one that opened new vistas for local popular control of land-use and development policy. Public policy is not self-implementing, however, especially when it dictates fundamental change in the policy-making system itself. Slow-growth leaders would soon have to decide whether to stop at the doors of city hall or to press forward and take direct control of local government itself. As leaders of a social movement, their successful initiative campaigns had illuminated the path—but could they now trust the city's politicians to walk it? Or would they have to move inside the system to become politicians themselves? For better or worse, as the next chapter shows, they decided to move inside.

5

From Social Movement
to Political Power:
The Election of Mayor Art Agnos

[The election of Art Agnos as mayor] demonstrates San Franciscans are not that concerned about being a world-class city. It is a populist revolt.
—Mervin D. Field

Those who have served the cause of revolution have plowed the sea.
—Simón Bolívar

INSTITUTIONALIZING SLOW-GROWTH REFORMS

Passage of Proposition M placed the burden of executing a comprehensive new policy on the shoulders of city hall politicians, planners, and bureaucrats. Parts of the policy were precise in their goal statements and implementation requirements—the numerical limits on high-rise office construction, for example, and the fixed developer fees per square foot for transportation and housing mitigation. These left little room for discretion or creative interpretation, although in some cases the minimum-square-foot fees served merely as baselines for bidding up developer concessions. Other parts of the plan, however, were considerably more vague and open-ended. The list of eight "priority policies," for example, broadly prescribed the "preservation" or "enhancement" of certain values, such as neighborhood diversity and affordable housing. It was left to the planners to define these goals more exactly and to decide when, where, how, and how much to convert them into action and results. But years of experience had taught the progressives not to trust the politicians and technocrats to do the right thing, especially not those who had espoused progrowth values, catered to developers, and fought slow-growth reforms every inch of the way. Proposition M gave the city a new compass and map, but the hands on the tiller were still those of Dianne Feinstein, Toby Rosenblatt, Dean Macris, and other defenders of the old regime.

84

As many progressive leaders saw it, neither protest nor citizen-mandated policy was sufficient to compel the city officials to proceed in a new direction. If the slow-growth movement was to have any lasting impact, if it aspired to do more than merely "plow the sea," its values and goals had to be welded fast to structures of government authority. In a word, slow-growth reforms had to be institutionalized.

As the term is used here, an *institution* is "a device for backing values with power."[1] Following Arthur Stinchcombe, it is assumed that "the social effect in the direction of a given value is a product of the depth of the commitment to the value by a decision-making apparatus and the resources and authority that apparatus controls."[2] The logic of the concept is multiplicative: If the value on some scale is ten and the power backing it is zero, then ten times zero is zero, which is a measure of how much influence that value has in society. By this logic, the progrowth regime became at least partially deinstitutionalized on the private-sector side when the unified downtown business elite crumbled into factions, dissipating the concentrated power that had once backed progrowth goals and values. On the regime's public-sector side, however, Mayor Feinstein still reigned, and city hall power continued to endorse progrowth values, even if those values had been pulled, degree by degree, concession by concession, in the slow-growth direction. As long as Feinstein and her appointed commissioners remained in office, new policy and old power would be negatively correlated. One could not reasonably expect a progrowth administration to implement slow-growth reforms. The inevitable result would be bureaucratic resistance and sabotage. But Feinstein would be stepping down soon. It was important to replace her with a mayor whose compass was set right, whose values were aligned with the slow-growth popular majority.

IN SEARCH OF A PROGRESSIVE MAYOR: THE CAMPAIGN FOR ART AGNOS IN 1987

In 1987, Dianne Feinstein's imminent departure from city hall, combined with Supervisor Quentin Kopp's election to the state senate and the deaths of Phillip and Sala Burton, created a power vacuum in San Francisco politics.[3] With the mayor's office up for grabs and no inner circle left to anoint a successor, progressive leaders saw their chance to capture city hall once again. Many of them shared Calvin Welch's view that the Feinstein administration had been merely a necessary detour into centrist politics brought on by the tragedy of assassination and prolonged by the turmoil of its aftermath.[4] The time was ripe to elect a progressive mayor to institutionalize slow-growth reforms and to complete the late George Moscone's unfinished agenda.

By the end of March 1987, the field of serious mayoral candidates had narrowed to four: Assemblyman Art Agnos, a liberal Democrat representing San Francisco's Sixteenth Assembly District; Supervisor John Molinari, a Feinstein ally and the front-runner in the mayor's race according to the polls; businessman Roger Boas, who had served for ten years as CAO under Moscone and Feinstein; and City Attorney Louise Renne, whose political career had begun in the wake of the assassinations when close friend Dianne Feinstein appointed her to the Board of Supervisors. On most issues, Molinari and Renne had established themselves as centrist progrowth candidates in the Feinstein mold. Molinari in particular had earned his reputation on the board as an effective conciliator and broker of interests, as a politician who could bridge the gaps between Asians and African Americans, gays and straights, and the neighborhoods and downtown. On the Right was Boas, a progrowth fiscal conservative with strong ties to the downtown business establishment. And on the Left was Agnos, the assembly's leading advocate of liberal social policies and gay rights legislation since 1976, when he won his seat against rival Harvey Milk. Of the four candidates, only Agnos had endorsed Proposition M in 1986. His championing of neighborhood interests, small businesses, labor unions, environmental groups, gay rights organizations, and low-income-tenant associations attracted progressive voters and repelled many downtown business elites. Going into the campaign, leaders of the city's corporate business establishment felt they had good reason to be alarmed by Agnos's candidacy. Between 1983 and 1986, for example, Assemblyman Agnos had opposed every major bill supported by the California Chamber of Commerce and other probusiness lobbyists.[5]

The First Election: Narrowing the Field

Many political observers at the time believed it was front-runner John Molinari's race to lose—and lose it he did. Perhaps lulled into complacency by the ease of Feinstein's reelection in 1983 and her continued popularity with voters, Molinari made strategic and tactical errors in running his own campaign. Strategically, he underestimated the degree to which the once-shattered elements of the Moscone coalition had solidified through the successive mobilizations of the slow-growth initiative campaigns. The city's ideological center of gravity had shifted distinctly to the left, and Molinari found himself out of step with public opinion. He compounded this strategic error tactically by adopting increasingly conservative public stands on the issues and by conducting a negative direct mail campaign attacking both Agnos and Boas. He characterized Agnos as a leftover radical from the sixties who was unfit to govern a world-class city like San Francisco. He also used the word "incompetent" to describe Boas's performance as CAO—a rhetorical mistake Molinari would later regret. As Molinari's support among moderates began to erode, his appeals to fiscal and social conservatives were biting on granite. Roger Boas's antiliberal views and his well-funded media campaign had received considerable support from downtown business leaders and from affluent white home owners living in the western part of the city. Meanwhile, Louise Renne's campaign attracted so little support that she decided to drop out of the race, vacating the wide niche in the center between Agnos and Boas. Molinari's conservative drift and his negative campaign tactics succeeded only in alienating many of his own supporters and pushing them through the void into Agnos's camp. In retrospect, it seems possible that Molinari could have won the election, but his blunders guaranteed defeat.

Art Agnos chose to wage an upbeat grass-roots campaign focusing on the issues.[6] This strategy violated the tested maxims of good campaign management as preached by the local experts. It was conventional wisdom that a focus on issues would turn off the voters; high-tech methods like direct mail would always defeat low-tech methods like precinct walking and rallies; and negative campaigning works. Many political observers were surprised, therefore, when Agnos began to organize an extensive precinct operation and moved his campaign into the streets. Agnos's campaign manager, Richie Ross, hired veteran political organizer Larry Tramutola to mobilize a citywide corps of Agnos volunteers, arrange hundreds of house meetings, conduct numerous public rallies, and establish a fund-raising network of small donors. Precinct leaders and assistants were set up in more than four hundred precincts, and phone banks were organized to canvass three hundred more. While Molinari relied mainly on direct mail and Boas on television spots to reach the voters, Agnos and his volunteer precinct workers made direct contact with voters where they lived in the neighborhoods. Further, the tone of the Agnos campaign was consistently positive. Tramutola explicitly instructed his field workers to avoid any kind of negative campaigning. The strategy was idealistic, old-fashioned, and risky, yet it worked brilliantly—despite a brief setback caused by media revelations that Agnos had failed to pay income tax on $65,000 he had received in a land deal with Sacramento developer Angelo Tsakopoulos.[7] Conventional wisdom was shattered.

Agnos also made inroads against Molinari in the competition for group endorsements from the city's elaborate network of neighborhood associations, labor unions, environmental organizations, and political clubs. Nearly all of the environmentalist groups involved in the slow-growth campaigns, including the Sierra Club and San Francisco Tomorrow, lined up on Agnos's side. He won an important victory when the San Francisco Police Officers Association endorsed his candidacy, an endorsement that many conservative voters found hard to reconcile with Molinari's portrayal of Agnos as a radical flake. Drawing on his legislative record in promoting gay rights, Agnos challenged Molinari's own strong ties with the city's gay and lesbian community. He won the backing of the more progressive gay political clubs and stalemated Molinari's attempt to garner support from the Alice B. Toklas Lesbian/Gay Democratic Club, the city's largest gay political organization.[8]

In the arena of newspaper endorsements, nobody was surprised when the progressive *Bay Guardian* came out for Agnos. Agnos was "out front on the key issues," especially growth limits, vacancy control, and district elections, while under the centrist Molinari "it would be a constant struggle to enforce Proposition M" and "all-but-impossible to win vacancy control."[9] Nor was anybody surprised when the *Chronicle* sided with Molinari. What was unexpected, however, was the *Examiner*'s decision to endorse Agnos, seconded by an endorsement from the *San Francisco Business Times*. These announcements came late in the campaign, long after the polls had christened Agnos as the new front-runner. Yet even taking into account the pragmatic realism of backing a winner, it was remarkable that such progrowth, probusiness publications would go on record in support of a neighborhood-oriented, slow-growth liberal who had been characterized by the opposition as the scourge of the business community.

Both editorial endorsements emphasized that the city's many problems called for strong leadership of the sort that Agnos could provide as opposed to the brokering of interests promised by Molinari. The *Examiner* argued that under Molinari's leadership "the priorities of the Feinstein administration would remain undisturbed. The trouble with the status quo: It's just not that swell." Agnos, on the other hand, had the "charisma to be a powerhouse for change and for conciliation," and he possessed "the kind of tireless energy and fresh ideas that San Francisco needs for the next four years."[10] The *Business Times* acknowledged that "business has every reason to be nervous about Agnos, who steadily throughout his public life has supported strongly liberal social causes and legislation, some of them viewed with alarm by business." Despite these reservations, the paper endorsed Agnos because "what we think San Francisco needs now is action," and Agnos as mayor offered the best chance of getting it "for reasons of background, firm convictions, determination, raw intelligence, and drive to seek solutions."[11]

Agnos's most spectacular campaign success came in September when he wrote an eighty-two-page campaign book, *Getting Things Done: Visions and Goals for San Francisco*, and had his small army of volunteers deliver copies to more than 200,000 households throughout the city.[12] The book detailed his positions on many key issues and stated exactly what he would do if elected as mayor. Most local experts were stunned by the audacity of this move, and many were skeptical to the point of derision. These professionals believed that the average citizen had a very short attention span for political messages—as short as two seconds in the case of direct mail. How could any politician realistically expect that voters would sit down and read a *book* that discussed the issues in detail? Yet thousands did read it and were impressed by it. (Exit polls on election day revealed that a majority of voters had received and read Agnos's book and that 64 percent of those who read it voted for Agnos.[13]) As his slogan, "Please read my book," became more familiar during the last weeks of the campaign, Agnos shot ahead of Molinari and Boas by more than twenty points in the polls.

On 3 November, election day, the Agnos campaign clinched victory by putting seventeen hundred volunteers on the streets in a massive get-out-the-vote effort. The best either rival could muster was about three hundred workers. After the ballots were counted, Agnos had won 48 percent of the vote, more than Molinari (25 percent) and Boas (22 percent) combined. Agnos needed a majority of votes cast to win outright, however, so final victory had to await a December run-off election pitting him against Molinari.

The Run-Off Election: Agnos versus Molinari

Molinari rejected pleas from the Reverend Cecil Williams and other advisors to throw in the towel and exit gracefully. He fired his campaign manager, hired a new one, and then took to the streets to denounce Agnos's radical thinking and fiscal irresponsibility. A prime objective of Molinari's strategy was to attract conservative voters from the Boas camp, now that Boas was defeated and his supporters presumably had nowhere else to turn. "I am not prepared to turn this city over to those who would bring it to darkness and doom," he declared. "I will not give it over to those who have a radical and dark vision of the future and visions more reflective of the '60s than the 1980s."[14] Using Agnos's now-famous book as a text, Molinari argued that Agnos's "attractive and clever" proposals would cost the city $310 million in new spending and lost revenues. Agnos's riposte was simple and effective: "The real question for Mr. Molinari is this— does he oppose what I'm proposing? If so, let him say so, and if not, let him explain how he'll pay for it."[15] Lacking a positive program of his own, Molinari had no reply.

Art Agnos, meanwhile, aggressively courted downtown business leaders by initiating one-on-one meetings with corporate executives and holding two press conferences devoted entirely to business issues and concerns. Even as Molinari was denouncing Agnos as a radical, six corporation leaders, including the Pacific Stock Exchange president, endorsed Agnos for mayor.[16] The *Business Times* reported that "the liberal Agnos, vociferously billed as 'anti-business' by opponents, is finding friends in the fragmented, balkanized business community of San Francisco."[17] But the crusher for Molinari came when Roger Boas announced on 16 November that he was going to vote for Agnos and urged his followers to do the same. Louise Renne followed suit a few days later. What had been merely a defeat now became a rout. On 8 December, Agnos won by a landslide, 70 percent to 30 percent.

The Agnos Campaign in Review:
Progressive Ends, Progressive Means

The election of Art Agnos was a progressive victory, not merely a victory for progressives. The campaign was progressive in its grass-roots style and issue content as well as its goals. It revealed the truth in Roberto Unger's remark that collective mobilization is "more than a weapon for the remaking of social life; it is the living image of society dissolved, transformed, and revealed, in the course of the fights that take place over what society should become."[18] The "bottom line" of getting Agnos elected was not the bottom line, because *how* it was to be done made a difference. The means justified the ends. In this vein, three features of the Agnos campaign stand out.

First, Agnos's campaign strategy assumed a high degree of political consciousness and cognitive mobilization among citizens. Voters were not seen as passive apolitical fools who needed to be fed bites of targeted pablum through the media or direct mail. "People don't want their intelligence insulted," explained Agnos campaign manager Richie Ross. "They don't want conclusions drawn. They'll evaluate character, thank you very much, and they'll arrive at their own set of conclusions."[19] The fact that Agnos's campaign book was so widely read and well received proves that a little respect from the politicians can go a long way—especially in San Francisco.

Second, the grass-roots style of the campaign tapped a reservoir of citizen activism and volunteer support, but it was not an amateur operation. Professionals were in charge from the beginning, and their organizing skills were needed through all phases of the campaign, not least to parry the opposition's media and direct mail barrages. If this was populism, it was sophisticated, shrewdly guided populism.

Third, the collective mobilization activated by the Agnos campaign reconstituted electoral alliances that had been torn apart by the Moscone and Milk assassinations. The slow-growth initiative campaigns had done much to rebuild these alliances, but the Agnos candidacy galvanized and expanded them to include more organizations representing the poor, the working class, and racial minorities. The inclusionary thrust of the campaign did not stop there, however, but reached still further to attract conservative refugees from the Boas campaign, moderate defectors from the Molinari campaign, downtown corporate executives, and many other groups and interests inclined to back a winner. The omnivorous quality of his campaign gave Agnos his landslide on 8 December, guaranteeing extra political capital to spend during his first year in office. But it also fattened his electoral coalition beyond the minimum size necessary to gain power without diluting or compromising his progressive agenda. As Agnos himself would discover later, the political carrying capacity of the city's progressive coalition was much smaller than the 70 percent vote he won in the run-off election. If he aimed to match that percentage in an eventual reelection campaign, he would risk alienating the ideological core of his grass-roots constituency.[20]

The Importance of Issues in the Agnos Campaign

In campaigning for mayor, Art Agnos focused on a wide range of issues and boldly stated his positions on them.[21] The content of his political discourse and programmatic agenda identified him as a genuine progressive candidate, one who articulated and defended Left positions as a liberal, environmentalist, and populist. As a liberal, he supported affirmative action programs for women and ethnic minorities, comparable worth programs for city employees, vacancy rent control, preservation of public housing, accelerated construction of affordable housing, shelters and case management services for the homeless, job creation for residents and ethnic minorities, and enhanced educational services. As an environmentalist, he backed rigorous enforcement of Proposition M growth-control guidelines, expanded recycling programs, acquisition and preservation of parks and open space, a "no" vote on home-porting the USS *Missouri*, and promotion of regional cooperation. And as a populist, he supported district elections, neighborhood "Mayor's Stations," increased citizen participation in the development planning process, promotion of small businesses, and preservation of neighborhood and cultural diversity.

Agnos's commitment to slow-growth reforms was strong and unequivocal. He promised to appoint a Planning Commission that would enforce Proposition M, particularly its guidelines on affordable housing, neighborhood preservation, and small business development.[22] He took issue with critics who saw Proposition M as antibusiness. "Prop. M was not anti-business," Agnos wrote. "It was anti-City Hall because City Hall has paid too much attention to *downtown* development and not enough to *neighborhood* development."[23] He argued that the San Francisco Redevelopment Agency (SFRA) "must never again be allowed to engage in wholesale clearance of neighborhoods" and that affordable housing should become SFRA's "number one priority."[24] He pledged that his appointees to boards and commissions would bring "dedication, independence and sensitivity to the concerns of neighborhoods."[25] He stressed that the planning process would be democratized under his administration and that the inner circles of wealth and privilege would call the shots no more: "Wealthy special interests, with high-priced lobbyists and big campaign contributions, should not hold more clout in the planning process than San Francisco taxpayers. Middle-income working families are being pushed out of our city. Under an Agnos administration, *that will stop*."[26] Finally, Agnos promised that, as mayor, he would "sit down with the private sector and community organizations to work out a plan which encourages balanced development. Balancing the needs of the business community with the concerns of the neighborhoods was a major goal of Proposition M."[27] This emphasis on "balanced development" is especially important because it would become the crux of many complaints voiced later by the more radical slow-growth progressives as they opposed Mayor Agnos's bid for reelection.

Neither in his campaign speeches nor in his book did Agnos delve very deeply into the priorities, linkages, or possible contradictions among these varied elements of his progressive agenda. But at least the different elements were there, and his commitments to deal with each formed an impressive portfolio of promises that his rival candidates could not match. Unfortunately for Mayor Agnos, as will be discussed later, the city's budget could not match them either. The problem of an overambitious "initial agenda" has caused the downfall of many new regimes.[28] It remained to be seen whether Agnos had promised too much in his campaign or written too much in his book for his own political good.

THE AGNOS ELECTORAL COALITION: AN ANALYSIS OF THE VOTE

If, as suggested earlier, institutions are values that are correlated with power,[29] the Agnos victory helped to institutionalize progressive reforms. Table 5.1 shows the correlations of the 3 November precinct vote for Agnos, Molinari, and Boas with selected indicators of voter support for progressive values and policies. The figures reveal that the vote for Agnos was positively correlated with the Feinstein recall vote in 1983, the vote for district elections in 1987, the vote for rent control in 1979, the vote for Proposition M in 1986, the liberalism index, the environmentalism index, the populism index, and the overall index of progressive voting. This profile of positive correlations is virtually the mirror image of those shown for Boas and Molinari. The results clearly identify Agnos as the "progressive" candidate, Molinari as the "centrist," and Boas as the "conservative"—at least in the eyes of the voters. Further, they demonstrate how discerning and issue-oriented San Francisco's voters are in choosing their leaders. Based on these correlations, if the voters were aiming to back progressive values with mayoral power, they made the correct collective choice: Art Agnos.

Multivariate analyses of the social base of the precinct vote indicate that (1) renters and Latinos voted overwhelmingly for Agnos, (2) gay and African American voters split their support between Agnos and Molinari, (3) Asian voters gave least support to Agnos and most to Molinari, and (4) *within* each ethnic group and housing tenure status, middle-class voters gave major support to Agnos, while

Table 5.1. Correlates of the Precinct Vote for Art Agnos, John Molinari, and Roger Boas with Selected Indicators of Progressivism: Mayoral Election, 3 November 1987

Correlates	Agnos	Molinari	Boas
Feinstein Recall Vote (1983)	.45	−.36	−.37
District Elections (P–1987)	.84	−.43	−.79
Rent Controls (R–1979)	.80	−.32	−.79
Growth Controls (M–1986)	.79	−.36	−.74
Liberalism Index	.89	−.26	−.92
Environmentalism Index	.32	−.43	−.13
Populism Index	.37	−.32	−.30
Progressivism Index	.79	−.47	−.69

Source: Analysis of precinct electoral data obtained from statements of vote published by the San Francisco Registrar of Voters.
Entries are Pearson zero-order correlation coefficients (n = 710 precincts).

low-SES and high-SES voters divided about equally among the three candidates.[30] The finding that middle-class voters were most supportive of Agnos within each ethnic and housing category runs against the grain of media portrayals of the Agnos victory as a "populist revolt"—at least if one interprets that phrase to mean an electoral uprising of the working-class poor. The Agnos campaign was populist in its grass-roots style and in its emphasis on people before profits. But in terms of its social base, if it was populist, it was a middle-class populism at its core.[31]

MAYOR AGNOS IN OFFICE: LAYING THE FOUNDATION FOR A NEW REGIME

After Agnos took office, new faces began to appear in city hall, and old ones vanished. Sue Hestor and Calvin Welch, virtual strangers to city hall during the Feinstein years, began to meet regularly with Mayor Agnos in his office to discuss growth issues. The Reverend Cecil Williams, Toby Rosenblatt, John Jacobs (Chamber of Commerce head), William Coblentz (developer lobbyist), and other Feinstein favorites found their access privileges downgraded or withdrawn.[32] City hall stirred with new blood. Progressive leaders' hopes were high, for they had passed through the portals and were insiders now.

The political situation facing Mayor Agnos was much rosier, in many ways, than that which had confronted his liberal predecessor, George Moscone, twelve years earlier. First, Agnos came to power on a landslide vote at the end of a campaign that had been waged on the issues. Both he *and* his progressive agenda won broad public support, and he entered office with lots of political capital and a community-certified mandate for change. Moscone, on the other hand, had squeaked to victory in 1975. His entire program had been bitterly contested by half the city. He had been given no mandate, no margin for political error.

Second, Agnos took office in a period of relative social tranquillity. Many conflicts still lacerated the city, but there were not the deep gashes of fear, hatred, and discord that had polarized citizens and paralyzed leadership in Moscone's time. The Feinstein administration had served as a nine-year recuperative journey that had given wounds time to heal.

Third, Agnos could look forward to working *with* a liberal/progressive majority on the Board of Supervisors, one that would actually expand and become even stronger over the next three years. Moscone had to fight *against* a predominately conservative board that opposed him and his policies at almost every turn.

Fourth, Agnos was the beneficiary of accumulated slow-growth policy bled from the Feinstein administration or imposed upon it by citizen initiative. Moscone had been expected to create such policy from scratch and to do so against the resistance of a unified downtown business elite. Agnos had the easier task of enforcing existing policy guidelines against weaker opposition from a fragmented, leaderless business community.

While enjoying these favorable conditions and political advantages, Agnos also faced some formidable obstacles. Number one was money—specifically, the lack of it. Former mayor Feinstein had bequeathed a revenue shortfall of $180 million and a budget that had to be balanced. Any checks Agnos might wish to write to pay for his ambitious social programs had been prestamped: "insufficient funds." This meant allocating burdens rather than benefits and saying no rather than yes, all against the background of rising expectations that the new mayor would "get things done" as promised in his book. "My curse is coming in as a liberal with no money to spend," Agnos complained.[33] Revenue shortfalls would plague him every year of his term as mayor.

A second problem for Agnos was the conservative climate of state and national politics. Compelled by Reaganomics, budget cutbacks, and privatization to fend more for itself, San Francisco had to dig into its own shallow pockets and to compete with other cities for private-sector investment.[34] Meanwhile, the property tax base was shrinking under the constraints of Proposition 13, and downtown business leaders were sounding increasingly mutinous as they publicly deplored the city's hostile business climate and its radical image in national media. The city seemed surrounded by rocks and hard places.

A third problem was the city's endemic government fragmentation and political disorder. This situation was not new, but it had gotten worse in recent years as groups and interests proliferated within broader, more stable constituencies. For instance, new groups forming in the gay and lesbian community, such as ACT UP and Queer Nation, were pursuing their own separate political agendas. Traditional power structures in the Chinese American community were crumbling as new groups and political leaders emerged from the network of social-service agencies. Non-Chinese Asian groups and clubs were beginning to flex their political muscle. Separate political organizations had arisen to represent the different interests of "citizen" and "immigrant" Latino communities. Schisms between older liberals and younger progressives were dividing the African American community, most recently around growth-control issues and domestic partners legislation. The downtown business community had fractured into several distinct clusters of interests. Organized labor was segmented by sector and politically disorganized. Neighborhoods and small businesses were spawning new organizations. The hyperpluralism of Joe Alioto's day had become "hyperpluralism-squared" under Art Agnos.

The city had made great strides in the political representation of social diversity. The Board of Supervisors, for example, no longer was a phalanx of white straight males, and even the most conservative agencies and departments (including police and fire) had made progress toward affirmative action goals. But these gains in the representation of increasingly fine-grained constituencies also complicated the task of coalition formation, leadership, and governance. "Getting things done" would be an awesome challenge in such a pulverized system.

Sisyphus with his boulder had it relatively easy; Mayor Agnos was condemned to push gravel.

As Barbara Ferman has shown, Mayor Moscone was unable to exercise strong executive leadership under these hyperpluralistic conditions. He lacked political skill in attracting resources and mobilizing support for his progressive vision. In Ferman's terms, he failed to convert his electoral coalition into an effective governing coalition.[35] Responding to the empowerment claims of the diverse groups that supported his campaign, Moscone made the mistake of ushering the whole lot of them into city hall with the idea of using this transplanted electoral coalition as an instrument of governance. Once leaders of these groups were ensconced in positions of authority on the city's boards, commissions, and agencies, many of them exploited their power and access by lobbying for their own constituencies from the inside while resisting Moscone's efforts to exercise central control. Moscone was unable to shield himself from these demands. He depleted his limited resources in reacting to them, often making more enemies than friends in the process.[36] Would Mayor Agnos make the same mistakes?

BUILDING A GOVERNING COALITION

Mayor Agnos's political challenge was to assemble an effective governing coalition from the building blocks of the electoral coalition that put him in office. To accomplish this he needed to empower both his own capacity to govern and those who had been excluded from city hall for over a decade. With limited formal authority, he had to create an informal power base capable of imposing some order and direction on a fragmented political universe. He had to do all this against the grain of an antipower bias in the political culture. His methods were threefold: to appoint loyal supporters to commissions and boards; to buffer himself with a cabinet government and use it as an instrument of surveillance and control; and to keep his grass-roots campaign organization alive and on tap to help him mobilize community support for his policies.

During the first weeks of the new administration, Mayor Agnos's fifty-one-member screening committee received over three thousand applications for the nearly two hundred seats on the city's thirty-one mayoral-appointed boards and commissions.[37] This "super commission" was "hailed as being representative of the city's diversity."[38] Agnos declared his hope to fill posts with people who had "Peace Corps hearts and linebacker eyes."[39] Making appointments to commissions was an opportunity, Agnos said, "for the mayor to empower the people, to make them partners in making policy."[40] Rhetoric aside, it was also an opportunity to pay back political favors and to construct a network of loyal followers in positions of authority. As noted in an investigative report on the city's commission structure, the "vast majority of Agnos appointees were vocal supporters during his bid for the city's top seat."[41] These were not hacks, however, and many had supported Agnos precisely because they shared his progressive vision to some degree. They included a number of African Americans, Latinos, Asians, gay men, and lesbians. At the level of bureaucracy, the political incorporation of minorities took another great leap forward under Agnos.[42] He also appointed environmentalists, neighborhood activists, nonprofit housing specialists, and slow-growth advocates to seats on the Planning Commission and the Redevelopment Commission, the two main centers of power in land-use and development policy. In reviewing Agnos's appointments, local political analyst David Binder commented, "These are people who had been on the outside during the Feinstein administration. These are the people that are going to be making decisions now and will be giving big developers and other people who had power a hard time."[43]

Unlike Moscone, who had given his commissioners free reign, Agnos kept close tabs on his charges and quickly dismissed those who crossed him in public or strayed too far from the team.[44] Unlike Moscone, who had failed to insulate himself from the internal pressures and demands of maverick commissioners, Agnos created a buffer in the form of a "cabinet" of six well-paid deputy mayors. By shrinking his span of political control, Agnos hoped to achieve greater executive leverage over his boards and commissions. He also imported experienced staff from his assembly office in Sacramento to help him run his new one in city hall. Managerially, these moves made good sense. But politically, as Agnos would learn later, they were a disaster. San Franciscans do not like their mayors buffered.

Early in his term as mayor, Agnos revved up the engine of the campaign organization that had brought him to power. He retained his top consultants as staff to run a permanent campaign of community organizing and political mobilization. His purpose in doing so, Agnos said, was "not to be some type of Tammany Hall power broker, but to use that power to solve [urban social] problems."[45] Seven months after taking office, Agnos and his aides restarted the network of precinct captains and loyal activists, sending 150 of them into the streets with ironing boards (a San Francisco tradition since 1983) and clipboards to rally support for the mayor's policies and to sample public opinion. Deputy Mayor Claude Everhart denied that this field organization was being used as a political tool. "This isn't some machine twisting and turning," he insisted. "It's not a machine at all." Yet several liberal candidates for local public office, including Angela Alioto and Terence Hallinan, were drawn to it as a valuable resource for their own grass-roots campaigns.[46] Even some of Agnos's political enemies admired the mayor's small army of precinct operatives. One of them was consultant Jack Davis, who would mobilize his own precinct army to help Agnos rival Frank Jordan unseat the mayor in 1991.

Mayor Agnos also pursued other strategies in building a power base to provide the organizational, economic, and political capacity to "get things done" in a fragmented system. He drew upon the resources and support of the Democratic party. He took steps to strengthen his ties with organized labor. He established friendlier relations with downtown business elites. And he worked closely with corporate executives to promote large-scale land-use projects in China Basin, Mission Bay, and the waterfront. These were the kinds of moves a tough liberal mayor might make to enhance the ability to govern. Unfortunately for Agnos, he had campaigned for office as a progressive. That is what his grass-roots supporters thought they were getting when they voted him into power. A progressive is not what they got.

6

Protecting Community from Capital: The Urban Antiregime

The people of San Francisco vote for liberal politicians, but when it comes to protecting the beauty of their city, they are hard-line conservatives.
—Mayor Art Agnos

"Just say no" is a fine slogan for fighting drugs, but it's not a good way to run a city.
—David Chamberlain
San Francisco Chamber of Commerce

THE ANTIREGIME

It is one thing to destroy an urban regime, quite another to create one. Although it might be accurate to say that San Francisco is currently regimeless, the city does have a regime of sorts—an antiregime. The ultimate function of the antiregime is to protect community from capital. It is a regime with the "power to" thwart the exercise of power by others in remaking the city. The primary instrument of this power is local government control over land use and development. In San Francisco, these growth controls have achieved unprecedented scope in the types of limits they impose on capital. They are used to suppress, filter, or deflect the potentially destructive forces of market processes on urban life as experienced by people in their homes, neighborhoods, and communities.

To use a phrase coined by Victor Thompson forty years ago in his study of wartime rationing, San Francisco's antiregime "regulates by impedimenta."[1] One indicator of the growth of regulatory impedimenta is the city's planning code, which tripled in size from 150 to 450 pages between 1985 and 1990.[2] Under the Agnos administration, these codes were strictly enforced. For example, in 1987, under the city's shadow ban regulations, the proposed height of a city-approved office tower had to be shortened by fifty-two feet because studies revealed the building would shade a small part of St. Mary's Square for three minutes in early morning twenty days of the year.[3]

The historical context has changed from when Thompson first used the term, but the rationing motive of regulation by impedimenta is the same: to protect and conserve scarce resources. In San Francisco, these resources include developable land, breathable air, sunlight, and affordable housing. The antiregime's regulatory hurdles and gauntlets are intended to discourage unwanted growth by a process of natural selection. Only those developers who have patience, charity, and down-sized visions will be given permission to build. Projects that leave big footprints are not going to fit into the glass slipper the city has become.

The antiregime is protective, defensive, and reactive. In the domain of land-use and development planning, its unwritten constitution can be reduced to a single word: no. The antiregime enshrouds the city in an integument of red tape. It protects a shrinking space of cherished urban values and guards against entry by predatory investors and their allies. Its defenders view the community within as a political chrysalis hanging by a single thread. The antiregime is a necessary stage through which San Francisco must pass if it is ever to evolve as a progressive urban regime, but antiregime leaders are as yet too proudly insular and too harshly negative toward the capitalist society in which their city is embedded. What they are learning now is how to say no to capital so that they can someday say yes in a more discriminating way.

The case studies in this chapter and the two that follow explore the impact of the antiregime on land-use and development planning and display the antiregime in its best light. The first study in this chapter looks at the effects of Proposition M on high-rise office construction in downtown San Francisco. The second examines Proposition M's priority policies at work in the Haight-Ashbury and Sunset neighborhoods.

THE END TO MANHATTANIZATION—
OR CLOSING THE BARN DOOR?

A major motivation behind San Francisco's slow-growth movement was to find some way to halt the Manhattanization of the city's downtown financial district. By the time citizens mustered the votes needed to clamp down on high-rise construction, however, the downtown district was largely built out with skyscrap-ers, and the pipeline was full to the brim with new ones to come. Moreover, the commercial real estate market (with help from the federal government) was finally regaining its sanity, and the signals were saying "Don't build." As business columnist Thom Calandra observed, "Low rents, a space glut and tighter credit requirements inspired by the S&L crisis—and not voter-approved Prop. M—will determine whether they [developers] pour their foundations."[4] In fact, in mid-1990 no fewer than seven *approved* office tower projects languished for lack of financing as developers hunted desperately for joint-venture partners and preleasable tenants with whom to impress the banks.[5] On several current project sites, the only signs of construction are steel beams protruding from bedrock to hold the soil until money arrives. Ridiculing these token efforts as "Steelhenge," city planning commissioners have taken steps to force developers to accelerate construction or risk losing their permits to build.[6]

In retrospect, those who questioned the timing and relevance of Proposition M in 1986 were quite correct: Imposing growth limits at this stage is like closing the barn door after the horse has left. What possible effects could growth controls really have in protecting the community from the scourge of Manhattanization? Unless one intended using wrecking balls, the high rises were there, a *fait accompli*. Therefore, what was the point of Proposition M? From a short-term, market-oriented business perspective, that is a sensible question to ask. From a long-term, community-oriented political point of view, the answer is: to protect community from capital, and capital from itself.

The Manhattanization of San Francisco provoked Proposition M but could not be prevented by it. Yet the time lag between the feverish pouring of concrete and the political response to it worked to the advantage of the progressive movement. Community became strong at precisely the moment capital was most weak in San Francisco. Progressive leaders seized that moment to enact slow-growth policies that were intended to have long-term and citywide repercussions in buffering San Francisco indefinitely against the cycles of capitalism. By implanting the policies in local government during the deepest trough of one of those cycles, progressive leaders increased the chance that those policies would take root and eventually spread to the level of political culture. Ironically, the collapse of the commercial real estate market and the continuing economic recession have all worked to strengthen the long-term effects of Proposition M by prolonging the nurturing trough. Commercial vacancy rates remain high (13 percent at this writing), rents are low, credit is tight, and the pressure to build in the city is minimal.

Business leaders continue to complain about Proposition M, but complaining and organizing are two different things. Planning Director Dean Macris recently declared that "in this city where everything already is built cheek to jowl and people want growth management, I don't see anyone stepping forward to say we need fewer rules with the political clout to back him up."[7] And Macris is correct that the people do want growth management. In a poll of 406 registered voters conducted during April–May 1989, 83 percent opposed (60 percent strongly) "a change in the City's Master Plan to allow more downtown highrise offices to be built."[8] Growth control in San Francisco will become routinized to the extent that Proposition M remains the unchallenged framework of land-use and development planning. It is a framework that gives ordinary citizens the institutional leverage they need to participate more actively in the planning process; indeed, as shown in later chapters, many citizens have grown accustomed to these new powers and are adept at using them. Some activists even view Proposition M as a kind of

citizens' bill of rights that protects grass-roots democracy in an arena once dominated by CEOs and technocrats. The deeper significance of Proposition M is that
it is the linchpin that couples polity and economy in the making of land-use
decisions. Its defenders want that coupling to stay intact, since there will always
be wild forces in the economy to keep penned. If growth control is a closed barn
door, then Proposition M is its strongest bolt.

Under Mayor Art Agnos—and sometimes against the grain of his own deal-
making proclivities and managerial style—Proposition M and the Downtown
Plan altered the decision premises that constrain planners and politicians in their
relations with capital. In some cases these new rules were almost "programmed"
into the planning machinery. For example, Proposition M's precise limits on new
office construction allow little room for discretion. Once installed, they had immediate and dramatic effects in reducing the annual square footage of new office
space approved by the Planning Commission. Figure 6.1 shows that the volume of
such approvals during the peak years of 1979–85 sputtered to a dribble in 1986 as
the Proposition M spigot was turned down hard. Further, the stringent annual
growth caps quickly altered San Francisco's competitive position relative to other
cities in attracting new businesses, particularly large corporations needing big
buildings with huge floorplates. For example, one San Francisco bidder in a
contest with Oakland for a Caltrans headquarters office employing fifteen hun-

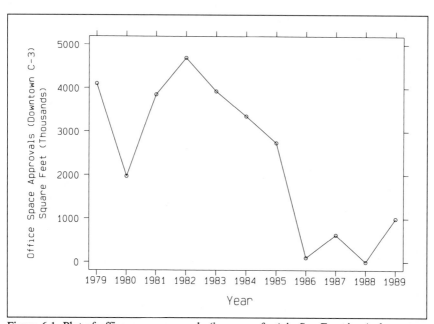

Figure 6.1. Plot of office space approvals (in square feet) in San Francisco's downtown
financial district, 1979–89. *Source:* Draft Growth Monitoring Report, San Francisco City
Planning Department.

dred workers commented: "The problem [for San Francisco] is that in Oakland they give away land and in San Francisco, we measure it by the teaspoon."[9] (Caltrans chose Oakland.) In other cases, Proposition M and the Downtown Plan narrowed and channeled discretion in ways that compel it to serve new social goals. The relatively few buildings approved since 1986 had to survive a difficult review process, known locally as the Planning Commission's "beauty contest." "This Planning Commission is demanding things that ten years ago, or even five years ago, were mentioned as social goals but were rarely attained," said one leading local architect about the new rules of the game.[10] Favored in the process are proposals with public amenities (on-site childcare centers, open space facilities, etc.), preleasing arrangements signifying high absorption rates, and building sites located in the less-impacted south financial district. Aesthetically, the new buildings are smaller, more delicate, and more architecturally consistent with the local urban design context and neighborhood character.

Yet there have been times when the city's planning bureaucracies demanded too much of developers. A particularly notorious instance of what can only be described as public-sector greed occurred in 1989 when the city's Redevelopment Agency rejected a proposal by the Wells Fargo Bank to construct a new building on city land at Third and Mission streets. That building would have housed a central office for the hundreds of data processors and other employees who were then working at scattered sites around the city. Mayor Agnos and his planning officials encouraged Wells Fargo executives to pursue the Third and Mission project because it would save existing bank jobs and add new ones for city residents. The Redevelopment Agency is not bound by Proposition M's rules, but the agency's director, Edward Helfeld, took advantage of the scarcity of land and the slow-growth milieu by encouraging a bidding war between Wells Fargo, Griffin Related Properties (a southern California firm), and other developers for permits to build on the Third and Mission site. In making its proposal for a twenty-eight-floor building with BankAmerica as its main tenant, Griffin offered lavish amenities and major concessions (including $5 million in fees above the minimum required). This was an offer that Wells Fargo could not match and the Redevelopment Agency could not refuse. Like the dog that dropped the bone in its mouth to fetch the one reflected in the pond, the agency dumped Wells Fargo and embraced Griffin. In the current harsh environment of finance capital, however, Griffin failed to muster the money needed to build. BankAmerica withdrew as a tenant. Wells Fargo spent its project money—$18 million—to buy 127 acres in Rocklin, California, for an employee business campus. And the city's hungry mouth was left empty.[11]

In sum, Proposition M could not roll back time and reverse Manhattanization. But in a soft commercial real estate market, the annual growth limits have helped to slow *new* high-rise construction to a trickle. Proposition M and the Downtown Plan have encouraged the city's land-use planners to be more demanding and selective—in the Wells Fargo case, too demanding and too selective—in choosing projects that serve new social goals. If public-sector greed can be bridled, the new growth-management rules also have the potential to reduce uncertainty and instability in local real estate markets. Most important, they alter the institutional and cultural context in which land-use and development decisions are made.

NEIGHBORHOOD POWER IN THE ANTIREGIME: THE CASE OF THRIFTY DRUGSTORE

This case study has the character of a before-and-after "natural experiment." What is the same both before and after the election of Art Agnos as mayor is Thrifty Corporation's desire to obtain a conditional-use permit from the Planning Commission under the Proposition M priority policies guidelines. The permits sought were for building chain drugstores in two separate neighborhoods, the first in the city's famous Haight-Ashbury, the second in the Sunset district. The Planning Commission's decisions were radically different in these two cases because the Planning Commission itself was different: The first was a Feinstein commission, the second an Agnos commission. The saga of the Thrifty Drugstore has many interesting aspects, but the most important point it demonstrates is that policy is only so much paper unless it is backed by power and authority. It matters who the decision makers are and what they think. What happened in the Haight helps to explain why the city's progressives decided to seek political power. What happened later in Sunset justified their decision.

Thrifty Drugstore versus the Haight[12]

In June 1987, Thrifty Corporation, a large national chain, sought permission to build a new drugstore covering 5,275 square feet on a leased lot in the Haight-Ashbury neighborhood commercial district. Neighborhood residents and merchants vigorously protested Thrifty's plans. Led by Calvin Welch of the Haight-Ashbury Neighborhood Coalition (HANC) and Jim Rhoads of the Haight-Ashbury Preservation Society (HAPS), the protestors gathered five thousand signatures on petitions opposing Thrifty's entry into the neighborhood. They also organized rallies and demonstrations to attract allies and to mobilize public sympathy for their cause. While freely (and proudly) admitting a "cultural animosity" toward chain operations in general, protest leaders argued that the proposed Thrifty store would drive out smaller, less competitive drugstores and shops, would increase car traffic and parking problems, and would "insult" the neighborhood's character and traditions.[13] The Haight-Ashbury's residents and merchants were by no means unanimous in opposing the new drugstore. Some of them, especially newer residents, viewed the anti-Thrifty campaign as a myopic attempt by radicals to resist needed change and to preserve the Haight as a historical museum. But the protesters did represent a very unsilent majority.

The Planning Department had just completed revising the elements of the city's Master Plan and neighborhood commercial zoning regulations to conform with Proposition M's priority policies. The critical changes focused on objective eight of the commerce and industry element, which required the city to "maintain and strengthen viable neighborhood commercial areas easily accessible to residents."[14] Nine new zoning policies replaced the five old ones for implementing this objective at the street level. These new zoning policies fused the slow-growth preservationist language of Proposition M's priority policies with progrowth text carried over from the old regime. For example, while Proposition M required that "the City's supply of affordable housing be preserved and enhanced," the new policies under objective eight required that the city "strike a balance between the preservation of existing affordable housing and needed expansion of commercial activity."[15] Although the new zoning regulations captured the spirit and some of the language of Proposition M's directive that "existing housing and neighborhood character be conserved and protected," the city was also instructed under objective eight to "promote high quality urban design on commercial streets."[16] Combined with neighborhood commercial-district planning codes that called for the provision within the Haight of needed goods and services, these "balanced development" and "urban design" hooks in slow-growth policy allowed Thrifty's representatives to justify construction of a large chain drugstore in the city's funkiest and most activist neighborhood community.

The rules required the Planning Commission to conduct a conditional-use permit hearing in this case because the proposed area exceeded the twenty-five hundred square feet allowed for business use on this site. The Planning Department's zoning administrator initially argued that such a hearing was not obligatory because the building had been approved with retail permitted on the first floor. But eventually, after repeated last-minute postponements of scheduled meeting times, the commission did hold a public hearing on 20 August before a large crowd. After listening to testimony from both sides (including speeches by Thrifty's senior vice president Robert Henry, Jr., Calvin Welch, and Jim Rhoads), and after hearing many impassioned pleas from long-time Haight residents to reject Thrifty's permit request, the Planning Commission voted six to one to grant the permit and to let work on the building begin. Only Sue Bierman voted against it, stating that "the small merchants are going to have a tough time. . . . There is not one business in the Haight that can afford the kind of advertising Thrifty can."[17] As one observer noted, "It was obvious that the intangible qualities about the Haight that so many people praised [at the hearing] were the least relevant for the Commissioners in analyzing the full issue. This was indicated by the remark made by [Zoning Administrator Robert] Passmore that 'you can't legislate over the character of a neighborhood.' The problems of traffic and parking congestion were passed off as 'problems that could be worked out later.' "[18] The announcement of the vote was not well received by those in attendance. Many of them "hurled wads of paper and shouted epithets" at the commissioners.[19] One

HAPS leader seized the microphone and yelled, "Listen to the people!" Another screamed, "What went through your mind? Did you listen to anything anyone said?" As Jim Rhoads walked by Thrifty's Robert Henry, he said, "Welcome to the neighborhood."[20]

The hopes that had been raised by Proposition M were dashed abruptly by the commission's decision. From the perspective of angry Haight activists, protest and policy were not enough to stop Mayor Feinstein's commissioners from giving big business a green light to destroy their neighborhood community. HAPS and other Haight groups soon filed a lawsuit challenging the Planning Commission's authority to grant conditional-use permits so contrary to the policy priorities expressed in Proposition M. Meanwhile, work on the Thrifty drugstore began. On 21 September 1988, however, a fire that was suspected to be arson burned the unfinished building to the ground. (The fire also damaged nearby buildings and displaced a dozen or so residents.) The political message of the act was transparent. HAPS leader Jim Rhoads, condemning the arson, said, "I would naturally rather have won in court." "This is bad business no matter how you look at it."[21]

In a letter to the city's new mayor, Art Agnos, Thrifty's Robert Henry wrote, "The message this conflagration gives out is that if one disagrees with how a permit process turned out, if the law of the city proves unsatisfactory to a given individual group, then all they have to do is burn the building down."[22] Mayor Agnos denounced the arsonous tactics, but he refused to meet face-to-face with Thrifty officials, delegating that task to James Ho, his deputy mayor for business. The meetings with Ho gave no assurance that the city could prevent sabotage of this sort in the future. The Thrifty Corporation decided not to rebuild in the Haight.[23]

Mayor Feinstein's Planning Commission could not have picked a worse place (the Haight) or a worse time (just months after the Proposition M victory) to sacrifice the spirit of slow growth on the altar of free enterprise. The whole episode corroborated what many neighborhood populists and slow-growth progressives already knew: The values and goals stated in Proposition M would have zero impact in reality unless they were upheld by local government power and authority. As long as Mayor Feinstein's appointed commissioners remained in office, the new policy priorities would be all gums and no teeth.

Thrifty Drugstore versus the Sunset District

In 1990, Thrifty Corporation requested another conditional-use permit from the Planning Commission, this time to expand a building in the Sunset district for a large drugstore. After a lengthy process of review and testimony under the Proposition M guidelines, the commission, now dominated by Mayor Agnos's neighborhood-oriented appointees, denied the request by a vote of six to one. The commissioners cited the project's incompatibility with Proposition M's priority policies and other Master Plan requirements.[24] Brett Gladstone, the attorney who represented Sunset residents and merchants in their fight against Thrifty, described the decision as a victory for Proposition M, commenting that "Prop. M is finally being enforced in our neighborhoods as well as downtown."[25] Thrifty's local lobbyists had invested a lot of money, time, and effort (including public opinion surveys) in an attempt to demonstrate the proposal's economic desirability and neighborhood compatibility according to the Proposition M standards. Their frustration with the new rules of the game under Proposition M was obvious. A month before the decision, one of them had exclaimed, "We suddenly find ourselves in the 'People's Republic of San Francisco.' "[26]

CONCLUSION

These case studies of land-use politics and planning in the antiregime focused on the familiar downtown and neighborhood arenas. They illustrate the power of the new slow-growth machinery to place clamps on the circuits of capital, to channel and divert its flow, and to prevent it from flooding into neighborhood communities. The studies also show that it matters very much who operates that machinery and that even the best operators can use it recklessly. Of all the people who make the machinery work, no one matters more than the mayor. The city's progressives had learned that lesson, and that is why they elected Art Agnos. As a candidate for office, Agnos had promised to enforce Proposition M and to appoint its advocates to positions of power. In the already-Manhattanized downtown financial district, the task facing Mayor Agnos as a slow-growth manager was relatively easy. The rules were clear, the district was built out, and the pressure of capital had dropped. In the neighborhoods, Agnos could trust his commissioners to do the right thing under Proposition M, which was to let the neighborhood residents have the last say in preserving and enhancing their communities. In areas outside the downtown and the neighborhoods, however, Agnos moved with a freer hand to pursue large-scale development projects that violated the spirit if not the letter of Proposition M. Those areas included the greater China Basin, the Mission Bay property, and seven miles of waterfront. It was in China Basin that Agnos first exposed his progrowth claws and began to alienate his slow-growth constituency.

7

Save Our Giants: Political
Hardball in China Basin

Ex ungue leonem.[1]

—Anonymous

In 1989, the city's voters rejected a proposal by Mayor Art Agnos and the San Francisco Giants to build a new baseball stadium at a downtown waterfront site in an area known as China Basin. The defeat of the stadium proposal meant that the Giants almost certainly would leave San Francisco after the 1994 season, perhaps sooner. The defeat also foreshadowed the struggles Agnos would face repeatedly in the months that followed as he tried to exercise progrowth leadership in a slow-growth political environment. Both in style and substance, Agnos's campaign for the China Basin stadium tarnished his reputation as a progressive politician and antagonized many former supporters. Yet, at the time, Agnos was proud of the "smart" deal he had struck in an effort to keep the Giants in San Francisco.

PANEM ET CIRCENSES ET BOB LURIE

In many U.S. cities, professional sports franchises provide jobs, revenue, entertainment, and national visibility. A city's big-league baseball and football teams foster intense fan loyalty, civic pride, and a strong sense of communal ownership. Beneath the rhetoric of public-private partnerships, however, almost all sports franchises are businesses organized to make profits, and the capital invested in them has become increasingly mobile. Team owners who believe they can get a better deal in another city will consider moving the franchise there—or they might threaten to do so to exact concessions from the host city.[2] Since the intercity competition for professional sports franchises is fierce, the threats often work. Owners can expect to be pampered by boosters and politicians who will do everything possible to "save our Raiders" or "save our Sox" or—the case in point—"save our Giants."

Millionaire Bob Lurie owns the San Francisco Giants baseball team. A life-long resident of the city, he purchased the club in 1976 to keep the Giants in San Francisco—and also, presumably, to make money. In the early 1980s, Lurie began complaining to Mayor Dianne Feinstein and other city officials about the inadequacies of Candlestick Park, which serves as the home field for both the Giants and the San Francisco Forty-Niners football team. Candlestick is located near the Bayshore Freeway on the southern edge of the city about five miles from downtown. It is the second-oldest baseball stadium in the National League and lacks many of the luxury accommodations, amenities, and concessions found in modern stadiums. It also has a well-deserved reputation for being cold and windy. Lurie informed Feinstein that his team would not play in Candlestick Park after the end of the 1994 season, when his lease with the city expired. He demanded that a new, smaller baseball stadium of modern design be built closer to downtown. He also invited offers from other cities to host the Giants. Leaders in the franchise-starved cities of San Jose and Santa Clara were quick to respond, and they began mobilizing boosters and advancing proposals as early as 1985. By mid-1986, the pressure on Feinstein was intense to find some way to build a new downtown stadium for Lurie's team or else face the ignominy of being known as the mayor who "lost the Giants."

Mayor Feinstein and her advisors faced formidable problems in trying to meet Lurie's demands. Selecting a downtown site for the new stadium would not be easy because of the increasing traffic congestion, growth restrictions, and scarcity of developable land. The financing of land purchase, site preparation, and construction of the stadium would be difficult, especially if substantial public subsidies were required. Politically, the stadium boosters could expect resistance from fiscal conservatives, neighborhood preservationists, and slow-growth progressives. A poll conducted at the time revealed that registered voters overwhelmingly opposed the idea of building a new stadium to replace Candlestick Park. A bare majority did agree, however, that building a new stadium was a good idea "if the taxpayers didn't have to pay for it."[3]

AN ILL-CONCEIVED WHITE ELEPHANT: PROPOSITION W

In 1987, Mayor Feinstein's stadium task force found a site for the new Giants ballpark near Potrero Hill at Seventh and Townsend streets. That location was close enough to downtown to satisfy Bob Lurie. The plans called for building a stadium seating forty-two thousand people at an estimated cost of $80 million. Santa Fe Pacific Realty owned the land but was expected to donate it. Most of the money to pay for construction would come from concessionaire companies, luxury box sales, advertising revenues, stadium rental fees, and private donations. Other possible funding sources included lease revenue bonds backed by private money and public subsidies from the city's hotel tax, paid by tourists.[4]

Lurie was prepared to endorse the Seventh and Townsend stadium proposal, but he insisted on a clear demonstration of public support before moving ahead. Given the passage of the Proposition M growth controls the year before and given the fact that San Franciscans composed only 15 percent of the Giants' fan base, political precautions seemed necessary. As Giants Vice-president Corey Busch explained, "We need to create momentum. This thing was on dead center, and we need to know the public will is there if we are to get private money. The best way to demonstrate that is a public vote."[5] Responding to this demand, Mayor Feinstein and the Board of Supervisors placed an official declaration of policy (Proposition W) on the 3 November 1987 ballot. It asked simply: "Shall a baseball park be built at 7th & Townsend on land at no cost to the city with no increases in taxes and all debt repaid with non-tax money?"

A major flaw in the Proposition W advisory measure was its lack of credibility. If taxpayers would not have to pay for the stadium, who would? Since traffic congestion was projected to increase on downtown streets even without the new ballpark, how would thousands of additional cars be accommodated for weekday games, especially at rush hour? Stadium supporters failed to provide clear answers to these kinds of obvious questions. Stadium opponents were free to assume the worst. When Potrero Hill residents learned that they would bear the brunt of traffic, noise, and commercial development spilling over from the stadium site, they mobilized in force to defeat Proposition W. They were joined by Assemblyman Art Agnos, then a mayoral candidate running a grass-roots campaign that stressed the importance of neighborhood preservation. Agnos attacked the proposed Seventh and Townsend stadium as "an ill-conceived, unneeded, unwanted, traffic-gridlocking, dollar-devouring white elephant that would not work, not help the Giants, is not downtown and affords practically no parking."[6] In his drive for mayor, Agnos said little to indicate support for a new stadium and wrote nothing on the topic in his widely distributed campaign book. Progressive voters had good reason at the time to believe that Agnos as mayor would stand up to Bob Lurie and not cave in to any unreasonable demands.[7]

On 3 November, San Francisco voters defeated Proposition W by 53 percent to 47 percent. To say the least, this was not the show of public support Lurie wanted. He quickly scrapped plans for the downtown stadium and challenged San Jose, Santa Clara, and other South Bay cities to make him a better offer. To prove he was serious, he contributed $200,000 to pay for a market study of a proposed stadium site in Santa Clara. Sunnyvale Mayor Larry Stone, head of the South Bay Stadium Task Force, said, "The message to us was, 'It's yours if you don't screw it up.' They [the Giants] said it was ours if we could make it happen."[8] In the summer of 1988, after the market study revealed that the Santa Clara site would attract fans from all over the Bay Area, Lurie publicly endorsed the South Bay planning efforts. The Santa Clara stadium boosters now had the inside track in luring the Giants away.

ENTER MAYOR AGNOS

Once in office, Mayor Agnos moved swiftly to organize a last-ditch effort to persuade Lurie to keep the Giants in San Francisco. In late September 1988, Agnos arranged a private meeting with Lurie to present plans for building a forty-five-thousand-seat baseball stadium at Second and King streets in China Basin. Impressed by Agnos's presentation, Lurie encouraged him to develop the China Basin proposal. But he was wary, knowing that one year earlier Agnos had opposed building a stadium at Seventh and Townsend, which was a mere five blocks from the China Basin site. Yet near the end of his mayoral campaign, candidate Agnos had assured downtown business elites that he was sympathetic to their interests and would seek their cooperation in promoting the city's economic development. Here was a chance for Mayor Agnos to act on that promise. Losing the Giants would be a severe blow to any development strategy—especially in a local economy so dependent on the hospitality and tourism industries. It was also clear that Agnos, like Feinstein before him, was anxious to avoid being labeled "the mayor who lost the Giants." Thus, despite Agnos's prior opposition and antibusiness reputation, his China Basin proposal appeared entirely credible to Lurie. Events would prove that his confidence in the mayor was not misplaced.

Lurie announced that he would choose between the South Bay and San Francisco stadium proposals in July 1989. That deadline allowed the two booster groups about a year to formulate detailed plans. Although the South Bay group had a head start in this leg of the race, Mayor Agnos's twelve-member Special Stadium Task Force moved quickly to place San Francisco in the lead once again. Two key members of the Agnos team were former planning commissioner Toby Rosenblatt and Planning Director Dean Macris. Their strategy was to sign on a developer at the very start of the planning process and to put together a complete package deal that Lurie would find irresistible. As one insider close to the deal making later recalled, "We brought all the parties together from the start—the tenant, the builder and the government. It was a critical decision that allowed us to pull far ahead."[9]

On 3 February, Mayor Agnos announced that his task force had selected Spectacor Management Group as the developer for the stadium project. Spectacor, a Philadelphia-based development firm, edged out two rivals in winning the bid because of its national reputation for making successful deals of this sort and because it had a plan to limit the city's financial liability in building and operating the China Basin stadium. Spectacor's track record was impressive. It had built Miami's Joe Robbie Stadium. The firm's architect, HOK Sports Facilities Group of Kansas City, recently had constructed a stadium in Buffalo and was working on ballparks in Baltimore and St. Louis. Spectacor's contractor, Huber, Hunt and Nichols, had built Cincinnati's Riverfront Stadium and the Louisiana Superdome. Spectacor also operated San Francisco's Moscone Center and therefore was well known locally. Spectacor's initial proposal called for building a baseball stadium and an indoor sports arena in the China Basin area at a cost of $200 million. (The indoor arena was later dropped from the plans.) The city would be required to supply land for the stadium site. Since the land was owned by the Port of San Francisco and the California Department of Transportation, arranging the land deal would be complicated but not impossible, especially if a land swap could be made with the approval of the state lands commission. Since the proposed site was located within one hundred feet of the waterfront, the city would need to obtain clearances from state and federal agencies. The city would also be required to issue $50 million in tax-exempt industrial bonds to be paid off over a thirty-year period. But Spectacor, not the taxpayers, would assume the risk of making payments on these bonds. The remaining financing details would be worked out later after the city entered exclusive negotiations with Spectacor to develop a final proposal.[10] If Lurie approved the deal, San Francisco voters would be given an opportunity to accept or reject it in the November election.

Even as Mayor Agnos and his group were negotiating with Spectacor, the South Bay Stadium Task Force began to stumble in the race for the Giants. Some members of the Santa Clara City Council were balking at the prospect of giving up one hundred acres of prime city land for a sports franchise considered to be economically marginal. Further, the proposed governance arrangement for the South Bay stadium—a joint-powers authority that would include representatives from Sunnyvale, Santa Clara, San Jose, and Santa Clara County—appeared complicated and unworkable. It certainly looked that way to Bob Lurie and his advisors. Reporter Thomas Keane wrote, "The Giants recoiled in horror [at the joint-powers authority idea], thinking that the bureaucratic entanglements would make the deal nearly as difficult as solving a jigsaw puzzle with a blindfold on."[11]

As the competition between San Francisco and South Bay wore on, some observers began to voice widely shared suspicions that Lurie was encouraging the South Bay planning efforts merely as a gambit to force San Francisco to build a downtown stadium on his terms. Santa Clara Councilman Dave Delozien remarked, "I have the feeling Mr. Lurie is using us as the old has-been date he can keep on a string."[12] Lurie and his aides always denied having such ulterior motives. Giants Vice-president Corey Busch insisted, for example, that "if we really wanted to light a fire under San Francisco, we would have opened our doors to Denver, Phoenix, and all those other places itching for a major league team."[13] Mayor Agnos also tried to quell such suspicions: "I can tell you that, in our negotiations, Bob Lurie never once played us off against Santa Clara. When we made our offer, he didn't try to take it to Santa Clara to see if he could get a better one."[14] Despite such protestations, speculation about Lurie's true motives would not cease.

LURIE CHOOSES

In July, as the day of Lurie's decision approached, suspense began to grow. Would Lurie pick San Francisco or Santa Clara? *Chronicle* reporters Ray Tessler and Thomas Keane framed the choice in the following terms: "Three decades after the Giants left Manhattan for the Golden Gate, a suspenseful countdown has begun that will determine whether the city of Willie Mays and Lefty O'Doul remains a Major League town."[15] Despite inside rumblings that the South Bay stadium deal was turning sour, editors of the *San Jose Mercury-News* exuded confidence that the decision would go their way: "While other kids were playing shortstop, [South Bay boys] were fiddling with vacuum tubes and slide rules. . . . And if they now ended up as owners of a big-league ball team—wouldn't that be the sweet revenge of the nerds?"[16] The Santa Clara Valley Giants Booster Club delivered a petition with fifteen thousand signatures to Lurie urging him to move the Giants to the South Bay. Meanwhile, San Francisco advocates of the China Basin stadium rallied their forces. Months earlier the San Francisco Ballpark Alliance had formed to seek endorsements and grass-roots support for the China Basin proposal. After years of internal division, the Chamber of Commerce closed ranks behind the plan, much to the delight of Barbara Bagot, president of the ballpark alliance: "We needed the business community out front on this issue and now we have it. We're on a roll."[17] Supervisor Wendy Nelder urged board members to give the China Basin proposal unanimous support, explaining that "Mr. Lurie has shown his loyalty to San Francisco, but he's a businessman, and he has to make a decision."[18] The Board of Supervisors voted eight to two to endorse the proposal, a strong show of support but not the desired unanimity. Supervisors Tom Hsieh and Richard Hongisto cast the two nays.

In explaining his dissenting vote, Hongisto conveyed the theme of fiscal populism that later would link progressives and conservatives in their opposition to the China Basin stadium: "In pursuit of the golden fleece, [the Giants] keep trying to fleece the city treasury. If we want to keep the Giants here, we've got to get hip to the fact that we already have a stadium. It may not be ideal . . . but it's bought and paid for."[19] Even as he spoke, Joel Ventresca and other opponents of the downtown stadium were gathering signatures to place an initiative on the November ballot (Proposition V) that would require the city to explore privately funded improvements in Candlestick Park as a positive alternative to the China Basin proposal.

Many former Agnos supporters were stunned by the mayor's dramatic about-face on the ballpark controversy. Some began to question his credentials as a progressive leader. San Francisco Tomorrow President Jack Morrison, a prominent critic of the China Basin proposal, commented, "At this stage, I don't think our support for [Agnos] is in any danger, but we're certainly very disappointed."[20] Elizabeth Boileau, who served Agnos as a precinct captain during his mayoral campaign, conjectured that the mayor "had to create some credibility with down-town interests and corporate interests. . . . I think he's responding to a different constituency now, and I think he's going to lose some [supporters] in this [China Basin stadium] effort, some people who really feel strongly about neighborhood issues."[21] Agnos's response to this kind of grumbling was to ask progressive critics to "wait until you see the details to make up your mind." The bargain he was negotiating would be made public soon, and patience would be rewarded. "I think we'll be able to put something smart to the voters," he said, "and I think we'll get a 75-to-25 percent vote."[22]

On 27 July, Mayor Agnos, Bob Lurie, and Spectacor Vice-president Don Webb announced that they had signed a formal agreement to build a forty-five-thou-sand-seat baseball stadium in China Basin. The deal called for the city to give Spectacor 12.5 acres of land for the site, $2 million a year for ten years to defray operating costs, and $1 million a year for ten years in the form of a loan to be repaid with interest in twenty-five years. Land owned by the city's Public Utilities Commission would be swapped for the needed port-owned and state-owned land at the site. The annual $3 million would come mainly from the city's hotel tax. The city also would have to build a fifteen-hundred-space parking garage, with the source of financing to be determined. In return, the city would receive 20 percent of the stadium's operating profits each year and would become owners of the ballpark when the forty-year lease expired. Spectacor would construct the $95-million stadium with funds obtained from developer-backed industrial rev-enue bonds and would also pay for some of the operating costs. In return, Spectacor would receive an undisclosed share of the ballpark revenues from VIP seating, advertising, luxury boxes, concessions, and choice of stadium name to please a corporate donor/sponsor. For his part, Lurie would give up an undisclosed portion of revenues from concessions, luxury boxes, and the like and would pay for ballpark security, ticket agents, players' salaries, and other employees. In return, he would have the use of a new downtown baseball stadium and would receive the bulk of revenues generated by ticket sales and television rights.[23] Lurie also would be exempt from property taxes on the stadium and would not be required to contribute any of his own money toward construction of the facility. Nor would he be compelled to divulge details of his separate agreement with Spectacor on issues such as profit sharing.

The race was over, or so it seemed, and San Francisco had won. San Jose, which had surpassed San Francisco years earlier by becoming the state's third-largest city, would have to make do with its single-A minor league baseball club, the San Jose Giants. The bitterness of defeat was palpable in Mark Purdy's front-page *San Jose Mercury-News* editorial: "Art Agnos' snake oil won. And the South Bay, once more, has had its face rubbed in that good old San Francisco superiority salad."[24] At the time he wrote those harsh words, Purdy did not foresee that mayoral snake oil can produce toxic side effects in a progressive body politic. The race was not over until the November election, and San Francisco voters, not Bob Lurie, would have the last say.

A "SMART" DEAL? THE PROPOSITION P CAMPAIGN

Shortly after the China Basin stadium deal was unveiled, an *Examiner* editorial concurred with Agnos that it was a "smart" deal—"the smartest one developed in North America." And the details of the plan—most of them, anyway—were there for all to see. "Two years ago, [San Franciscans] voted against an ill-defined proposal for a downtown stadium. This one will be *well-defined*, full of specifics, lacking in liabilities."[25] Stadium opponents would agree that the China Basin proposal was relatively well defined but would dispute the claim that it lacked liabilities. Indeed, revelation of the particulars exposed the specific drawbacks that critics would seize upon in organizing the opposition campaign: increased traffic congestion, raids on the hotel tax fund, and ruination of long-established plans to develop the China Basin area for light industry and affordable housing. Perhaps most troubling to progressive critics was the underlying issue of *who* defined the "well-defined" deal. Mayor Agnos's nonconsultative style of secret, backroom negotiations with Lurie and Spectacor smacked of elitist deal making for the people but not by the people. Jack Morrison commented, "We're sorely disappointed that the mayor went ahead with this project. This proposal goes against all the mayor's previous commitments to community consensus and responsible land-use goals."[26]

On 9 August, at Mayor Agnos's request, the Registrar of Voters placed a proposed ordinance (Proposition P) on the November ballot that would ratify the city's agreement with Lurie and the Spectacor Management Group. Also on that ballot were Proposition V, the citizen-initiated declaration of policy for improving Candlestick Park, and Proposition S, a citizen-initiated referendum on the recently passed domestic partners ordinance. As a further demonstration of the city government's official resolve to meet Lurie's demands, Agnos and a majority of the Board of Supervisors amended the Candlestick lease to allow the Giants to leave San Francisco immediately if the voters rejected Proposition P. This action had the effect of burning bridges to prevent voters from procrastinating on the false hope that Lurie might change his mind about Candlestick before his original lease ran out in 1994. To some observers this was blackmail, pure and simple, and it was certain to backfire among resentful voters.[27]

Mayor Agnos threw himself into the campaign for Proposition P with a fervor that was noticed by supporters and opponents alike. A *Chronicle* editorial endorsed the stadium proposal, calling Agnos a "real champion" who was "campaigning just as hard for the park at China Basin as he did for the mayoral office more than a year and a half ago."[28] Fortified by his landslide victory in the mayoral run-off election, Agnos had surplus political capital to invest in responding to the demands of a rich baseball club owner, even at the risk of losing some of his progressive support. Downtown businesses, corporations, and other donors would contribute plenty of their own kind of capital to the Proposition P campaign: over $880,000, including $86,539 from Spectacor Management Group. Opposition spending amounted to $130,000.[29]

Apart from emotional appeals to fans and voters to "save our Giants" and preserve San Francisco's big-league standing among cities, the major theme of Agnos's Proposition P campaign was economic development. If San Francisco lost the Giants as a Candlestick tenant after 1994, the city would forfeit an estimated $700,000 annually in revenues.[30] If the Giants could be enticed to stay and play in the new ballpark, however, the city eventually would receive an estimated return of between $170 million and $2.1 billion on an investment totaling less than $101 million.[31] In addition to the jobs generated by constructing and operating the new stadium, the projected net revenues would help secure the city's long-term fiscal health and also expand the resources available for fighting AIDS, building affordable housing, and meeting other social needs. Any deal that promised these kinds of economic benefits for the city seemed smart to Mayor Agnos, especially at a time of budget deficits and shrinking federal assistance. This economic development motif would appeal not only to downtown business elites but to ethnic minorities and working-class voters. Joe Alioto, Dianne Feinstein, and other mayors had used such progrowth arguments in the past to win popular support for large-scale development projects. Perhaps these same arguments would work for Agnos, too.[32]

Leading the "No on P" campaign were Jack Morrison and Jim Firth of San Franciscans for Planning Priorities (SFPP), an umbrella organization comprising many of the same environmentalist and neighborhood groups that had supported Proposition M in 1986 and defeated Proposition W in 1987. Among those joining SFPP in opposing Proposition P were San Francisco Tomorrow, the Coalition for San Francisco Neighborhoods (representing fifty-seven neighborhood groups across the city), various Potrero Hill neighborhood and merchant associations, the San Francisco Taxpayers Association, the organizers of the "Yes on V" (Candlestick improvements) campaign, well-known civic leader James Haas, and Supervisor Richard Hongisto.

Familiar slow-growth and neighborhood preservation themes dominated the early stages of the antiballpark campaign, tempered by the fiscal conservatism of older home owners who saw no compelling reason to trade in the worn but functional Candlestick Park for a new-model stadium just to please Bob Lurie. Ballpark opponents quoted Planning Department studies that projected traffic gridlock in the stadium area on game days even if 20 percent of the fans used public transportation. The demand for parking would swamp the proposed parking garage and spill over into the streets of surrounding neighborhoods.[33] Columnist Warren Hinckle's nickname for the proposed stadium, "Gridlock Park," conveyed the gist of these concerns.[34] Mayor Agnos and Planning Director Dean

Macris responded that these traffic and parking nightmares were based on worst-case scenarios and that the planned development of nearby Mission Bay would be accompanied by improved public transit serving the China Basin area.[35] But many stadium critics felt that such optimism was unwarranted, especially since the Mission Bay Plan was known only to Agnos and a few others and would itself require voter approval.

Unable to rebut arguments that the China Basin stadium would cause severe traffic and parking problems, ballpark advocates characterized such concerns as small-minded and provincial. Dean Macris, for example, declared that "great cities—Paris, Rome, San Francisco—always have parking problems because we give the highest priority to an active, built-out city—not to parking lots."[36] Agnos was equally dismissive: "If you want a bucolic existence, move to [the small rural town of] Bolinas."[37] As these remarks revealed, radically different conceptions of the city were at odds here. One responded to the imperatives of capital in building out the city, the other to the imperatives of community in preserving neighbor-hoods and the quality of life. China Basin became a new battleground for the continuing conflict between progrowth and slow-growth perspectives on land use and economic development.

Agnos and other ballpark supporters attacked the "No on P" campaign as anti-growth and antibusiness. In response, "No on P" leaders stressed repeatedly that they favored development of the China Basin area—but not the blockbuster type of development envisaged by the ballpark proposal. What the Proposition P advocates did not see or chose to ignore was that a process of planned and disci-plined development had been taking place in the greater China Basin area for fifteen years. As stadium opponent James Haas observed, the "question before the voters was not whether to build at China Basin, but what."[38] Over the years a consensus had emerged among community groups, business leaders, and city planners regarding development priorities for the area. Top priority had been given to building moderate-priced housing to accommodate the growing numbers of downtown workers. A redevelopment district had been created at South Beach for that purpose and also to allow construction of a seven-hundred-berth marina. Rincon Hill had been rezoned to promote housing uses. By late 1989, Forest City Development and other residential developers had built over twelve hundred units of housing in the area at a cost of more than $150 million. Plans had been approved to reconstruct the Embarcadero as a roadway with light rail transit in the median. Attracted by these endeavors, investors such as the Harper Group, a transportation company with more than $350 million in sales, were entering the area to purchase, convert, and rehabilitate older buildings for use as inexpensive office and commercial space. The Rincon Point–South Beach Advisory Commit-tee had been organized to counsel the Redevelopment Agency on planning in the area and was now promoting construction of affordable housing in the South Beach district.[39]

In sum, China Basin was not a neglected, empty space just waiting to be filled by ambitious politicians pursuing visions of world-class city grandeur. It was one of the city's prime growth centers, a source of new housing, a magnet for entrepreneurs, and a model of planned and rational development shaped by citizen participation. Before the city's deal with Spectacor, Haas noted, "the greater China Basin area was developing nicely according to the established plans. Then, out of the blue, the planning director announced that a 15-story, two-block long baseball stadium would be located on the publicly owned land at China Basin. This decision was made without consultation with the advisory committee or the South Beach property owners. It was made in the face of 15 years of planning calling for residential development to occur in the area."[40] In this context, it is understandable why many "No on P" leaders viewed the proposed stadium as a destroyer rather than a creator of growth and business in the area. It seemed ironic that Mayor Agnos would want to bury this vibrant, expanding community under tons of stadium concrete, all in the name of growth and economic development. The feelings of perplexity, anger, and betrayal among former Agnos supporters were captured in the remarks of Joel Blum, leader of a coalition of business owners located at the former MJB coffee building near the stadium site: "That the same municipal government which has encouraged the economic growth of this important neighborhood can make itself liable for the destruction of those businesses it has helped to nurture, will be an unforgivable paradox."[41]

In devising his campaign strategy for Proposition P, Mayor Agnos must have anticipated this strong opposition from the neighborhood activists and environmentalists who made up the slow-growth wing of his progressive electoral coalition. That would explain the unusual logrolling tactic he employed to reinforce his resurrected progrowth coalition with support from the gay and lesbian community.[42] Agnos promised to campaign hard for Proposition S, a citizen-initiated referendum on the new domestic partners legislation. Passage of Proposition S was of paramount importance to the city's gay and lesbian residents, most of whom tend to vote progressive across the board. In return for his active support of Proposition S, Agnos asked leaders and members of the city's gay and lesbian political clubs to endorse Proposition P. As progressives, most gay and lesbian voters would be inclined to oppose such a measure in alliance with environmentalists and neighborhood activists. But Agnos's pledge of extra campaign effort on behalf of Proposition S enticed at least some gay and lesbian leaders to suspend their opposition. Agnos's campaign slogan, "Vote for one another," was heard often early in the campaign. Later, however, this direct-democracy back scratching began to break down. For example, the gay and lesbian Stonewall Democratic Club initially gave its endorsement to Proposition P but later withdrew it when Agnos refused to push Proposition S with the socially conservative Black Leadership Forum.[43] By election day, it appeared that Agnos had failed to pry loose this particular wedge from the progressive coalition.[44]

THE LOMA PRIETA EARTHQUAKE

On 17 October, three weeks before the election, nature threw politics a curve. The Loma Prieta earthquake, measuring 7.1 on the Richter scale, rolled through the Bay Area leaving behind widespread physical destruction, dozens of deaths, and the dislocation of thousands of families. At the time the earthquake hit, thousands of fans were packed into Candlestick Park to watch game three of the 1989 Giants-Athletics World Series. The temblor jolted the old stadium but caused only minor structural damage and no major injuries or loss of life. Elsewhere in San Francisco, however, 500 buildings were lost, more than 150 of them in the South of Market area. The Central and Embarcadero freeways were severely damaged and had to be closed. Worst hit was the residential Marina district, built on landfill, where many structures collapsed or burned. Total damages in the Bay Area were between $5 billion and $6 billion, with an estimated $2 billion in San Francisco alone.[45] The earthquake turned a national spotlight on Mayor Agnos as he exercised his leadership skills and emergency powers in coping with the crisis. He suspended all campaign activities, reassigned staff and resources to disaster relief efforts, and took command of a difficult situation. He earned praise even from his critics for a job well done. It was the mayor's finest hour.

As the dust settled from the earthquake, however, and as normal politics resumed only days before the 7 November election, it became obvious that the "Yes on P" campaign was in trouble.[46] Shaken residents were still digging out of the rubble, assessing damage, and counting the dead. They were preoccupied with safety concerns, transportation problems, and needs for assistance. In this context of ruin, it would take quite a political sales pitch to convince voters that now was the time to spend city revenues on a new baseball stadium to be built on landfill in China Basin. Mayor Agnos accepted that challenge.

In the short time remaining before election day, "Yes on P" leaders initiated what one reporter described as "a final series of subdued appeals to skittish voters."[47] Agnos and others argued that building the China Basin stadium would accelerate the city's recovery from the earthquake, both financially and symbolically.[48] An *Examiner* editorial exhorted that "approval of Prop. P will send an international message that San Francisco is back."[49] Opposition leader Jim Firth was disturbed by this effort "to place the stadium in a pivotal point of the city's rebuilding, when in fact there are many other existing buildings that will need millions and millions of dollars put into them, just so that they can be re-opened and used."[50] To rebut these charges of misplaced priorities, Agnos held a news conference in Glide Memorial Church to introduce the Reverend Cecil Williams, Mitchell Omerberg, Roberta Achtenberg, and other well-known social-services leaders who came to endorse Proposition P as a source of new funding for city programs, "for the homeless, for those who are suffering, for all those that we care about in San Francisco."[51] To counter arguments that the proposed stadium's landfill site was unsafe, "Yes on P" leaders noted that many high rises in the financial district were also built on fill but had survived the earthquake intact because they rested on supports driven into bedrock. These same modern engineering techniques would be used in constructing the China Basin ballpark.[52] While accepting such claims, "No on P" skeptics wondered why this stadium's estimated price tag was actually lower than that for similar stadiums which did not require this complicated and expensive engineering.[53] *Bay Guardian* editorialists recapitulated many of the postquake antistadium arguments and used them to reinforce a broader attack on the progrowth version of economic development: "The overall Agnos/Ex/Chron line—that San Francisco's future ought to be linked to big new construction projects like a downtown stadium—represents a basic denial of reality . . . [The earthquake] reminded us that some parts of town aren't terribly well suited to full-scale development, that money and political power may move city planning commissioners but they are useless against plate tectonics."[54]

HIT PIECE HIJACK

Four days before the election, a new group called the "No on P/Yes on V" committee materialized to distribute an antiballpark mailer to voters citywide. The mailer bore the message "Now is not the time" and showed scenes of earthquake destruction. The existence of the "No on P/Yes on V" committee came as a complete surprise to leaders of the other campaigns. The mailer identified historian Kevin Starr as chairman and treasurer of the new committee, but little else was known about the group. No papers had been filed with the registrar of voters. The group's origins, sponsors, and funding sources were a mystery. When informed about the "No on P/Yes on V" committee and its mailer, SFPP leader Jack Morrison replied, "This is news to me."[55] Ed McGovern, manager of the "Yes on P" campaign, said, "It smells," adding that he believed the piece probably violated California fair political practices laws requiring financial disclosure.[56]

Ballpark supporters were outraged to learn a short time later that half of the $25,000 paid to produce and distribute the "No on P/Yes on V" mailer came from Gregg Lukenbill, a Sacramento developer and part-owner of the Sacramento Kings basketball team. Lukenbill had built the Kings' arena and was constructing a multi-use stadium in Sacramento to lure a big-league football or baseball franchise to that city.[57] On election day, a front-page editorial in the *Examiner* condemned the mailer as "a scheme by Sacramento promoters who want to hijack the Giants" and as a "contemptible, inflammatory and highly inaccurate hit piece."[58] Mayor Agnos was furious and lashed out at Lukenbill and his supporters: "There was no looting after October 17—until now. What we're seeing is a Sacramento developer, Gregg Lukenbill, and his cohorts, trying to loot San Francisco of its baseball team."[59] This attempt to portray sponsors of the mailer as outside agitators struck some ballpark opponents as hypocritical in view of the fact that Philadelphia-based Spectacor had contributed more than $86,000 to the "Yes on P" campaign. By the time voters cast their ballots on election day, the "hit piece" controversy had festered into a boil of angry accusations and ugly rhetoric. Just how angry and ugly would become clear in the eruption that followed the final counting of votes.

THE VOTE AND ITS AFTERMATH

In a surprisingly high-turnout election, Proposition P was defeated 49.5 percent to 50.5 percent, losing by fewer than two thousand votes. The China Basin stadium would not be built. *Examiner* reporter Eric Brazil wrote, "If Bob Lurie was bluffing about moving his National League champion Giants from Candlestick Park as soon as the 1991 season, the electorate called him on it."[60] The voters also defeated Proposition S by less than two thousand votes, thus rescinding the city's pioneering domestic partners ordinance.[61] The combined defeat of propositions P and S underlined the futility of Agnos's attempt to forge a tactical alliance between stadium supporters and gay rights advocates.[62] Proposition V, which Agnos had dismissed during the campaign as a "deleterious, frivolous measure designed to defeat Prop. P,"[63] passed with 51.4 percent of the vote. Mayor Agnos's best-laid backroom deals were dust. Accustomed to winning, he was not a gracious loser.

In conceding Proposition P's defeat, Agnos expressed bitter disappointment and said, "I don't know what'll happen next, and I'm not going to think about it." He was not inclined to put such a proposal before the voters again: "How many times can you go to the well? I don't know if we can do it again. We've taken our best shot, and now the future is in someone else's hands." Bob Lurie commented that "we did not . . . lose Prop. P because of the earthquake. Most of the people who voted 'no' are not baseball fans and don't go to Candlestick." As if to emphasize that he had not been bluffing, he reiterated that Candlestick Park "cannot serve as the long-term home of the Giants."[64] As far as Lurie was concerned, passage of Proposition V was meaningless—a point underscored later by Giants Vice-president Corey Busch: "Even if you were to tear down Candlestick Park and build an entirely new facility, that site would not be acceptable."[65] Mayor Agnos also shrugged off the Proposition V victory: "Who in their right mind is going to spend money to improve Candlestick for a team that won't be playing there?"[66] Following the election, Bob Lurie retreated into seclusion to await new proposals from the jilted South Bay boosters. Agnos, meanwhile, had scores to settle with those who had dared to play hardball with a hardball politician.

Prompted by the mayor's outrage at the last-minute antiballpark mailer distributed by Gregg Lukenbill and associates, District Attorney Arlo Smith began a four-month criminal probe of campaign activities by Lukenbill, his aide Maurice Read, Sacramento political consultant David Townsend, and San Francisco political consultants Richard Schlackman and Jack Davis. Smith and his deputies then sought indictments against these men, who became known as the "Ballpark Five." After hearing evidence from twenty-five witnesses, the grand jury charged members of the Ballpark Five with misdemeanor violations of campaign reporting laws. Defending himself and Arlo Smith against claims that such charges were overblown, politically motivated, and a waste of taxpayers' money, Agnos declared, "The most important thing is to protect the integrity of the voting process. Whether it's a presidential election or a local election, voters have a right to know if their vote was fairly or illegally influenced."[67]

On 22 June 1990, as still-angry ballpark supporters carried signs outside the Hall of Justice that read "Lock up Lukenbill" and "Fair election in S.F.," municipal court judge Philip Moscone dismissed all charges against the Ballpark Five on grounds that there was "no evidence" showing a conspiracy to evade campaign reporting laws.[68] Commenting on the decision, Jack Davis said, "This case was an attempt to send a chilling message to those who dare disagree with the mayor."[69] Mayor Agnos and District Attorney Smith had succeeded in giving the public rare insight into the squalid details of how political campaigns are run, but the media portrait of unsavory characters that emerged included Agnos and Smith themselves. It was politically embarrassing to Agnos that months of righteous accusation and zealous investigation had yielded nothing more than bad publicity.[70]

One year after San Francisco voters rejected the downtown China Basin ballpark, South Bay voters approved a Santa Clara site for a new Giants stadium. At the same time, they nixed a proposed utility tax to finance its construction, so the deal was off. Even as the thrice-disappointed South Bay Giants boosters trudged back to their political drawing boards, San Francisco boosters began swinging into action once again. By this time, however, San Francisco voters had rejected a proposal endorsed by Mayor Agnos to exempt the Mission Bay project from Proposition M's growth limitations, and they also had imposed restrictions on waterfront development (see chapter 8). These actions eliminated any further consideration of a downtown stadium site. Perhaps more important, both Agnos and Lurie had grown extremely wary of proposing any kind of deal to the electorate that would involve public financing or use of downtown property. San Francisco voters in particular were to be shunned. "If something is put together on land in San Mateo County," Agnos asked, "do you put it on the ballot there or here?" He made it clear this was a rhetorical question. "Leadership is making decisions and moving forward while respecting the right of citizens to participate in those decisions when it involves their money. If it doesn't, why do I have to put it to a vote?"[71] Strong executive leadership and grass-roots democracy were not mixing well in San Francisco. By the summer of 1991, Mayor Agnos had taken the lead in mobilizing support among South Bay politicians for building a privately financed stadium on 180 acres of vacant city-owned land across from the San Francisco International Airport. Perhaps capital would prove easier to muster than votes.[72]

MAYOR AGNOS'S FIASCO

The China Basin ballpark controversy was an important chapter in San Francisco's changing political life. As a candidate for mayor, Art Agnos had presented himself as a true progressive and a worthy successor to George Moscone. He had raised hopes that a progressive regime was at hand. With his domineering management of the China Basin ballpark campaign, however, Mayor Agnos began to dash those hopes and to alienate the grass-roots constituency that had elected him into office.[73]

Agnos's model of executive leadership appeared to rest on four assumptions that ran counter to the city's newly empowered progressive constituency. First, leaders are supposed to lead and should be judged by the results achieved rather than by the leadership style that produced them. Second, in a fragmented, hyperpluralistic polity, only the mayor is in a position to responsibly define strategic goals for the city as a whole and to make the trade-offs necessary to attain them. This is particularly true in regard to economic development policies, which have citywide impact, as opposed to social policies (such as domestic partners) that concern specific interests and constituencies. Third, like it or not, business leaders control the economic resources needed to finance an ambitious social agenda. An effective mayor is one who can deliver golden eggs to the progressives while keeping the business goose that laid them happy and well. Finally, citizen participation is important in electing leaders and ratifying policy but should not be allowed to disrupt delicate negotiations by experts in making deals and implementing plans.

Unfortunately for Agnos, he underestimated the political power of the city's environmentalist and neighborhood movements, and he overestimated his own skill and acumen as a deal-making politician. Leadership traits that had served him well in the cloakrooms of the California legislature ultimately backfired in the fishbowl of San Francisco politics. He damaged his reputation as a progressive mayor by rushing to placate millionaire Bob Lurie, by currying favor with downtown business elites, by spouting progrowth rhetoric in selling a new ballpark to the voters, by angrily and vindictively attacking those who had defeated his proposal, and by abandoning environmentalists, neighborhood preservationists, and housing activists on their small beachhead of social change in China Basin. Many former supporters felt deceived and betrayed by these actions. If Mayor Agnos learned anything from this fiasco, however, it was not evident in his handling of the Mission Bay project or in his approach to waterfront development.

8

The Politics of Urban Deals:
The Mission Bay Project
and the Waterfront

In many cities mayors must be careful not to give the impression that they are grabbing power. In San Francisco, mayors must avoid giving the impression that they are using power.

—Barbara Ferman

Harvey Molotch, in his study of "urban deals," writes, "While often explicitly oriented toward limiting the amount of development, the primary thrust of growth control has probably been to alter the ratio of public to private benefits from the projects that are built."[1] Illustrating Molotch's point are the urban deals made by San Francisco in planning the Mission Bay development project and in guiding commercial development of the waterfront. By conventional standards, the ratio of public to private benefits achieved in these transactions with the private sector would be considered outstanding, perhaps even spectacular. But it was growth control that altered those ratios so favorably, and that thrust did not come from city hall. The deals were good ones for the city because the citizens intervened in the deal-making process, said no to developers and investors, and prevented Mayor Agnos from selling the city short. As these cases show, the public sector truly has become more public in its interaction with the private sector. A deal is more than a deal in San Francisco; it is also an occasion for democracy.

THE MISSION BAY DEVELOPMENT PROJECT

The idea behind the collaboration between San Francisco and the Catellus Development Corporation (formerly Santa Fe Pacific Realty, and before that, Southern Pacific) was to build a "city within a city" on 315 acres in the greater China Basin district. Known as the Mission Bay project, the original Southern Pacific proposal

123

in 1980 called for the construction of three forty-story towers and several twenty-
to thirty-story buildings, creating 11.7 million square feet of office space to hold
more than forty-six thousand workers. The development scheme provided housing for only twelve thousand workers, dumping the problem of housing and
transporting thousands of new workers into the laps of San Francisco and other
Bay Area cities.[2] Devoid of public amenities, this was a project made in developer's heaven. The ratio of private to public benefits was very high, to say the
least. Yet officials in many financially troubled U.S. cities would have accepted
such an offer with gratitude. Here was a wasteland of old railyards and ware-
houses, and here was the owner proposing to convert it into jobs for residents and
revenues for the city. How could responsible city officials rationally turn it down?
In San Francisco they did so because they were forced by the citizens to bargain
tough. What the city got in return was a much better deal.

In 1984, following the merger of Southern Pacific and Santa Fe Industries, the
developer announced a revised Mission Bay proposal and began negotiations with
Mayor Dianne Feinstein and her planners in drafting a development agreement.
Feinstein's bargaining position was strengthened by the recent passage of Proposition K (the shadow ban ordinance), the Downtown Plan, and the near victory of
the San Francisco Plan Initiative in 1983. The slow-growth movement at the time
was still gathering steam, and the rule of anticipated reactions dictated that the
original proposal had to be scaled down considerably to appease potential opposition. The maximum height of Mission Bay office buildings would now be eight
stories. Total constructed office space would shrink to 4.1 million square feet.
More housing would be built (7,577 units instead of 7,000), and subsidies from
the developer and city would make 30 percent of the units affordable. There
would also be more parks and open space.[3] Although city ordinance required
citizen participation in hammering out development agreements, the negotiations
with Santa Fe Pacific Realty were conducted over the next six years by Mayor
Feinstein (and later Mayor Agnos) and officials from the city attorney's office, the
Planning Department, and the CAO's office.[4] Out of that process came the Mission Bay Plan in 1987, soon followed by the Mission Bay Draft Environmental
Impact Report (EIR), which was prepared by the Planning Department at the
developer's expense.

The Planning Department released the three-volume, seventeen-hundred-page
draft EIR in 1988.[5] As summarized there, the Mission Bay Plan now proposed
construction over a thirty-year period of "7,700 to 7,960 residential units; 2.6 to
4.1 million square feet of offices; 2.3 to 2.6 million square feet of service, light
industrial, or research and development space; 200,000 square feet for community
use; 500 hotel rooms; a ballpark; and up to 78 acres of open space."[6] This would
be the single largest development project in the city's history.

Public hearings were held on the plan and on the draft EIR as these documents
made their way through the planning channels toward final approval (at the city/
county level) by the Board of Supervisors and the mayor. Dozens of groups

Aerial view of the Mission Bay development project and greater China Basin area. The San Francisco–Oakland Bay Bridge and the downtown financial district are shown in the background.

participated in the process, many of them organized in a consortium called the Mission Bay Clearinghouse. Citizen critiques of the Mission Bay Plan focused on six substantive issues: the jobs/housing balance, housing affordability, traffic congestion, open space, toxic cleanup, and financing.[7]

The Mission Bay project was designed to create twenty-three thousand jobs but only about eight thousand housing units. Community leaders demanded more housing, fewer jobs, and/or a greater fraction of jobs earmarked for residents to relieve commuter traffic. Representatives of Latino, African American, and other ethnic communities pressed for affirmative action and job training programs. The plan proposed that three thousand of the eight thousand housing units be affordable by federal standards keyed to median incomes. Leaders of tenant groups insisted that half or more be made affordable. The plan made what many regarded as unrealistic assumptions of increased public transit use by commuters. It also assumed that somehow a second Bay Bridge or a second BART tube or a new highway and other transit improvements would be built before the project was completed in the year 2020. The proposed creation of forty-eight hundred parking spaces at Mission Bay office buildings would reinforce an excessive reliance on the automobile and add to the Bay Area's traffic congestion.[8] The plan offered no answers to the question of who would undertake and pay for the cleanup of toxic wastes in the area, a well-known "hot spot" for uncontrolled solvent-using facilities.[9] Nor did the plan consider how the subsidized affordable housing and various public amenities would be financed. Presumably the city would pick up the tab through revenue bonds, later to be repaid by anticipated increases in real estate taxes generated by the Mission Bay project. For those short on faith or averse to gambling, this posed a unwelcome risk, especially at a time of budget crisis.

Another issue raised by the Mission Bay Plan, one critical to the *politics* that swirled around it and the big money at stake, was the possible impact of the project on the already-soft market for downtown commercial real estate. The story here is rather complicated, but it explains why Walter Shorenstein, the city's leading commercial landlord and the nemesis of the slow-growth movement, would later join forces with Calvin Welch, the city's leading slow-growth advocate and the nemesis of the downtown business elite, in fighting the developer's bid to exempt the Mission Bay project from Proposition M's annual growth limits. Shorenstein was "running scared," according to some property experts, because he feared that the expected low rents and huge floorplates (forty thousand square feet per story) in Mission Bay office buildings would lure corporate tenants away from downtown buildings, including Shorenstein's Bank of America office tower.[10] There was no development timetable, and the fact that this one corporation (renamed Catellus Development Corporation in 1990) would exercise sovereign control in deciding how and when the "city within a city" would be built did not sit well with Shorenstein and other downtown business people.[11] Mayor Agnos dismissed these worries, claiming that Shorenstein saw Mission Bay "as front-office, corporate headquarters space, and so it's competition," while he, Mayor Agnos, was "selling it as back-office space for clerical workers."[12] Other downtown business leaders, including Chamber of Commerce President Donald Doyle, defended Catellus's dominant role in the project because "a prime developer needs to be a long-term player, with the resources and commitment to see the plan through."[13] These arguments and assurances did not assuage Shorenstein's fears, and it was he who bankrolled the campaign by arch-progressive Calvin Welch and others to derail the Mission Bay Plan.[14]

It would be hard to overestimate the importance of Proposition M in shaping the final outcome of the Mission Bay deal. As noted earlier, the mere prospect of growth controls had led the developer to make major concessions in revising the original proposal to win community support. With the passage of Proposition M in 1986, stringent growth controls became a reality, and they applied to Mission Bay. The whole context of development planning and deal making had changed. A critical new constraint was the annual limit of 475,000 square feet on high-rise construction, a limit that applied citywide and from which projects could be exempted only by voter approval. With 4.8 million square feet of office space to develop, Catellus executives had a choice. They could develop the Mission Bay project piece by piece, year by year, entering each element separately in the Planning Commission's annual "beauty contest" to compete with other proposals for the precious few permits to build. Or they could seek voter approval of an exemption from Proposition M's annual limits which, if granted, would spare Catellus the expense and uncertainty of repeated battles with rival developers. Proposition M allowed no escape: It was the frying pan or the fire. Catellus chose to seek the exemption; at least the fire was quicker. On 8 August 1990, supervisors Angela Alioto, Harry Britt, Terence Hallinan, Bill Maher, and Doris Ward placed an ordinance on the 6 November ballot that would exempt the Mission Bay project from the annual office-space limits. This initiative, Proposition I, put matters in the hands of the voters.

Proposition I lost 49 percent to 51 percent. The voters turned down the deal, one reason being that they did not know exactly what the deal was.[15] Not even the Board of Supervisors had been given an opportunity to read the text of the proposed development agreement. The "No on I" leaders seized on this fact, warning voters against giving Catellus a "blank check." In a brilliant op-ed piece written for a business audience, Calvin Welch wrote, "It's not over until the fat development agreement sings, and the sheet music is still being written."[16] Playing on the fears and suspicions of downtown business leaders, Welch noted that if Proposition I passed, Catellus would get "a city-sanctioned development monopoly on a single 315-acre parcel of San Francisco for up to 40 years." He asked, "Is this good for business at this time? How will this whole thing work?"[17] While acknowledging that many business people were still opposed to Proposition M, he pointed out that at least it "created certainty in the wildly uncertain marketplace of San Francisco commercial office development."[18] That stability would evaporate with the passage of Proposition I. San Francisco Tomorrow counseled its members: "If there is no signed agreement by the election, then voters should defeat Proposition I. Defeating Proposition I does not mean that Mission Bay will go away. It just means that voters can vote on a Proposition M exemption later on when we see what is provided for in the signed development agreement."[19] The "No on I" campaign sent out a mail piece emblazoned with a picture of a bright yellow lemon. Without a text of the contract to read, many voters would wonder if that was what they were getting in Mission Bay.

To developers accustomed to handshake deals with city elites and the grateful embrace of trusting citizens, the spectacle of this campaign must have come as quite a shock: San Francisco voters wanted to see the fine print—otherwise, no go. Commenting on the Proposition I vote, Planning Commission President James Morales said that "we can still be choosy, even fussy about what we approve. I think we're still in a position where we can refine some projects and even say no to some."[20] This particular demonstration of the city's capacity to exercise its discretion brought quick results.

Soon after the 6 November election, Catellus revised its proposal to address some but not all of the concerns raised. The Mission Bay Plan now would include 250 additional units of affordable housing. Half the subsidies would be paid by the developer, the other half by the city through sale of revenue bonds. Catellus still planned to seek an exemption from Proposition M limits but only for half of the

4.8 million square feet. Catellus promised a firm start date of two years after approval of the development plan.[21] The company also agreed to conduct a thorough toxic cleanup of the site and to pay an independent consultant to monitor the process, a concession viewed by San Francisco Tomorrow as "a major area of victory for the people of San Francisco."[22] On 19 February 1991, the Board of Supervisors approved this latest deal ten votes to one. The citizens and their leaders had played a good hand.

ON THE WATERFRONT: VETO BY INITIATIVE

Mayor Agnos viewed the waterfront as the city's "last frontier."[23] The case for developing the waterfront, particularly the seven-mile stretch controlled by the city's Port Commission, was about as strong as one could make, for the following reasons. (1) The port infrastructure was in sad shape. Many of the piers were rotting. Terminals for cruise ships were dilapidated and second-class. Cargo-handling machinery and facilities were hopelessly obsolete in an age of container-cargo shipping. The fish-processing facilities on Pier 45 were antique. The Loma Prieta earthquake only made things worse, causing $20 million in damage to the port.[24] (2) The city's port, once the hub of the Pacific shipping industry, now controlled less than 4 percent of West Coast cargo shipping. The Port of Oakland, with its superior container-cargo handling equipment, had eclipsed San Francisco years ago in capturing the lion's share of business. Even the small Port of Richmond had moved past San Francisco in terms of tonnage.[25] But more important than the local competition was the fact that the Bay Area as a whole was losing its portion of the rapidly expanding West Coast shipping market to Seattle, Tacoma, Portland, Long Beach, and Los Angeles; that share dropped from 27 percent to 17 percent between 1980 and 1990.[26] (3) The Port Commission, required by state law to be financially self-supporting, received more than half its revenues from retail leases to waterfront shops, restaurants, and parking lots, most of them located on or around Fisherman's Wharf and Pier 39. Tourists enjoyed these amusements, but residents, particularly the old-timers, were embarrassed by them. As business columnist Thom Calandra observed, "To make ends meet, the Port has become a Shrimp Louis affair, a purveyor of quiche rather than cargo."[27] (4) As charged in a civil grand jury report in 1987, the port's managers lacked leadership skills, planned poorly, and approved "sweetheart" deals with tenants that lost the city money.[28] (5) Finally, and perhaps decisively, the waterfront area under Port Commission authority was exempt from Proposition M controls on development. To gain access to most other parts of the city, including Mission Bay, developers now had to jump through Proposition M's many hoops and pass muster with the citizens—but not so with the waterfront. This "last frontier" was wide open and ripe for development; the pressures of competition, economic rationality, and civic pride compelled it. Smooth sailing seemed likely—or so Mayor Agnos might have thought.

In early 1989, Agnos appointed Michael P. Huerta as the new port director. Huerta had served three years as commissioner of New York City's Department of Ports, International Trade, and Commerce. During that period he solved many of the same problems now facing the Port of San Francisco, and in doing so he earned his reputation as a financial wizard and aggressive competitor. Supported by Agnos's appointees to the Port Commission, Huerta quickly set about to formulate a strategic plan for waterfront development, reorganize his staff, scrutinize tenant lease agreements, hustle contracts, and learn the ways of San Francisco politics. One of the first things he discovered was that San Francisco is not New York City. "I think the process is sometimes a little more contentious here than in New York. You're really in a fishbowl here. You spend a lot of time explaining to people what exactly you're doing."[29] He also found it is hard to make deals under those conditions, particularly ones involving high rises and hotels.

High-rise office buildings were the bête noire of the slow-growth movement, but hotels were only a notch below on the list of potential threats to the community. More hotels meant greater economic dependence on tourism. Hotel construction disrupted neighborhoods and displaced populations.[30] Proposals to build hotels on the waterfront combined these negative attributes with threats to the Bay, obstruction of views, traffic congestion, and blockage of public access to the shorelines. No hotel had been built on any city pier since the mid-1800s, and if slow-growth leaders had their way, that tradition would continue. Unfortunately for them, the Port Commission was a semi-autonomous *state*-chartered agency, and its land-use decisions were immune to Proposition M controls. As Agnos and Huerta began inviting proposals for waterfront projects, vigilant slow-growthers dusted off their trusted weapons: protests, lawsuits, and initiatives.

During Mayor Feinstein's last year in office, protest by outraged citizens smothered one ill-conceived waterfront project at the outset. That scheme would have planted a hotel on Pier 45, displacing the fish processors and fishermen who worked there. All four leading candidates for mayor that year condemned the proposal, which was quickly withdrawn. Neither protests nor lawsuits, however, could prevent final approval in September 1990 of the $22-million joint-venture proposal by Questar of New Zealand, Pier 39 Limited Partnership, and Chronicle Ventures. The centerpiece of the project, known as Underwater World, was a forty-foot-high aquarium and pavilion at the entrance of Pier 39. Although Underwater World lacked a hotel component, it was high on the slow-growth hit list because it would dig holes in the Bay, draw patrons away from the city's Steinhart Aquarium, congest traffic, and compound the carnival atmosphere of Pier 39. The slow-growthers' defeat on this project was especially vexing because the negotiations that produced it bristled with charges of influence peddling and conflicts of interest.[31] Even the supporters of Underwater World might concede that the decision-making fishbowl in this case was murky with intrigue. But out of it, they argued, would come badly needed private-sector revenues to finance redevelopment elsewhere on the waterfront. That same argument, compelling to many in a time of economic drought and budget deficits, would also be used by Agnos, Huerta, and their allies in late 1989 to justify development schemes on the city's long-neglected Piers 24–26 and Piers 30–32.

Under pressure from Agnos, the Port Commission put development of Piers 24–26 out to competitive bid, despite the fact that an earlier proposal (sans hotel) by Robert D. Scott's Gateway Pacific had already received informal approval. On 11 December 1989, Gateway Pacific's proposed marina and conference center was rejected in favor of the Koll Company's proposed $58-million waterfront hotel and sailing center. Commission President James ("Jimmy") Herman cast the lone vote against the Koll proposal. Herman, also president of the International Longshoremen and Warehousemen's Union and a close friend of Art Agnos's, warned that the commission's selection of the Koll Company's proposal would invite developers to turn the waterfront into a "wall of hotels."[32] Fellow commissioner Arthur Coleman, who had earlier expressed similar concerns, switched his vote and gave the project a green light. Bottom-line arguments addressing the port's need for money evidently swayed his thinking. Clearly he was not moved by Robert Scott's question to the commission: "Are we going to send a message to the world . . . that says, 'Let's go for the fast buck'?"[33] The answer, it appeared, would be yes, which surprised and dismayed many slow-growth leaders who had counted on Coleman to deadlock the process.

Following the commission's three-to-one vote for the Koll Company's project on Piers 24–26, San Francisco Tomorrow (SFT) took the lead in drafting a new citizen initiative to prevent the commission (renamed the "Pork Commission" by *Examiner* columnist Rob Morse) from doing to the waterfront what the progrowth coalition had done to downtown. The final version of that initiative was submitted eight months later to the registrar of voters with over fourteen thousand valid signatures attached. It was placed on the 6 November ballot as Proposition H, the Waterfront Land Use Plan Initiative. Proposition H called for a ban on hotels as an unacceptable nonmaritime use of waterfront property. It also required the city to prepare a waterfront land-use plan and prohibited it from taking any action on development proposals until the plan was completed and made public (a process expected to take about eighteen months). This last provision in particular reflected growing disgruntlement among former Agnos supporters with the mayor's deal-making propensity and nonconsultative style.[34] His populist rhetoric to one side, the mayor seemed intent on restricting the citizenry's vocabulary to just two words, "yes" and "no," to be uttered passively at the *end* of the planning process in voting *his* deals up or down. As a candidate for mayor, Agnos had promised in 1987 to "halt all new [waterfront] projects until guidelines for future planning are developed."[35] Yet it was now clear to many slow-growth leaders that Mayor Agnos was impatient to move ahead on waterfront development without such guidelines in place and without citizen input on the strategic plan that Huerta and his staff claimed to be preparing. The mayor would have to be blocked and his unilateral policies vetoed by citizen initiative.

With Jack Morrison as the campaign committee chair, SFT was joined in its sponsorship of Proposition H by San Franciscans for Reasonable Growth, the Coalition for San Francisco Neighborhoods, the Save the Bay Association, the Sierra Club, the San Francisco League of Conservation Voters, and other organizations and civic leaders (including Joe O'Donoghue, president of the Residential Builders Association, a familiar opponent of previous slow-growth measures). Gathered against them was a coalition led by Jimmy Herman and Fritz Arko, president of Pier 39 Associates. Although not in favor of Koll, Herman did not view Proposition H as the answer. The "No on H" forces included Mayor Agnos, the San Francisco Chamber of Commerce, the Koll Company, the San Francisco Labor Council, the Hotel and Restaurant Employees and Bartenders Union Local 2, the Metropolitan California Stevedore Company, and leaders of the black and Hispanic chambers of commerce. Herman also persuaded the Democratic County Central Committee to reverse its original support of Proposition H and join the opposition.[36] A glance at these rosters suggests that the progressive coalition had unraveled on this issue. Environmentalists and neighborhood populists tended to support Proposition H, while liberals aligned with business and labor in opposing it. Not surprisingly, the local Democratic committee vacillated between these two electoral coalitions.

In most respects, the content of debate on Proposition H was a rehash of previous slow-growth initiative campaigns: concerns about the environmental and aesthetic impact of development versus concerns about the business, jobs, and revenues that would be lost if development were stopped. For example, Margaret Verges, president of the Coalition of San Francisco Neighborhoods, said that "we know what Hong Kong and Rio de Janeiro look like—we don't need that."[37] On the other hand, Fergus Moran, vice-president of California Stevedore and Ballast Company, the port's oldest tenant, described Proposition H as "very dangerous" because it would "handcuff the port" in its attempt to modernize and compete with other cities.[38] The *Bay Guardian* endorsed Proposition H and urged voters to "send an unmistakable message to the modern-day Robber Barons: If you're going to build in our town, you're going to build to *our* standards, not yours."[39] Ironically, Jimmy Herman's warning about the "wall of hotels" was used repeatedly by Proposition H leaders in rallying support for the initiative. Herman's response was to ask: "If the proponents of Proposition H only wanted to halt hotels from being built on the Waterfront, why didn't they write an initiative that did just that?"[40] Proposition H, he argued, was a "rigid, all-encompassing, extreme approach" that halted waterfront development across the board.[41] What Herman and other opponents missed or ignored, however, was the critique of *process* conveyed by Proposition H's planning requirements. An editorial in the *San Francisco Independent* made that aspect explicit: "What is especially attractive about Proposition H is that port executives would be required to develop a detailed plan for each parcel of port property. Such a plan would be available to the public and designed with public input, something the public hasn't been accustomed to lately."[42] Business deals involving public land and property were too important to be decided by business leaders and planners. The process had to make room for citizens as active participants; traditional methods of deal making had to be discarded.

It was in the middle of this campaign that Scandinavia Center Inc. submitted a preliminary proposal to develop Piers 30–32 as an international cruise terminal with a hotel attached. The developer at that time viewed the hotel as a financial and practical necessity.[43] Leaders of the Swedish-American, Danish-American, and Norwegian-American chambers of commerce declared that Proposition H "*kills the project* because the hotel is an integrated and essential part of the cruise terminal and without it the cruise terminal and public access could not be built."[44] This kind of take-it-or-leave-it argument was typical of private-sector development proposals in the past. Many San Franciscans badly wanted that cruise terminal, but it seemed they would have to accept the developer's nonnegotiable terms—and reject Proposition H—to get it.

When the ballots were counted on 6 November, Proposition H squeaked by with 51 percent of the vote. The Koll Company withdrew its proposal for Piers 24–26. Construction of the Underwater World aquarium was stopped, despite protests by developers that Proposition H did not apply to their project (a point still being argued in the courts at this writing). Meanwhile, Scandinavia Center presented a revised proposal to develop a $200-million cruise terminal on Piers 30–32 *without* the waterfront hotel deemed so essential in the original plan. Because the project would be financed entirely by private-sector funds, a hotel was in fact included to make the development more attractive to investors. But the hotel would be constructed across the street, 175 feet from the cruise terminal— a design change obviously intended to assuage environmentalist concerns and gain community support for the project. Even Jimmy Herman, who had earlier raised the specter of a "wall of hotels," described this proposal as "spectacular."[45] Hearing news of the revised plan, Ed Emerson, a leader of the "Yes on H" campaign, declared, "We'll go out there with sledge-hammers and nails and help them build it, now that there's no hotel."[46] San Francisco's citizens, it appeared, were better than the mayor at driving hard bargains and making good deals. The secret of success was in learning to say no without blinking.

CONCLUSION

The case studies presented here illustrate in different ways the power of San Francisco's antiregime to protect community from capital, whether capital takes the form of a developer seeking permits to build high rises, a chain store seeking conditional-use permits to build in the neighborhoods, a homegrown millionaire seeking to build a baseball park on city land, a real estate combine seeking to build a city within the city, or a foreign investor seeking to make profits on a waterfront hotel. In all these cases, what capital sought had the capacity to injure communities. Capital's potential to cause harm is the primary concern of the antiregime. By raising standards, imposing restrictions, and erecting regulatory hurdles, the antiregime lays down a very crooked and exhausting path that businesses must traverse to reach the community. What arrives at the city gates and is allowed to pass through are the best and safest enterprises that capital can offer. In an age of exploited and downtrodden cities, this is a remarkable accomplishment for San Francisco's antiregime.

But opposite each of the antiregime's strengths are its weaknesses. San Francisco's antiregime can protect community but cannot create it. It can filter out the chaff, but in doing so, it filters out much wheat. It can block and deflect the power of capital to do evil, but it cannot generate and harness the power of capital to do good. The antiregime can keep those who try to govern in check by punishing their mistakes, but it cannot provide a positive model of progressive governance for new leaders to follow. It can choose among competing plans, but it cannot make them and propose them. It is a reactive regime, wary of power, isolated, and doomed by its principles to tolerate and protect the status quo. What the antiregime must acquire in order to become a progressive regime is a strong political center to establish and enforce progressive priorities and a source of economic power to accomplish positive goals.

9

Creating a Progressive Urban Regime: The Architecture of Complexity

As flourishing as it is in many of its component parts, San Francisco seems to have lost its hold on its public identity. We have neighborhoods, and competing ethnic groups, and various categories of the aggrieved and/or oppressed; but do we have, any longer, San Franciscans?

—Kevin Starr

During the [Paris] Commune, many preferred to defend their quarters rather than the city walls, thus giving the forces of reaction surprisingly easy access to the city.

—David Harvey

In exploring the relationship between complexity and evolution, Herbert Simon tells a parable of two watchmakers, Hora and Tempus. Both make fine watches consisting of a thousand parts each, and both are interrupted from time to time as they work. But Hora is much more successful than Tempus in terms of watches produced and money made. Hora makes a watch from ten subassemblies, each containing ten sub-subassemblies of ten parts each. When he is interrupted, his work falls to pieces, requiring reassembly. But the worst he faces is the task of reassembling the ten parts of a single subassembly or sub-subassembly. Tempus, on the other hand, makes a watch part by part, using no subassemblies, until the whole watch is done. When he is interrupted and his work falls to pieces, the worst he faces really could be the worst, namely, the task of reassembling 999 parts from scratch.[1] Simon formalizes this parable as a mathematical model, and from it he concludes that Tempus will take on average four thousand times as long to assemble a watch as Hora. He later generalizes that "complex systems will evolve from simple systems much more rapidly if there are stable intermediate forms than if there are not. The resulting complex forms in the former case will be hierarchic."[2]

134

In San Francisco's polity of a thousand parts, the progressives are inclined to think like Tempus. True democracy resists subassembly; each part in the process is a jewel by itself. Since hierarchy concentrates power and negates true democracy, slow evolution seems a small price to pay to avoid it. But interruptions loom and time flies.

REGIME TRANSFORMATION AND
THE PROBLEM OF HYPERPLURALISM

Over the last two decades, San Francisco has become more socially and ethnically diverse. The communities of labor and business have dissolved into smaller constituent parts. Formal structures of government authority have remained diffuse and decentralized. And the progrowth regime, that powerful subassembly of political and economic parts, has fallen to pieces. The antiregime is the protective container of this fragmented political universe. Clumps of power can be found in it, but overall it is basic and primordial. From its swirling parts many new kinds of political order can evolve, including a progressive urban regime.

In the literature on urban regimes, the main focus has been on the informal arrangements that exist between a city's political and business elites—arrangements that facilitate governance and social production in the area of economic development. Drawing on that literature, H. V. Savitch and John Clayton Thomas recently conceptualized four "ideal types" of regime, each defined by the strength of its political leadership and the cohesion of its business elite.[3] "Corporatist" regimes have strong political leadership and a cohesive business elite. "Elitist" regimes have weak political leadership and a cohesive business elite. "Pluralist" regimes have strong political leadership and a dispersed business elite. "Hyperpluralist" regimes have weak political leadership and a dispersed business elite.[4] Observing the increasing fragmentation of urban political environments over the last thirty years, Savitch and Thomas conclude that many corporatist and elitist regimes have become pluralist or hyperpluralist in character and that some formerly pluralist regimes, such as Los Angeles, have joined San Francisco as hyperpluralist. Thus, in many U.S. cities, the overall trend in regime transformation appears to be one of increasing political disorder. Political fragmentation and "centrifugal forces," argue Savitch and Thomas, are "defying efforts [in some cities] to build effective central authority" and are reducing "governing capability." Governing regimes in both San Francisco and Los Angeles, they warn, "teeter on the edge of collapse."[5] Although it is not clear what the authors mean by "collapse," one can agree that San Francisco's governing coalition under Mayor Agnos did teeter, particularly in the area of economic development, where Agnos was repeatedly blocked or outflanked by slow-growth opposition.

Within the framework of Savitch and Thomas's analysis, the implied solution to the problem of ungovernable disorder is to find some way to strengthen a regime's central authority, so that it can exert a centripetal pull on the centrifugal forces that are tearing the regime apart. This kind of solution is ancient. It can take many forms, some of them unpleasant. In San Francisco, one benign proposal along these lines comes from Kent Sims, former head of the city's now-defunct Economic Development Corporation. Sims urges leaders of the city's Democratic and Republican parties to develop "comprehensive programs that help the city establish strong competitive positions" and that focus on the "big picture, the long-term well-being of our city." He believes such partisan programs are needed to overcome the "entropy" of single-issue politics.[6] Another proposal, less benign, is hinted at in historian Kevin Starr's lamentations about San Francisco's loss of "public identity," which he believes is most fully expressed in grand development projects, high-rise office towers, and *fête imperiale*.[7] Starr recognizes that these Brobdingnagian aspirations are doomed in the political land of Lilliput, thwarted at every turn by the city's pesky environmentalists, conservationists, tenant unions, ethnic groups, and neighborhood activists. Acknowledging that it "would be naive, even proto-fascist, to long for a man on a white horse such as [shipyard developer and hotel builder William Chapman] Ralston," Starr nevertheless wishes "that at least the public consciousness, the public will of Ralston would reassert itself in this city."[8] Such frustration recalls the biblical men of Shinar, whose own grand project, the Tower of Babel, was sublimely disabled by a multiplicity of tongues. For those who aspire to build towers, the temptation to restore unity of purpose through strong central leadership is almost irresistible.

Inviting as they may be, these solutions to the problem of political disorder rest on two key assumptions that no longer hold in San Francisco—namely, that the primary function of an urban regime is to increase system governability in promoting economic and physical development; and that political order requires imposing the will of elites on the masses to whip or cajole them into shape.[9] San Francisco's progressives do have problems of political disorder to solve, but they arise only in the context of their own progressive aspirations and human development goals. The first is the difficulty of establishing the spatial boundaries of citizenship in a new progressive regime. For some San Franciscans, these boundaries have contracted to the size of their neighborhoods, while for others they have expanded to encompass the entire Bay Area region and beyond. The second is the need to reconcile competing materialist and postmaterialist values within the progressive ideology that informs such a regime. These two problems compound each other, as illustrated in the Potrero Hill case discussed next. The third and fourth problems for San Francisco's progressives are how to create an economic base for the new regime that is supportive of community rather than a threat to it, and how to build structures of citizen participation and accountable public authority that are mutually compatible rather than mutually interfering, as seems to be the case now.

NIMBYISM, REGIONALISM, AND
THE TAFFY PULL OF CIVIC SELVES

The Dangers of Thinking Too Small:
NIMBYism and Enclave Consciousness

The neighborhood movement is both a fount of inspiration and the Achilles heel of the progressive movement in San Francisco. Writing in 1985, a year before passage of Proposition M, Stephen Barton assessed the neighborhood movement's unique qualities and strengths: (1) It is "actively inclusionary rather than exclusionary"; (2) it "seeks to provide all citizens with rights to residential security and stability rather than relying on property ownership as the basis of citizenship"; and (3) it "links neighborhood concerns with the economic development of the city as a whole and seeks to assert democratic control over the whole process, rather than restricting its concerns to neighborhood protection and leaving control over development to business."[10] If ever there was a picture of neighborhood parochialism, this is not it. With the passage of Proposition M, however, the goals of the neighborhood movement were incorporated if not enshrined in the city's restrictive development guidelines. Neighborhoods were considerably empowered, particularly with the election of Art Agnos as mayor. It was then that residents of some neighborhoods began, in Castells's phrase, to "shrink the world to the size of their community."[11] The city's Potrero Hill neighborhood offers a case in point.[12]

A developer wanted to build ninety-one units of housing, including twenty-nine low-income residence/work spaces for artists, on a steep hillside lot in Potrero Hill. A group of Potrero Hill residents delayed the project for months to keep the lot the way it was "when the Indians roamed around here."[13] The group repeatedly invoked a discretionary review provision in the planning code that gives residents the right to file an objection to any project on any grounds at any time during the approvals process, even if the project meets code requirements. When that tactic failed, the group stalled the project three more months by claiming that the site was a possible habitat for the harvestman spider, a rare species protected under national and state law. After surveys by an entomologist yielded negative results, the project was finally approved. The developer had to absorb $60,000 in carrying costs because of the delay. Noting that the ravine was used mainly as a dog run, the frustrated developer asked, "What're we going to have next, environmentally-endangered doo-doo?"[14] In almost any other U.S. city that would have been considered a rhetorical question.

The Potrero Hill case illustrates the kind of textbook NIMBYism (Not In My Back Yard)[15] that can arise from what Sidney Plotkin has called "enclave consciousness."[16] What makes the case especially interesting is that, based on precinct voting trends over the last ten years, Potrero Hill is one of the most progressive neighborhoods in the city. Yet progressivism became protectionism when local turf was threatened by a project that would serve affordable housing needs and the interests of low-income residents. This Potrero Hill group used expanded citizen powers under progressive rule to subvert the progressive agenda. Their actions demonstrate that regulation by impedimenta can succeed in rationing scarce resources, but the resources rationed are often what the haves have and the have-nots need.[17] In the current antiregime, the "power to" impede tends to negate the "power to" create—even the power to create a handful of affordable housing units in a vacant ravine.

The Potrero Hill incident is not an isolated case.[18] In the Bernal Heights neighborhood, scene of the "city's last sizable store of buildable lots,"[19] two resident-run design review boards have been empowered informally by the city Planning Department to stop residential development projects that fail to satisfy their interpretation of what the zoning rules allow.[20] Bernal Heights residents are used to getting their way. In early 1991, neighborhood activists formed a group called Save the Market Task Force to block plans by the Bernal Heights Community Foundation to build a 120-unit affordable housing project for low- and very low-income families in an area directly adjacent to the city's well-known Farmers Market. The foundation is a nonprofit, multiservice agency that has a strong interest in enhancing the stock of affordable housing. Task force activists, backed by Supervisor Bill Maher, attempted what has been described as a "hostile takeover" of the foundation by joining en masse as members with the aim of electing a sympathetic majority to the foundation's board of directors.[21] The power grab failed, but the task force did manage to exact concessions from the housing plan sponsors—fewer than 120 units of housing would be built, the housing complex would be set back sixty feet from market stalls rather than the twenty-five feet originally proposed, and farmers would be compensated by the developer for loss of sales because of increased traffic and construction. Further, the Board of Supervisors directed the foundation to begin a "conciliatory process with its critics" using the mediation services of Community Boards, a neighborhood-based conflict-resolution agency.[22]

Administrators of the mayor's Office of Housing predict that neighborhood groups will make increasing use of Proposition M and the city planning appeals process to challenge all types of projects deemed undesirable in their communities. Since in some neighborhoods such projects include the construction of affordable housing units for low-income families, there may be many more cases like Potrero Hill and Bernal Heights in the future.[23] This internal conflict within the progressive coalition between the city's "power to" achieve affordable housing production and the neighborhoods' "power to" block such production is one that progressive leaders must resolve if they wish to establish a progressive urban regime.[24] If they respond by decentralizing power to neighborhoods to do as they please, one perverse outcome could be the forced exit of low-income families and individuals who must go elsewhere for affordable housing. Given San Francisco's overheated housing market and high cost of living, such an implicit policy of benign neglect could channel the city's poor into a housing market in which they cannot compete. Meanwhile, middle-class residents living securely in semisovereign neighborhoods retain their regulatory "monopoly" privileges.[25]

To resolve this dilemma coercively by restricting neighborhood autonomy would extinguish authentic local democracy at its source. Coercive solutions also would entail vanguardist usurpation of collective control of the progressive movement. Educational programs designed to raise progressive consciousness in the neighborhoods and to produce "structurally informed coalitions" have greater chance of success.[26] But even these purely ideological answers must harness rather than suppress the energies of neighborhood activism. Enclave consciousness per se is a natural defense against forces that work to flatten places into spaces and to dissolve communities into aggregates of individual citizens. Plotkin, for example, prefaces his plea for a "transenclave consciousness" and greater linkage between class and community by applauding the "functional unruliness" inspired by enclave mentality and its disruptive effects on the workings of the capitalist state.[27] Sheldon Wolin, an antistatist democratic theorist, is even more accepting of enclave consciousness and streetfighting NIMBYism. He finds an overlooked but solid theoretical foundation for such arguments in the writings of the Anti-Federalists and also in Montesquieu's *Spirit of the Laws*, which defended the virtues of decentralized power as a barrier against encroachments by the centralized state. In Wolin's reading of Montesquieu, the function of local institutions and local laws and customs was "not simply to defend or mediate between state and civil society but to complicate power. At [Montesquieu's] hands feudalism became a term to designate an alternative to the centralized state. It stood for the periphery against the center, for the diversity of local institutions and practices against the uniformizing tendencies of administrative rule, in short, for political polytheism against political monotheism."[28]

In the context of San Francisco's antiregime, one might characterize the more exclusionary elements of the city's neighborhood movement as a kind of latterday urban feudalism that preserves local diversity by complicating the exercise of centralized power. One challenge facing progressive leaders is to find a way to incorporate the antistatism of San Francisco's neighborhood movement into progressive ideology without undermining the legitimacy of a progressive *local* state. To some extent this must involve expanding the territorial boundaries of "enclave consciousness" to encompass the city as a whole.

The Dangers of Thinking Too Big: A Regional Progrowth Coalition

The issue of regionalism poses another challenge to San Francisco's progressive leaders. There has been a revival of interest in regional government in the Bay Area.[29] Many of the parties involved include groups that battled one another during the growth-control wars in the 1980s. Regional perspectives on urban problems are an important part of the progressive ethos, particularly at a time when transportation gridlock, urban sprawl, housing shortages, and population growth affect all nine counties, ninety-eight cities, and 721 special districts in the greater Bay Area. Art Agnos, in his 1987 campaign for mayor, issued a "Declaration of Interdependence" calling for greater cooperation among local governments in dealing with regional problems. Environmentalist and conservationist organizations that had participated in the slow-growth movement (including the Greenbelt Alliance and Sierra Club) have been actively mobilizing support for regional government proposals advanced by the Bay Vision 2020 Commission, a blue-ribbon citizens' group recently formed to recommend regional solutions to Bay Area growth problems.[30]

In its final report, the Bay Vision 2020 Commission proposed (1) effective *state* growth-management policies (especially ones that "reduce the tax pressures that 'fiscalize' land use" and provide "financing methods for the infrastructure needed to serve a growing population"); (2) a *regional* agency that would consolidate existing regional government structures and develop specific growth-management plans; and (3) "strong" *local* governments "acting consistently within approved regional plans."[31] The commission also recommended that a governing board of the proposed regional agency be *appointed* for a three-year term and that it have the authority to "allow or deny developments of regional importance" during that period.[32] Not least because of its threat to local control and its nondemocratic governance structure, the commission's proposal has failed to inspire significant political backing in the Bay Area. Joseph Bodovitz, project manager of Bay Vision 2020, candidly admitted the shallowness of its support: "What the coalition amounts to is the large corporations that tend to support the Bay Area Council, some government officials who see the handwriting on the wall and those environmentalists in the Greenbelt Alliance who are primarily concerned with preserving open space. As a coalition, it's holding—but at present, it isn't very deep."[33] One advocate of Bay Area regional government, Revan Tranter, executive director of the Association of Bay Area Governments (ABAG), explains the opposition by what he calls the "NIMEY syndrome"—Not In My Election Year.[34] Most local elected government officials simply are not willing to take the political risks of relinquishing home rule to an appointed regional body established to implement state-level growth-management policies.

The looming threat to local power is a strong factor motivating recalcitrant local officials to consider voluntary creation of regional government. Some critics of regional government read that message between the lines of the Bay Vision 2020 report, and they resent it. "Basically, the commission is telling us they'll go to Sacramento and shove a regional government down our throat," said Randy Hamilton of the University of California Institute of Governmental Studies.[35]

Among those ready to applaud state intervention are some of the state's leading corporate executives, real estate investors, commercial and residential developers, and business-oriented think tanks such as the Bay Area Council. Frustrated by the rising flood of local growth-control initiatives, many California business leaders have sought to curb local government discretion in growth management by assigning new power and authority to a different (and potentially more responsive) set of public officials at a higher political level. Some of these executives have urged the state government to "punish" local governments that implement growth controls.[36] Unusually blunt was Dick Wirth, a leader of the Southern California Building Industry Association, who declared that "if the people in a certain place want to close off growth, then they should be shut off from state tax dollars, because they're just being greedy little clowns."[37] One might debate endlessly which types of "clowns" are more worrisome: those who seek to close off growth completely or those who chaff at any growth restrictions. But there is no question that many local governments throughout the state have used local growth-management policies as a pretext for shirking regional responsibilities and as a means of class and racial exclusion.[38] These abuses of home rule provide rhetorical opportunities to business advocates and their state-level political allies in pushing for state intervention in local land-use and development policy-making. More than fifty growth-management bills were introduced in the state legislature in 1989, for example, and the volume of such measures has grown steadily. One expert's analysis of these bills revealed a common theme: "All of the proposals are designed to zap the control that local officials have over development decisions."[39]

Taken as a whole, these trends suggest that moves are afoot locally and statewide to create a much broader progrowth coalition at the regional and state levels. Business elites and their environmentalist and state government allies would likely dominate the formulation of growth policy at this higher tier. As Michael P. Smith writes, "Commercial elites, banks, the mass media, utility companies, and corporate executives have consistently been among the chief backers of various plans for the creation of regional planning and metropolitan government. This is not at all surprising. These interests are well equipped to influence government decision making at that level."[40] While some form of regional growth management in the Bay Area seems necessary and inevitable, the prospect of state-mandated regional government is a potentially divisive issue within San Francisco's progressive coalition, particularly between the environmentalists and the neighborhood populists.[41] Under different political scenarios, regional government could either fulfill or undermine the progressive agenda.

The Spatial Boundaries of Progressive Citizenship

A troublesome aspect of both NIMBYism and regionalism is that they complicate the task of defining primary territorial allegiance and local citizenship under a progressive regime. Just as the neighborhood populist wing of the progressive movement tends to shrink citizenship to fit neighborhood boundaries, the environmentalist wing tends to expand citizenship to encompass the entire region. This taffy pull of civic selves could disrupt efforts to create a new urban regime. In their sophisticated analysis, Robert Dahl and Edward Tufte suggest that "rather than conceiving of democracy as located in a particular kind of inclusive, sovereign unit, we must learn to conceive of democracy spreading through a set of interrelated political systems, sometimes though not always arranged like Chinese boxes, the smaller nesting in the larger."[42] Nevertheless, a Chinese-box conception of democratic citizenship could end up slicing the progressive movement into distinct spatial domains of political action. In his detailed study of the Paris Commune of 1871, for example, David Harvey notes that many cleavages divided the communards, including those "between loyalties to *quartier*, city, and nation, between centralizers and decentralizers, [which] all gave the Commune an air of incoherence and a political practice riddled with internal conflict."[43] San Francisco is not the Paris Commune nor can it be. But in guiding the transition from antiregime to progressive regime, the city's more visionary leaders might do well to emphasize *city* boundaries in defining the "we" that citizens will become in the new political order.

RED-GREEN FUSIONS AND FISSIONS

A significant political accomplishment of San Francisco's progressive leadership was its coalignment of the three Lefts in mounting attacks on the progrowth regime. Middle-class environmentalists, neighborhood populists, and working-class liberals all worked together tactically to pursue common political goals. Three historical conditions made this fusion possible. First, federal government cutbacks in urban aid programs dumped national social problems into the kettles of cities, there to let them stew. Local political pressures that once diverged upward and outward in search of solutions now converged on city hall. Second, inside San Francisco, citizen demands pressured the local progrowth regime to produce. As many progressives saw it, what the progrowth regime had been producing were skyscrapers for speculators, jobs for commuters, housing for the upper middle class, and a big environmental mess. The trickle-down of housing, jobs, and services for low-income residents was very thin indeed. Increasingly disgruntled, leaders of constituencies within the three Lefts began to depend less on the progrowth regime and more on each other. Third, the city's progressive leaders—Calvin Welch, Susan Hestor, Nancy Walker, Tim Redmond, and many others—seized that historical moment and exploited it politically by welding the three Left agendas into an *inclusive* slow-growth coalition that eventually changed public policy and captured city hall. Materialist and postmaterialist goals overlapped; development was made to serve redistribution; environmentalist and neighborhood concerns were linked; working-class and community needs were joined. These novel fusions were only partial, mainly tactical, and possibly temporary. But political practice had given the theorists something to think about: A progressive coalition was possible because it existed in at least this one city. The most important and difficult fusion achieved in building a progressive electoral coalition was the one that linked the interests of working-class and ethnic minority liberals with those of white middle-class environmentalists—the materialist Left and the postmaterialist Left, "red" and "green."[44] It was important because it demonstrated that such a fusion was politically possible and because, if it proved durable, it might be replicated in other cities and at the national level. But it entailed the difficult task of bridging the gulf of differences that separated the two groups. The liberals as a group were nonwhite, working class, less educated, less cognitively mobilized, elite directed, and motivated by material concerns about safety, jobs, and housing. The environmentalists as a group were white, middle class, more educated, more cognitively mobilized, elite directing, and motivated by postmaterial concerns about environmental protection, urban aesthetics, and the quality of life.[45] Mayor Feinstein attempted to exploit these differences in organizing her campaign against Proposition M in 1986. Although that maneuver ultimately failed, the confrontations that took place between the Reverend Cecil Williams and white middle-class progressives during the campaign illuminated the stark contrasts that exist between two distinct life-worlds. Progressives were able to forge political links between those two worlds based on the premise and the promise that a new regime would improve the quality of life in both. In the antiregime, however, signs of fission and breakdown have begun to appear in this formative red-green alliance.

African Americans and Redevelopment: New Rules, Same Game

The clearest signs of disappointment and discontent with the antiregime are seen in the city's African American community. Many African American leaders participated in the slow-growth movement because the progrowth regime had not delivered on its promises of decent jobs and affordable housing for African American residents. With the passage of Proposition M and the election of Art Agnos, the prospects for African Americans looked better. Encouraging were the words of Buck Bagot, an Agnos appointee to the Redevelopment Commission: "The old-style project-area clearance, which to a large extent was 'Negro removal,' is never going to happen again."[46] Yet some of the city's African American leaders judge redevelopment under Agnos as just more of the same. The grand opening of the Redevelopment Agency's Fillmore Center in 1990, for example, gave the city's African American residents little to cheer about. Located in an area that had once been the business hub of an African American community, the Fillmore Center project constructed a largely market-rate residential complex complete with street-level boutiques and recreation facilities that, according to one observer, "would be the envy of the most exclusive private club."[47] The Reverend Hannibal Williams, Housing Authority administrator Mary Rogers, and other African

American leaders objected to what they perceived to be a continuation of city-sponsored gentrification. Although the project actually started under Mayor Feinstein, Mayor Agnos received much of the blame. "This isn't being built for those of us in the community," said Rogers.[48]

A year later, the Planning Department announced its South Bayshore plan to rezone and redevelop portions of the predominately African American Bayview–Hunters Point neighborhoods. The proposal called for building market-rate apartments, eliminating many liquor stores, and cleaning up "the unattractive physical appearance and seedy economic character" of Third Street, a major center of drug dealing in San Francisco.[49] Many neighborhood leaders and residents protested in testimony before the Planning Commission, one of them declaring that it was "obvious you intend to piecemeal our community," another claiming that the plan would "move all African Americans out of San Francisco."[50] Pastor Eddie Welborn warned, "We let it happen in the Western Addition, but we're not going to let it happen in the Bayview–Hunters Point neighborhoods."[51] The New Bayview Committee and the Bayview-Hill Residents Association mobilized to block the plan, which Planning Director Dean Macris later withdrew for further study.

Responding to these kinds of concerns in the city's African American community, Mayor Agnos appointed an African American task force for economic empowerment to advise the Redevelopment Agency. The Redevelopment Agency set aside $5 million to support African American goals.[52] Some African American leaders have not been satisfied by these efforts, however, including New Bayview Committee President Sam Murray, who called the $5-million pledge a "scam" after the Redevelopment Agency spent $777,500 of it on a white-owned supermarket to be located in Hunters Point.[53]

The Battle of the "Richmond Specials"

Another sign that the red-green alliance is falling apart is the continuing battle between neighborhood preservationists, affordable housing groups, and residential developers over zoning regulations that limit or prohibit demolition of single-family dwellings. At the root of this conflict is the city's chronic housing shortage, which has induced home owners and developers to tear down single-family houses and replace them with boxy multiple-unit structures (known locally as "Richmond specials") that maximize allowable floor space under city codes. Although Richmond specials are pedestrian in appearance, leaders of many tenant groups welcome them because they add to the housing stock. Market-rate developers like them because they increase the volume of their real estate business. Many Asians in particular favor them as affordable living space for extended families. Many home owners claim the right to develop their own property in this way and profit from it under reasonable restrictions.

Most of the city's neighborhood and historical preservation groups oppose Richmond specials as if they were the plague, to the point of organizing neighbor-

A typical "Richmond special"—the boxy, multiple-unit housing opposed by San Francisco's neighborhood and architectural preservationists.

hood watch patrols to look for construction violations, screening building permit applications, and engaging in related surveillance activities. Led by San Francisco Tomorrow, leaders of these groups have mounted campaigns to outlaw construction of Richmond specials and to block the demolitions that make room for them. They argue that the ugly buildings destroy the charm and character of the city's neighborhoods, permanently diminish the supply of precious single-family homes, and replace it with housing not all that more affordable.[54] They deny the recurrent charge of racism toward the city's Asian community. In 1987, Richmond-specials opponents succeeded in getting the Planning Department to impose a demolition moratorium, followed a year later by a three-tiered system of interim zoning regulations that made it harder for home owners in some neighborhoods to get demolition permits, and easier in others. In late 1990, when the Planning Department proposed a new set of permanent rules to deal with the problem, nearly all parties to the controversy objected.[55] Ever persistent, the Planning Department in 1991 offered yet another set of rules (including the requirement that all demolitions be replaced with units of comparable price and size), but even these "compromise" rules have been attacked from all directions.[56]

The demolition issue appears to be unresolvable in the antiregime, and the politics swirling around it provide a model of "street-fighting pluralism" in the literal sense. At the center of all this scrimmaging, however, is the concept of property itself, which is being fundamentally contested in San Francisco.[57] The essence of the neighborhood preservationist view of property is captured in the claim made by Lois Miyashiro, Richmond Residents Council president and demolition opponent: "Communities as well as individuals have rights." The community rights implied here are consistent with C. B. Macpherson's expanded concept of property as a "right to a set of social relations, a right to a kind of society," which means a "new property in the quality of life."[58] In this view, regulation by impedimenta is necessary to protect a community's rights, not just at the level of the semisovereign city but also at the level of the increasingly semisovereign neighborhood. Red tape is "what's going to keep San Francisco San Francisco," as one preservationist put it.[59] Those who cling to the Lockean notion that individual liberty and property are linked and that property ownership "is rightly understood in terms of rights over resources which the individual can exercise without interference" are likely to feel very unfree in San Francisco and to see their property as imprisoned by the burgeoning restrictions of community.[60] Those who lack property altogether and who define "quality of life" in terms of basic shelter needs and housing opportunities are likely to feel even less free in a city that worships red tape.

The broader point of these examples is that there is a bias in the antiregime that protects the interests of only two of the city's three Lefts: environmentalists and neighborhood activists. Zoning restrictions, red tape, prolix discretionary review procedures, a community-rights doctrine of property—all of these tend to preserve not merely neighborhood character and fine Victorian homes but also the status quo. In this context, the antiregime can be considered conservative and exclusionary. The progrowth regime excelled in its ability to cut through red tape and to get things done; the antiregime excels in its ability to create red tape and to prevent things from getting done. In a word, the outstanding strength of the antiregime is its power to say no. But this is not a message that ethnic minority and working-class liberals want to hear. There is a danger under the antiregime that this third Left will be left out.

The disintegration of the red-green (liberal-environmentalist, materialist-postmaterialist) alliance has had electoral consequences. For example, where city-level battles are still being fought on land-use and development issues (Mission Bay, the waterfront), working-class and ethnic minority liberals tend to vote progrowth in opposing the bans and restrictions advocated by environmentalists and neighborhood preservationists. Voters in African American and low-income precincts, for example, strongly opposed Proposition H (waterfront hotel ban) and gave majority support to Proposition I (Mission Bay exemption from Proposition M).[61] A graphical snapshot of the widening gap between materialist and postmaterialist aspirations is shown in Figure 9.1, which plots the precinct "yes" vote on Proposition H against the precinct "yes" vote on Proposition J—a failed 1990 initiative that would have required the Board of Supervisors to appropriate at least $15 million each year to the city's Housing Affordability Fund. Highlighted in the

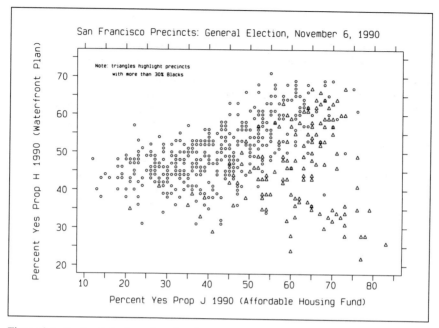

Figure 9.1. Scatterplot of precinct "yes" vote on Waterfront Hotel Ban Initiative (Proposition H, 1991) by "yes" vote on Affordable Housing Initiative (Proposition J, 1990). Precincts with a high percentage of African Americans are highlighted (triangles) (N = 710 precincts). *Sources:* See appendix A.

plot are precincts that have a high percentage of African Americans. The pattern is clear. Many precincts (by definition "progressive") supported both the materialist Proposition J and the postmaterialist Proposition H. The "liberal" African American precincts, on the other hand, tended to support J but to oppose H.

It is possible that the red-green fusion achieved during the slow-growth battles was in fact nothing more than a fleeting tactical alliance, a loose knot in time that briefly joined two divergent political trajectories but that is now beginning to unravel. Just as a good thrashing of oil and water can produce an impression that the ingredients are mixable, the solidarities formed in political battle can deceive observers into thinking they are permanent. But in the calm aftermath, unmixable things will separate. If red and green (and black and white) are politically unmixable, if constant thrashing through collective mobilization is required to keep them fused, then San Francisco's progressive movement becomes much less interesting. It is my contention, however, that a more enduring progressive coalition is possible, *especially* in San Francisco. If the poor, the workers, and the ethnic minorities turn their backs on the progressive movement, progressive leaders will have mainly themselves to blame for their neglect of the working class and for their failure to look at the big picture of progressivism on a national scope. A postmaterialist political agenda arises naturally in a postindustrial city like San Francisco. But the materialist foundation of postmaterialist values must not be ignored. Abraham Maslow, whose theories of motivation inspired Ronald Inglehart's work on postmaterialist politics, writes, "To complain about rose gardens means that your belly is full, that you have a good roof over your head, that your furnace is working, that you're not afraid of bubonic plague, that you're not afraid of assassination, that the police and fire departments work well, that the government is good, that the school system is good, that local politics are good, and many other preconditions are already satisfied."[62] To prevent San Francisco politics from drifting down the rose garden path, the city's progressive leaders must address working-class needs and must view ethnic minorities as more than mere ornaments of social diversity. Inglehart's own words of warning are relevant here. He praises the postmaterialists for helping to "correct a course that tended to sacrifice the quality of life to one-sided economic considerations." But he goes on to add that "Postmaterialism can be equally self-defeating. The anti-industrial outlook of some of the movement's ideologues could lead to neglect of the economic base on which Postmaterialism ultimately depends."[63]

In sum, the novel political fusion achieved by San Francisco's progressive movement in the 1980s seems now to be in a state of dissolution. Neighborhood activists and environmentalists are pulling the movement apart spatially, while the materialist Left and postmaterialist Left are pulling it apart ideologically. The springs and gears of the meticulously built progressive electoral coalition seem to be popping out all over the place. The political carrying capacity of the progressive movement's *governing* coalition appears quite limited relative to the inclusive sweep of the *electoral* coalition that passed Proposition M and put Art Agnos in power.[64]

The Imperative of Redistribution

Some of the city's progressive leaders argue that these limits do not arise from ideological contradictions, but rather from a lack of collective political will. It is a mistake, in their view, to chastise neighborhood residents for wanting to preserve and protect what they have worked so hard to build. It is a mistake to rebuke environmentalists for caring so much about the city's ecological health and the aesthetic qualities that define San Francisco. And it is also a mistake to think that these values and concerns must be sacrificed to respond to the needs of the city's have-nots. It only appears that such a sacrifice is necessary because the city's chronic budget crisis produces a zero-sum situation that inevitably breeds conflict within the progressive movement. There simply is not enough money to go around.

The reason for this deficiency is that city officials have failed to move aggressively in extracting more revenues from the city's large corporations and businesses. If these large firms paid the city in full for the municipal services actually received, the needed resources would be there to finance an admittedly ambitious social agenda. Redistribution, therefore, is essential. Unfortunately, although re-distribution from the local private sector to the local public sector is economically feasible, it is extremely difficult to achieve politically. As a *Bay Guardian* edito-rial put it, "There are ways to fund such programs without placing an undue burden on the poor or the middle-class, but politicians are loath to tax the politi-cally powerful individuals and corporations that would be affected by progressive taxes."[65] Indeed, elected officials can avoid paying the political costs of redistri-bution by pursuing "big ticket" development projects, such as baseball stadiums and waterfront hotels. Although these projects generate new revenues, they do so only by imposing unacceptable social costs on the city's environment, neighbor-hoods, and low-income populations. Even worse, such projects increase rather than decrease dependence on big business and outside capital, thus undermining the local autonomy and homegrown economy that the city's progressives have worked so long and hard to achieve.[66]

In the context of the theory of urban regimes, the redistribution argument raises the question: Can San Francisco's business community change so as to provide an economic base for a progressive regime that can (1) sustain a high level of social production in serving human development goals and (2) insure distributive justice in allocating jobs, housing, and employment opportunities, but do so without (3) diminishing the city's social diversity or (4) violating environ-mental and neighborhood standards of the quality of life?

BUSINESS NOT AS USUAL IN SAN FRANCISCO POLITICS

In the wake of Proposition M and the progressive capture of city hall, San Francisco's business community has been riven with conflicts and changing in ways that eventually could support the formation of a progressive regime. Several trends are clear. First, downtown business elites are divided and no longer speak with a single voice regarding development strategy or public affairs. Second, threats of business disinvestment have done little to reverse slow-growth policies, intimidate public officials, or induce a more hospitable "business climate" as defined by business elites. Finally, the small business community in particular has acquired elevated status and influence because of its growing size and anticipated pivotal role in a reconstituted public-private partnership.

Urban Misfortunes: Downtown Business and Proposition M

San Francisco's downtown business community is a microcosm of the general political disorder that characterizes the antiregime. If Atlanta provides the model of a unified downtown business elite, San Francisco is the archetype of its oppo-site. The transition from a progrowth to a slow-growth political environment continues to engender discord and turmoil among the former master builders of the city. Their responses fall roughly into the categories of fleeing, fighting, and adapting.[67]

Fleeing: Privatization of urban policy has made many cities vulnerable to the threat of private-sector disinvestment. Failure to cultivate a good "business climate" can induce local businesses to relocate elsewhere, taking needed jobs and tax dollars with them. In San Francisco, however, the void created by privatization has enlarged local autonomy rather than diminished it. On balance, the city's fragmented business community may be more dependent on local government (for permits, approvals, and clearances) than the other way around. Moreover, the accumulated fixed capital investment in San Francisco's built environment and human resources is simply too substantial. Business analyst Michael Pitre points to the Bay Area's service economy and "diverse and educated work force" as reasons for businesses to stay, adding: "With [San Francisco's] capital investment in buildings, transportation and communications, it provides corporations with logistical advantages that cannot be easily duplicated elsewhere."[68] Favored by its "place luck," its specialization in advanced corporate services, its proximity to the Pacific Rim, and its scaled-down development objectives, San Francisco is one of those cities that is "strategically located to drive harder bargains than others" in making deals and forming partnerships with the private sector.[69]

It is difficult to measure just how many firms have actually left the city or, of those that left, how many of them would have relocated anyway even without Proposition M's restrictions. In 1988, one survey of San Francisco downtown businesses reported that 9 percent of them (representing about eleven hundred companies) planned to move from the city within the next two years. High rents and occupancy costs and "the anti-business attitude of the city government" were the most frequently cited reasons.[70] Firms wishing to expand their office facilities or work spaces probably will have to relocate elsewhere given the growing scarcity of large floorplate buildings. One study by the Chamber of Commerce attempted to estimate the financial (tax and business fee) losses to the city resulting from Proposition M's restrictions. The figure arrived at was a surprisingly small $9 million, and even that amount was disputed by slow-growth activists.[71]

No systematic evidence has been presented to document the claims that firms are deserting San Francisco to escape the city's hostile business climate. Even granting that significant disinvestment has occurred, however, what is bad medicine for most cities could be good for San Francisco. Indeed, voluntary exit through disinvestment provides a natural mechanism for selectively replacing disgruntled and potentially antagonistic business leaders with ones more sympathetic to slow-growth policies and more dependent on and loyal to the local economy.[72] In the long run, to the extent business flight actually occurs, it could work to secure a progressive urban regime, both economically and politically, rather than to undermine it.

Fighting: San Francisco's downtown business community has engaged in very little active fighting of city hall and the progressives since 1986. In part this is a strategic defensive posture, a form of burying one's tanks in the sand until the worst winds of slow-growth progressivism blow over. Following the Proposition M victory, many business leaders counseled patience in mounting a repeal campaign, predicting that the time would be ripe sometime after 1991 when commercial office vacancies would be down, rents up, and the market pressures for growth revived. In any case, until very recently, the downtown business community has not been in shape to fight, lacking both central leadership and political influence. The Chamber of Commerce remains the city's foremost business association, but it no longer exercises public leadership in the broader sense of the term. A business columnist recently observed that "the overwhelming impression the Chamber leaves at the moment . . . is that of an organization not fully in control of its own destiny"; the Chamber's image has been "battered by complaints that it has been ignoring the needs of small business, losing political clout—and losing vital political battles—in San Francisco."[73]

The inner circle of the Chamber of Commerce, the city's so-called "Big Seven"—Pacific Gas and Electric, Levi Strauss, Pacific Telesis, BankAmerica, Bechtel, Chevron, and Transamerica—showed fighting spirit in organizing a business coalition that helped to defeat a business tax initiative sponsored by Mayor Agnos in the June 1988 election. But that victory was short-lived. Soon after the election, Mayor Agnos "played political hardball" by threatening to mobilize another grass-roots initiative campaign unless the Big Seven executives agreed to endorse his proposed increase in the city's payroll tax.[74] They gave in and did as he asked—much to the dismay of other downtown business leaders, some of whom felt they had been sold out. One inside witness to the quiet surrender noted, "The nagging fear was that Agnos would lead a populist holy war and they would be made out as the bad guys. They didn't think it was worth it."[75]

Stung by such criticisms, the chamber recently hired a public relations firm to refurbish its image.[76] It has begun mending fences with the small business community, and it emerged from its bunker to mount offensives against the new progressive establishment in city hall. In February 1991, the chamber launched its national ad campaign attacking the city's sanctuary policies and antiwar stance. This drew venom from one of the city's leading progressives, a good sign that the chamber was being taken seriously again.[77] A more significant indicator of the chamber's revived political clout was its recent success in dissuading the city's small business leaders from endorsing a divisive business tax increase (see below).

Adapting: Some business leaders have abandoned progrowth ideology almost entirely and are beginning to think about the development process from a slow-growth perspective. One reason is that prophecies of economic doom have not come true—in particular, the predictions of many business executives that the city would suffer economic disaster if Proposition M passed.[78] In mid-1991, five years after passage of Proposition M, commercial office vacancy rates in the financial district remained moderately high at about 13 percent and rents low ($18 to $40 per square foot for Class A space); tourism and visitor spending were increasing; and unemployment rates were lower than state and national averages.[79] This stubborn tendency of the city's economy to remain healthy has eroded cherished maxims. For example, the traditional progrowth argument that high-rise construction holds the key to the city's economic vitality has lost credibility even among some high-rise developers. Although most downtown business leaders continue to view growth controls as toxic to the city's business climate and economic health, there are those who accept them as inevitable and even desirable. This adaptive "second generation" thinking about growth controls[80] is clear in the remarks of developer Matthew Witte: "Although the trend for new and higher urban development standards can claim its origins in San Francisco's unique geographic constraints, I think developers everywhere are soon going to have to play by similar rules. . . . As citizens begin taking a more active role in the development process, developers will be forced to treat local government policies and community concerns as goals to be met, rather than as obstacles to be overcome."[81]

Norman T. Gilroy, managing director of China Bridge, has used the term *entrepreneurial planning* to describe recommended business practices that are socially responsive, politically adroit, and economically profitable in the new slow-growth environment. At a recent business conference in San Francisco focusing on real estate issues, he argued:

> In the tradition of the martial arts, if you can use the momentum of the barriers that have been built against you . . . , if you can use that momentum to work for you, often the path to approval is much quicker . . . . Perhaps there's a better way. Perhaps if you can plan strategically from the very beginning, go in, take the pulse of the community, develop some sensitivity to the inter-cultural aspects—you can avoid both the courthouse and the ballot box . . . and you can arrive at something that goes much quicker, much cheaper, and I believe is done better and is maybe more lasting in its form; it's more a part of the community it's in.[82]

San Francisco architect Jeffrey Heller also spoke at this conference. Probably no business leader in San Francisco can match Heller's success in working within the structure of the new regime. He is said by some observers to have "Hellerized" the San Francisco skyline with his smaller and more delicate buildings, several of them constructed under the new rules of Proposition M. He commented that

> projects are getting much, much more sensitive to the areas that they're put into. And I think in the end, for the public, that's good. The danger, of course, and the danger of Prop. M and other things is that they will drive the markets away. I frankly don't see that. I would tell you that the last year in San Francisco I've seen more energy and excitement than I've seen in quite a

while. . . . People ultimately don't want to choke on the air they breathe and they want to be able to move from A to B in their car. And places that are a little more lax about these things get into those kinds of issues and drive people to places like this.[83]

New types of entrepreneurial-planning businesses have emerged in San Francisco to guide other businesses (especially developers) through the city's increasingly labyrinthine planning review process. A good example is the recent formation of The GCA Group, which teams Bob McCarthy (one of the city's leading land-use attorneys and Democratic party influentials), Debra Stein (a community-relations and environmental specialist), and Will Chang (a local developer) in helping businesses cope with what McCarthy describes as "the most sophisticated and complex building-approval process in the United States."[84] A number of new law firms and environmental law specialists have gravitated to San Francisco with the same goal in mind, many of them replacing corporate law practices that had to close shop because of the collapsing commercial real estate market.[85]

Donald Keough, publisher of the *San Francisco Business Times*, acknowledges that "business, as a whole, lost touch with the rapidly changing and culturally diverse community that was going to dominate in a changing San Francisco."[86] Arguing that "civic and political clumsiness" isolated business leaders from the community, he urges the business establishment to "forgo the notion that it will call the shots" and to work harder in selling itself as a friend rather than an enemy. Failure to do so, he writes, will have political consequences: "The Nancy Walkers, Calvin Welchs and Sue Hestors of this world are winning the battle of the streets and the 'x's of the voters."[87]

This reshaping of business ideology and practice in response to progressive social objectives is a trend that bodes well for the possible founding of what Elkin calls a "commercial republic" in San Francisco—that is, an urban regime in which people and places have power and business power is put in its place (or puts itself in place) to serve social goals.[88] It is true that all of those quoted here have been successful in their efforts to work within the system and thus what they say might not apply to those who have tried and failed. But most have not tried, and others have withdrawn or are hunkering down in strategic retreat waiting to squash the new regime. What remains to be seen is whether a process of natural selection is at work winnowing out detractors from the business community while enticing and keeping those whose citizenship roles have been broadened by San Francisco's new planning institutions. This kind of restructuring of and by business is very difficult to study empirically, but it is precisely the type of change that must be understood if the "commercial republic" is ever to become more than just an ideal type.

Despite the Chamber of Commerce's recent shifts in community posture and the encouraging emergence of a second-generation business approach to issues of growth, San Francisco's downtown business elites remain ideologically divided, politically disorganized, and not yet capable of exercising unified leadership in the realm of public affairs. The contrast with Atlanta's business-dominated urban regime is striking. In Atlanta, the city needs the unity of downtown business leaders to facilitate local government in achieving large-scale development objectives. The regime serves collective goals; economic means are consensually adapted to political ends. In San Francisco's antiregime, on the other hand, progressive leaders believe they have good reason to fear the solidarity of downtown business elites. The old progrowth regime was a means for attaining ends that are no longer collectively pursued. That is why Proposition M and other slow-growth measures were deliberately thrown up as policy barricades to block business power and cut it down to size. San Francisco needs business—but not big business.

Petty Bourgeois Radicalism in the Antiregime

For many progressives, small business is the answer to building a progressive urban regime in San Francisco. The city requires a healthy economic base, one that can generate jobs for residents, construct needed affordable housing, and sustain local commerce without damaging the environment, disrupting neighborhood communities, or destroying the city's architectural heritage. Many progressive leaders believe that only a small business economy can support new social goals without violating slow-growth constraints. The *Bay Guardian*, for example, has advocated this small business strategy of economic development for years. *Guardian* editor Tim Redmond argues that "a diversified base of small, locally owned companies would provide jobs for the community, encourage local reinvestment and avoid inappropriate, environmentally detrimental development that would harm the city's quality of life."[89]

Jane Jacobs's *The Economy of Cities*[90] is a crucial text supporting the economic logic of this approach, particularly regarding the importance of diversification in a homegrown local economy.[91] In terms of its political logic, Roberto Unger's concept of "petty bourgeois radicalism" captures the essence of a small business strategy and its linkage to progressive reforms.[92] Unger argues that much of the historical radical challenge to dominant forms of governmental and economic organization "came from skilled workers and artisans, technicians and professionals, shopkeepers and even petty manufacturers, rather than from the proletariat or the lumpen that have played so prominent a role in traditional leftist historiography."[93] Generally rejected by centrists and Marxists alike on grounds that it forfeits economies of scale and is economically and politically unstable, petty bourgeois radicalism has been "repeatedly suppressed rather than defeated in an impartial Darwinian competition."[94] Denied a chance to succeed during the age of industrialization, an emerging form of petty bourgeois radicalism may now be put to a test in postindustrial San Francisco.

San Francisco is a nationally recognized mecca for small businesses. One business analyst writes that San Francisco is "on the leading edge of a rapid and dramatic transformation taking place in many major U.S. cities—a transformation from the corporate era to an era that is dominated by the entrepreneurial aspirations of a new class of white-collar artisans."[95] Susan MacCracken, a researcher with Cognetics Inc., describes San Francisco as "an entrepreneurial kind of place. Between the universities, Silicon Valley and a good quality of life, it has a lot of things going for it."[96] In 1988, 97 percent of the city's 30,500 business firms employed fewer than one hundred workers, 88 percent employed fewer than twenty workers, and 64 percent employed fewer than five. Of the 26,800 firms employing fewer than twenty workers, 46 percent were specialized in business and professional services—the two sectors experiencing most rapid growth.[97] A study by job creation expert David Birch shows that small businesses produced virtually all of the city's new jobs between 1981 and 1985, and 75 percent of those jobs were in companies employing less than twenty workers.[98] The city's new small businesses often occupy niches in downtown office buildings vacated by larger firms, such as Chevron, BankAmerica, and Southern Pacific. Real estate analyst Mark Buell estimates that 78 percent of the businesses working in downtown office buildings employ ten or fewer people.[99] As suggested by this sampling of statistics, small business is big in San Francisco.

Many of the city's new small businesses are socially enlightened high-tech service companies meeting the changing needs of an informational society. A good example is Abacus Inc., which provides a variety of services for microcomputer and minicomputer systems and is one of northern California's leading suppliers of advanced computer graphics. Ranked as one of the country's fastest-growing companies, Abacus closed 1990 with $14 million in sales.[100] Way Konigsberg, the firm's founder and executive vice-president, views Abacus as a "feminist-oriented business dedicated to growth and generation of jobs, and ultimately to progressive social change." In her eyes, Abacus is a "business-driven Peace Corps" and a "force for advancing global and social issues."[101] In San Francisco's booming garment industry, the Jeanne-Marc apparel manufacturing firm is an exemplary small business that combines financial success with environmental sensitivity and progressive social values. Workers in Jeanne-Marc's huge but "environmentally friendly" factory operate energy-efficient sewing machines, practice water conservation, and recycle all materials. The firm's owners, Jeanne Allen and Marc Grant, helped to create the Green Ribbon Panel of the San Francisco Small Business Advisory Commission. The panel's mission is to "promote environmentally sound practices among small businesses and to publicize small companies run with ecological efficiency."[102]

Immigrant enterprise also is a major source of small business growth in San Francisco, particularly in sectors with low entry barriers, low capital-to-labor ratios, and products and services that cater to ethnic consumer tastes.[103] The

Chinese Chamber of Commerce and the Hispanic Chamber of Commerce have been active in promoting the spread of small business in their ethnic communities. Under the direction of Harold Yee, Asian Inc. has played an important role in nurturing entrepreneurial talents and sponsoring small business start-ups in the Asian American community. One small stretch of the city's Tenderloin district has more than one hundred Vietnamese-owned businesses serving the ten thousand Vietnamese who live in the neighborhood. Residents and merchants hope to transform the area into a "Little Saigon" that will rival Chinatown, Japantown, and North Beach in attracting tourists and dollars.[104] Scattered throughout the city are an estimated 520 Arab grocers (mainly Palestinians), who have formed their own trade group, the Independent Grocers Association.[105]

These examples illustrate the diversity and vitality of small businesses in San Francisco. As the small business sector has grown in size and complexity, new layers of organization have formed to coordinate its economic and political activities. The most important of these is the San Francisco Small Business Network, which now represents eleven thousand firms. Current president Scott Hauge and other network leaders have formulated a citywide perspective on small business issues and have joined forces with the Council of District Merchants, neighborhood merchant associations, and multicultural business groups in fighting proposed increases in business taxes, mandated health-care benefits, and bureaucratic red tape.

Small business owners are in a position to assume a much more visible leadership role in San Francisco politics because, first, public opinion favors it, and, second, established leadership groups on all sides—progressives, downtown business, and city hall—are courting them as allies. In a 1989 voter survey, 79 percent of the city's respondents said that small business firms "should be given more power and influence than they have right now in making city policies." Only 14 percent said the same about large business corporations. Two out of three voters (67 percent) felt that *only* small businesses should have more input.[106] Support of small business and support of slow-growth policies are linked. The stronger the opposition to "a change in the city's Master Plan to allow more downtown high rises to be built," the greater the support for small business power. Fully 73 percent of those who strongly opposed high-rise construction also favored more clout for small business. This last finding demonstrates that San Francisco's slow-growthers are not "antibusiness" per se, as many downtown business leaders have charged, but are quite selectively anti–big business and pro–small business.

The political stock of the small business community has gone up in recent years; nearly all of the city's political leaders place a rhetorical halo over small business enterprise and seek to enlist small business owners as allies. Downtown business elites have responded to small business interests by admitting small business representatives into some of the outer, if not the inner, leadership circles. Progressive leaders have rallied to protect neighborhood businesses from displacement by franchise operations, have protested increases in small business taxes (while at the same time demanding increases in taxes on large corporations), and have written explicit mandates for small business preservation into the eight priority policies of Proposition M. For his part, Mayor Agnos established the Small Business Advisory Commission and promised to cut the red tape and costs involved in small business start-ups.[107]

For progressives, the motives for seeking an alliance with small business run deeper than the desire to achieve merely tactical political goals. Small businesses must provide the economic foundation for a new progressive regime. It remains to be seen, however, whether small business owners can perform as reliable partners in a coalition with slow-growth progressives. The streaks of individualism and preindustrialism in small business ideology are compatible with an antiregime, but they might prove corrosive in a more centralized progressive regime.[108] Labor demands, treatment of the homeless, mandatory health benefits, and business taxes are only a few of the issues that could become divisive in such a partnership.[109] An important demonstration of the small business community's unreliability as a progressive political ally was the recent decision by the Council of District Merchants and other small business organizations to join the Chamber of Commerce and downtown business associations in opposing Supervisor Harry Britt's 1991 proposal to increase payroll taxes on medium- and large-sized businesses. What makes this decision worrisome to progressives is that Britt's plan would also have eliminated the city's $150-business-license tax, which small business owners have resented and resisted. Britt's proposal obviously was intended to split the business community, but the stratagem did not work. Indeed, if anything, the maneuver only drove small business leaders into a closer alliance with chief executives of the city's largest corporations and the downtown business establishment.[110] This anti-progressive drift among small business leaders was reinforced by growing dissatisfaction with Mayor Agnos's management of business issues.[111] Scott Hauge of the Small Business Network, for example, complained that "to this day, [Agnos] has not talked to anyone in the small-business community. It appears to me that the mayor is making a conscious effort to split the small-business and big-business communities."[112] In view of the intellectual and political investment that progressives have made in cultivating small business as an ally, these developments are ominous.

Another problem with exclusive reliance on a small business economy is that it downplays the economic importance of larger firms, which many of the small businesses are set up to serve. Further, a recent local survey indicated that many small businesses provide dead-end jobs, pay lower-than-average wages, and have poor or nonexistent benefits packages and pension plans for their employees.[113] Another survey found that smaller businesses in San Francisco were much more likely than larger firms to be ignorant of the immigration laws and to violate the rights of immigrants and native workers in their employment and hiring practices.[114] These findings, taken together, hint at the danger of relying solely on small business to resolve contradictions between materialist and postmaterialist goals in the progressive agenda.[115]

ART AGNOS AND THE FAILURE
OF RIGHT-WING PROGRESSIVISM

Expectations that Art Agnos would become the long-awaited political architect of a new progressive regime died early in his administration. Shortly after his inauguration, Mayor Agnos was besieged at city hall by community activists demanding affordable housing and neighborhood preservation: "They'd become so accustomed to fighting City Hall," Agnos recalled, "I think they forgot who they were talking to. I told them, 'Hey, you don't have to convince me, we own this place now.' "[116] This sense of collective political ownership quickly evaporated, however, and near the end of his fourth year Agnos found himself in trouble with his progressive constituency. Disillusionment with Agnos had increased to the point that separate progressive factions were recruiting rival candidates to challenge his bid for a second term in the November 1991 election.

Progressive critics viewed Agnos as a bait-and-switch political con artist who got himself elected as a slow-growth progressive but then governed the city as a progrowth liberal. They saw him as secretive in his deal making with business elites; inaccessible and nonconsultative in his relations with progressive constituencies; and mediocre at best in fulfilling his campaign promises. Many progressives were especially distressed by Agnos's campaign to build the China Basin ballpark, his support of hotel construction on the waterfront, and his private negotiations with Catellus Corporation to develop Mission Bay. They had grown tired of having to block Agnos's development proposals at the ballot box through the channel of direct democracy. In commenting on their report card evaluating Agnos's mayoral performance (overall grade: C-), the *Bay Guardian* editors expressed a widely shared feeling of anger toward Agnos and disappointment with his policies: "There's a basic lesson of San Francisco politics here, one that Agnos seems unwilling to learn. The progressive voters who make up the majority of this city never expected much from the Joe Aliotos and Dianne Feinsteins, so they were pleased when those mayors did anything decent at all. Agnos promised to be something different—and if he can't live up to that promise, he's going to generate nothing but anger."[117] Lurking beneath these complaints was a deeper sense that Art Agnos had betrayed the progressive cause by lowering his aspirations and abandoning his grass roots.

During his years as mayor, Agnos showed no interest in assembling the many, tiny elements of his electoral coalition into a stable governing structure. The complexity of that task was daunting. Agnos was a politician, not an architect of dreams. His experience was in using regimes, not inventing them. Once elected, he gravitated instantly to the larger clumps of power that still survived in the city's fragmented polity. Faced repeatedly with budgetary crises, he made deals with big corporations, local millionaires, and outside investors to bring fresh capital to the city. He probably spent more time in Washington, D.C., seeking grants and federal assistance than he did in the neighborhood communities that had elected him. To generalize, Mayor Agnos preferred to use power that was already assembled and to mobilize resources already at hand. He had neither the inclination nor the patience to collaborate with grass-roots supporters in building new structures of power on the foundations they had laid over the previous twelve years. His strategy of working through established power centers and elites to attain progressive goals is one that I characterize as right-wing progressivism. It was a strategy destined to fail in San Francisco's antiregime.

As a right-wing progressive, Agnos followed what he perceived to be the path of least resistance in pursuing his agenda. It was easier for him to promote a few huge development projects as a way to create jobs and increase revenues, for example, than it was to nurture a small business economy more consistent with neighborhood preservation and slow-growth goals. Stone, Orr, and Imbroscio capture the political logic of such a strategy in suggesting that "possibly urban regimes devoted to and capable of pursuing redevelopment are easier to build than regimes devoted to and capable of pursuing human-capital development. It may well be that, other things being equal, what is easier to assemble is able to crowd out what is harder to construct, especially given the short time frame that elected politicians operation within."[118] In San Francisco's antiregime, however, this kind of logic led Agnos unwittingly down the path of greatest resistance. His proposed development projects were blocked at every turn by angry progressives who would not be crowded out by stadiums or hotels. Agnos had underestimated the obstructive force of the slow-growth coalition that had helped to put him in power.

Deaf to his own campaign rhetoric, Agnos learned too late that democratic process and citizen empowerment were integral to the progressive agenda. To achieve progressive ends by nonprogressive means was a contradiction in terms. George Moscone had seen this; Agnos had not. In the refrain used often by his progressive critics, Agnos did not "get it." What he did not "get" was that he had become part of the problem rather than part of the solution in the effort to create a progressive regime. Only near the end did it dawn on Agnos why many of the same progressives who had voted for him in 1987 worked so hard to defeat him in the 1991 mayoral election: They dumped him to clean the slate for new and better leadership. In doing so, however, they caused factional strife that divided the ranks. And they created another problem for themselves in the person of Mayor-elect Frank Jordan, a probusiness moderate who had little sympathy for growth controls, social reform, or left-wing progressivism.

10
Postscript: The 1991 Mayoral Election and Beyond

So too, T. E. Lawrence's organizing of the Arabian revolt against the Turks was limited by the character of his largest stable building blocks, the separate, suspicious desert tribes.
—Herbert A. Simon

On 10 December 1991, former police chief and progrowth moderate Frank Jordan defeated incumbent Art Agnos in a close run-off election to become the next mayor of San Francisco. How and why did this happen in a city described by some as the "capital of progressivism"? What are the long-term implications of this transfer of power for the future of progressive politics in San Francisco? The following account focuses mainly on the progressive side of the campaign and sketches some very preliminary answers to these questions.

SETTING

By August 1991, Art Agnos was facing an uphill battle for reelection. Prolonged recession continued to dampen the local economy and to saddle Agnos with yet another revenue shortfall—the fourth since he began his term of office. Many downtown business leaders were dismayed by Agnos's meager success in keeping and attracting businesses and jobs. Many small business leaders felt neglected by Agnos and complained of taxes and red tape. The city's more conservative residents continued to feel estranged from the liberal/progressive establishment that had run city hall for nearly four years. In the eyes of many, San Francisco's quality of life had deteriorated during the Agnos administration. Some native San Franciscans still viewed Agnos as a Sacramento outsider who showed little respect for the city's history or traditions. His aggressive tactics, abrasive personality, and imperious leadership style grated on citizens and mocked their populist aspirations. Many disappointed progressives who had once supported Agnos now were turning against him. Mayor Agnos's accomplishments were invisible to most voters: his tough and effective lobbying for urban assistance funds in Sacramento and Washington, D.C.; his travels around the country and to the Far East to promote San Francisco as a tourist and convention center and as a place to do business; his long-range multiservice shelter program for the homeless; his precarious behind-the-scenes balancing of budgets year after year. In late summer 1991, what most voters wanted was a friendly, homegrown mayor who could solve street-level problems with visible, immediate results. Widely perceived as unfriendly, inaccessible, and ineffectual, Mayor Agnos no longer fit that bill. Pollsters now found that only 35 percent of the city's registered voters rated him as a good or excellent mayor; 28 percent rated him poor.[1] Agnos was in trouble.[2]

Agnos's fall from grace was hard but not sudden. It had taken him nearly four years to become unpopular with most voters, despised by many, and vulnerable to attack from both Right and Left. It would be difficult if not impossible to repair all that damage in a few short weeks. Commenting on his campaign strategy, Agnos assessed the situation correctly: "I see myself as my main competitor."[3]

THE PRIMARY ELECTION

Tom Hsieh, Agnos's most outspoken conservative critic on the Board of Supervisors, announced in late 1990 that he would challenge the incumbent mayor in the November 1991 election. He thus became the first Chinese American in the city's history to run for mayor. Agnos's former police chief, Frank Jordan, announced his candidacy in early January 1991. Jordan's campaign manager, Jack Davis, had directed Molinari's disastrous run-off campaign against Agnos in 1987. Former supervisor Richard Hongisto announced his candidacy in March. This move surprised many political observers because Hongisto had just been elected as city assessor five months earlier, had served barely three months in that new position, and had sworn publicly that he would never run against Agnos. Aware of Agnos's vulnerability and goaded by *Bay Guardian* editors and other Agnos-hating progressives to "run, Dick, run," Hongisto apparently believed he enjoyed a genuine ground swell of support and had a real chance to win.[4] But others, including *Examiner* columnist Bill Mandel, were more skeptical: "It's hard to believe that the anti-Agnos left is sufficiently desperate to pick the steadfast-as-quicksilver Hongisto as its hero."[5] Agnos formally announced his own candidacy for reelection in July. A month later, Supervisor Angela Alioto, daughter of former mayor Joseph Alioto, threw her hat in the ring. Angela Alioto had been Mayor Agnos's closest political ally on the Board of Supervisors. As the only female candidate among the serious contenders, Alioto perhaps felt that her chances would be as good as or even better than Hongisto's to unseat the weak incumbent.[6] Although Hongisto claimed to have "a constituency that sticks to me like glue," many supporters abandoned his sinking campaign when Alioto announced.[7] By late summer, the political stage was set for the 1991 mayoral campaign. *Guardian* reporters Kathleen Baca and Craig McLaughlin summarized the plot succinctly: "Agnos ran as a progressive, so the conservatives don't trust him. But he never carried out his progressive mandate, angering progressives. That means he's now facing two challengers to his left and two to his right."[8]

On San Francisco's left-shifted ideological spectrum, the five major mayoral candidates had much in common. All were registered Democrats, for example, and all supported women's rights, endorsed the city's domestic partners legislation, expressed concern for people with AIDS, and emphasized the need for affordable housing.[9] Frank Jordan, portrayed by some critics as an extreme conservative, wisely framed his candidacy in a comparative perspective: "I've been painted as an ultra-conservative, right-wing chief of police. In any other city, they'd call me a liberal."[10] To differentiate themselves from other challengers, some candidates staked out positions regarded by observers as bizarre. Hsieh, for example, railed against the San Francisco school district's court-imposed school busing program. This stand pleased constituents who favored neighborhood schools, but debate on the matter was pointless because school issues fell completely outside the control of the mayor's office. Hongisto proposed limiting the number of people living in the city and billed himself as the "one candidate for mayor [who] will stop the Manhattanization of San Francisco."[11] Mindful of the skyscrapers already piled high in downtown San Francisco, even the editors of the progressive *SF Weekly* scratched their heads over that one: "It's disturbing that Hongisto seems more comfortable playing to the outdated notions of reactionary anti-growth advocates than dealing with the city's pressing needs to take care of all its residents."[12] Alioto made special appeals to women, ethnic minorities, and gay and lesbian voters. Although her candidacy injected energy and excitement into the campaign, her championing of minorities could become patronizing, as when she promised: "I will appoint minorities. But not like this mayor. I'm going to appoint *real* minorities—*real* African Americans, *real* Latinos."[13]

Of all the challengers, it was Frank Jordan who found and pressed the "hot buttons" in San Francisco's restless and discontented electorate. Jordan staked out his territory early in the campaign: the mean streets. As he saw it, under the Agnos administration, the streets of San Francisco had become a kind of Hobbesian hell: dirty, dangerous, crowded with homeless, and menaced by pushy panhandlers. At one point he posed for reporters near a dead rat in a gutter and said, "I think you all know that San Francisco has a foreign policy and can't even keep its streets clean."[14] This message struck a responsive chord with many voters, and it defined the focus and theme of the entire campaign. If the streets were mean and neglected, Jordan suggested, perhaps that was because Mayor Agnos was mean and neglectful. It did not matter that street-cleaning duties fell mainly to the Department of Public Works, outside the mayor's direct control. The underlying message was that the mayor did not seem to care about these nuts-and-bolts issues of city management and had let the city slide into disrepair and disrepute.[15] *Examiner* columnist Rob Morse wrote: "Agnos has never had a firm grasp of San Francisco symbolism. People complain about dirty streets knowing full well that we have bigger problems. But for San Francisco to have dirty streets is like [the movie actor] Julia Roberts walking around with axle grease on her face. It's all wrong. Politicians should know that symbolic issues are the most real issues of all."[16]

Jordan also exploited Agnos's vulnerability on the issue of homelessness. One poll reported that an estimated 40 percent of registered voters ranked homelessness as the number one problem facing the city.[17] Liberals and conservatives disagreed about *why* it was a problem; some viewed the homeless as needy casualties of a sick economy, while others saw them mainly as an aesthetic problem on a par with litter and grime. But nearly everyone agreed that Agnos had failed miserably in his efforts to cope with the situation, despite his early boasts that he would make San Francisco the first city in America to end homelessness. Business leaders and conservatives criticized Agnos for having allowed the homeless to camp out for a year in civic center plaza while multiservice shelters were being built to implement his "Beyond Shelter" plan. But when finally he directed police to clear the plaza and move the homeless into the waiting shelters, homeless advocates and many of the homeless themselves complained bitterly because the facilities and services were inadequate—a fact that Agnos found hard to accept and at first denied.[18] Only 2 percent of voters thought Agnos had done an excellent job in addressing the plight of homelessness; 49 percent thought he had done a poor job.[19] Frank Jordan, who made hay of this, offered no real solution for the problem of homelessness. (Early in his campaign he proposed moving some of the homeless to work camps near the city's jail in San Bruno, a draconian scheme he later abandoned.[20]) But he did offer voters a solution for the problem of Agnos: himself.

Times were hard, and Mayor Agnos found that incumbency was more a liability than an asset in running his campaign. Columnist Bill Mandel called him the "Velcro mayor" because "everything sticks to him. People hold him accountable for the rotten weather this summer."[21] Agnos complained that he was the target of "heat-seeking missiles" from challengers and critics. Unhappy voters could not reach the president or the governor, he said, "but they sure can get to me." While defending his policies and programs, he conceded that his mayoral style left much to be desired: "I need to improve my bedside manner. My medicine and healing has been good, but my bedside manner needs to get better."[22] He apologized for having lost touch with his supporters, and he also tried to explain himself: "No one can make the major, important decisions in a big American city and keep everyone happy. The mayor makes decisions every hour, on the hour, that will offend somebody."[23]

Certain that a run-off election would be necessary and that he would be in it, Agnos ran his initial campaign at half-throttle. He wrote and distributed another campaign book, this one a twenty-four-page pamphlet called *Things to Be Proud Of.* One-third the length of his 1987 book of promises, *Getting Things Done*, this new text made few waves with the voters. His field director, Larry Tramutola, restarted the engines on Agnos's long-dormant precinct operation, gathering 250 precinct captains to a rally in mid-September. Agnos pledged to them that he would "maintain regular communications, every two months at least, in the next four years."[24] In public debates and campaign appearances, he kept a low profile and adopted a soft-spoken manner. Along with his fence-mending measures and gestures of humility, however, Agnos also conveyed a prickly sense of betrayal at being challenged by disloyal former allies. In one candidate forum, for example, when asked what he would have done differently in his first term, Agnos replied, "One thing I would change the most is who I trust on the Board of Supervisors, or in the assessor's office, or in the police chief's office."[25] In a speech at Glide Memorial Church, he applauded the Reverend Cecil Williams as a model loyal supporter: "Because he's my friend, he comes to help me when I'm in trouble, rather than run against me."[26]

Agnos found himself in a lose-lose situation of his own making. On the one hand, Chamber of Commerce leader Jim Lazarus condemned Agnos and the Board of Supervisors for placating the city's "far left wing" and for leaving the downtown business community high and dry.[27] On the other hand, members of that "far left wing" (who had sabotaged Agnos's efforts to appease the business community) felt that *they* were the ones who had been left high and dry. Supervisor Harry Britt, for example, attacked Agnos as "an outsider who doesn't listen to us. Gays, in particular, are sensitive to bullies, and Art Agnos is the quintessential political bully."[28] Recalling Agnos's unsuccessful attempts to cut deals with big business in China Basin, Mission Bay, and the waterfront, Susan Hestor remarked that Agnos had not learned "a basic lesson of San Francisco civic life: Don't cut deals in secret and expect them to fly with the voters."[29] Ridiculing Agnos's claim in an endorsement interview that he was "the most progressive mayor—with the possible exception of George Moscone—that this city has ever had," *Bay Guardian* editors blasted Agnos because he "failed to deliver on the style of leadership he promised this city."[30] Their most scathing attack focused on Agnos's relationship with Pacific Gas and Electric and his failure to push for public ownership of utilities. The battle for public power was a "litmus test," they argued. If candidates failed that test, they had to be told that "they can no longer get away with running as progressives only to move to the right as soon as they get elected."[31] Agnos was caught in a political double bind. Business leaders were abandoning him because he had not delivered; progressives were abandoning him because he had tried. And nobody liked his style.

As conservatives converged on the Jordan bandwagon, progressives diverged into separate trajectories of support for Agnos, Hongisto, and Alioto. Agnos backers blamed Hongisto and Alioto for causing the fission; Hongisto and Alioto backers blamed Agnos. The *Bay Guardian*'s Tim Redmond blamed just about everyone for the "ugly dilemma" progressive voters faced: "Do you vote your conscience or do you hold your nose and vote pragmatically?" Perhaps with tongue-in-cheek, he groused, "Maybe anyone who wants to be mayor as badly as Art Agnos, Frank Jordan, and Angela Alioto should be immediately disqualified. Maybe the sort of person who would make the best mayor is someone who doesn't really want the job."[32] Witnessing this self-destructive melee, editors of the progressive *SF Weekly* counseled readers to expect less from Art Agnos: "The idea that Agnos turned his back on his progressive ideology once he was elected mayor is absurd. Art Agnos is a former social worker turned liberal hardball politician. He never espoused a progressive ideology to begin with." They pointed to the more dangerous threat posed by Frank Jordan, a candidate who in their eyes resembled Frank Rizzo, the right-wing ex-cop who once served as the mayor of Philadelphia. They urged progressives to unify tactically and pragmatically behind Art Agnos. "Art Agnos hasn't been perfect," they conceded, "but he has been a whole lot better than Dianne Feinstein."[33] This advice was cool, calculated, and practical: Agnos was the half-loaf, Jordan was the none. Many of those who dismissed such reasoning felt certain that Agnos would make the run-off. There would be a second opportunity then to make compromises. Meanwhile, at minimum, Agnos needed a good scare; he needed to be punished for his transgressions and forced to make amends.

As the November election day approached and as the progressives continued to fire shots at one another, Frank Jordan's field operation laid track into the neighborhoods west of Twin Peaks and rolled heavy organizational machinery into action. Designed by Jack Davis, fueled by two-thirds of Jordan's entire campaign fund, and run by former Feinstein aide Jim Wunderman, the field operation mobilized a ten-thousand-member volunteer network, targeted 410 precincts, identified sixty thousand likely Jordan supporters, and issued election-day marching orders to fifteen hundred get-out-the-vote workers. As Jack Davis said, "Four years ago, when Agnos shocked everybody with the immense vote nobody saw coming, that's where it came from, and that's where Frank's vote is coming from."[34] Jordan had other assets: downtown money, statewide real estate money, the *Chronicle*'s endorsement, an assortment of club endorsements, and the backing of State Senator Quentin Kopp, to name a few. But mainly he had workers and voters, and the voters he worked on were the types most likely to vote.

On 5 November, following the most expensive mayor's race in the city's history ($3.5 million total), Frank Jordan took first place with 31.5 percent of the votes, followed by Agnos with 27.7 percent, Alioto with 18.7 percent, Hongisto with 9.5 percent, and Hsieh with 9.4 percent.[35] The top two vote-getters, Jordan and Agnos, now would compete in the 10 December run-off election. The overall voter turnout rate of 46 percent was about average for an off-year election. However, neighborhood-level turnout rates varied considerably, ranging from very low in the lower-income Bayview–Hunters Point, Ingleside, and Fillmore districts to very high in the well-heeled Pacific Heights and Marina districts. Jordan won the lion's share of absentee ballots, beating Agnos by two to one. These turnout rates and absentee tallies were cause for concern in the Agnos camp.[36]

Although most political observers agreed that Jordan had scored a great upset, there was much debate about whether or not the results signaled a genuine conservative turn in the electorate. Arthur Bruzzone, a Jordan supporter and also vice-chair of the San Francisco Republican Central Committee, left no doubt about his opinion: "Some have called it a populist revolt or anti-incumbency sentiment. It is not sentiment and it is not just anti-incumbency. It is a grass-roots, sometimes fanatical, repudiation of 15 years of liberal reign and political correctness. Along with it, the demise of the nationally celebrated San Francisco Democrat."[37] Impressed by the number of first-time Asian American voters and by Hsieh's strong showing in that constituency, Bruzzone sketched a bright future for the city's conservatives: "If the other quiet minority, the City's Asian Americans, become politically active, the Jordan-Hsieh vote could reach a majority by the 1995 supervisorial campaign."[38] In the short run, however, even if the predominately Asian American vote for Hsieh was counted as a conservative bloc and then added to the Jordan vote, the conservatives still came up short of a majority.

Voting on ballot propositions further complicated an ideological interpretation of the mayoral election results. The voters overwhelmingly rejected yet another attempt by religious conservatives to repeal the city's domestic partners legislation. They ratified ordinances restoring collective bargaining rights to city workers along with concessionary civil service reforms. They rejected an initiative opposed by affordable housing advocates that would have eased restrictions on condominium conversions. And they approved an initiative supported by liberals to earmark city funds for spending on children-assistance programs. On the other hand, perhaps mainly because of massive campaign spending by real estate interests, the voters rejected the city's recently passed rent-control ordinance that tenant groups had sought for years. And they also approved an initiative endorsed by Hsieh, Kopp, Jordan, and others to eliminate deputy mayors. As pollster David Binder commented, "The liberals and progressives get the publicity, but there is a high proportion of moderate to conservative voters who actually vote. I don't necessarily think [the election result] means San Francisco is shifting to the right because it is not as far to the left as everyone believes. It's a divided city."[39]

With the run-off election only six weeks away, perhaps the most important signal sent by the November results was that voter support for Agnos was weak— weaker than anyone had thought. A city lobbyist observed, "By finishing second, Art has lost the mantle of invincibility. People now sense there is blood in the water."[40] Dick Pabich, Alioto's campaign manager, spelled out the implications for Agnos: "Art has to win the left back. If he doesn't, he loses. . . . The problem is he's burned all his bridges with those people."[41]

THE RUN-OFF ELECTION

In launching his run-off campaign, Jordan continued his earlier attack on Art Agnos, only now more confidently and with sharper focus: "For the past four years, we've had vindictiveness, arrogance and closed-mindedness. We've had an 'anything goes' philosophy that has made our streets dirtier, our neighborhoods more dangerous and our city less livable. And we've had a mayor who has tried to blame everyone but himself for the failures of his administration."[42] With his first victory under his belt and with good coaching by consultant Dee Dee Myers, the amateur politician Frank Jordan was beginning to look and sound like a winner. The Jordan campaign became a money magnet—especially for real estate money. The San Francisco Building Owners and Managers Association contributed $20,000, and the California Housing Council raised funds for Jordan throughout the state. Preston Cook, chair of the San Francisco Association of Realtors Political Action Committee, exclaimed, "This is the easiest money I've ever raised for a political campaign."[43] The defeat of rent-control advocate Art Agnos, Cook reasoned, would send "a politically negative message [about rent control] that will reverberate throughout the state and the nation."[44] Housing activists such as Randy Shaw, executive director of the Tenderloin Housing Clinic, took such threats seriously and warned that a Jordan victory might spell disaster for San Francisco tenants. The Rent Board under Mayor Agnos had placed caps on the rent increases landlords were allowed to charge in order to pay for capital improvements, so rents had been fairly stable. With Agnos out of the picture and a new Rent Board in place, however, real estate speculation might reach the levels observed during the Feinstein administration.[45] If real estate interests stood to gain so much from a Jordan victory, then the progressives stood to lose from an Agnos defeat.

Agnos had looked forward to the run-off campaign. Now that it was Agnos versus Jordan, the mayor predicted a better result: "This is no longer a tag-team match with four candidates ganging up on one candidate."[46] He began to shift to full-throttle and to change his tone. In an early speech, he said, "Frank Jordan is a nice guy, but this isn't a contest about Mr. Congeniality. It is a conflict over the future of the city."[47] Rather than apologizing for his tough demeanor, he began to reframe this trait as a leadership virtue in the demanding world of American urban politics. For example, in a debate with Jordan, he argued, "We need leadership that's strong enough and tough enough—that's the word—tough enough to go to Washington. We need someone who knows how to work Washington. Someone who knows how to work Sacramento. . . . Not a novice."[48] Responding to charges that he was an outsider who spent too much time away from the city, Agnos said, "More and more, the fate of this city's budget is intricately involved with state and federal budgets. You'd better be an expert in those milieus or you're going to get wiped out by those who are from other cities. . . . San Francisco has 2.3 percent of the state's population and is getting 20 percent of the state's money. That's not

Immaculate Conception, that's not because a Republican administration likes San Francisco. It's because we are smart and are on top of our game."[49] As proof of his lobbying and grantsmanship skills (and good sense of political timing), Mayor Agnos and Congresswoman Nancy Pelosi announced five days before the election that San Francisco had received an additional $188 million in federal and state funds, including $35 million to complete the Embarcadero Freeway replacement project, $4 million for a new detoxification center to be constructed as part of the "Beyond Shelter" homelessness program, and $21 million for AIDS services, nearly double what the city had received the year before.[50] These statistics no doubt impressed at least a few Agnos-haters, but probably not those whose geopolitical universe was confined to the city's 46.4 square miles and who viewed their peninsula as an island.

As the run-off campaign built toward its climax, Jordan and his advisors made some shrewd moves. One of them was to announce that Hadley Roff would become chief of staff if the voters elected Jordan. Roff had served as Mayor Feinstein's chief of staff and also held another position in the Agnos administration for a brief time. A knowledgeable and respected veteran of San Francisco politics, Roff knew his way around city hall and the bureaucracies. By promising to place Roff second in command after the election, Jordan reassured many voters who were nervous about Jordan's lack of political experience and his reputation as a hands-off administrator. Jordan also kicked sand over his earlier work-farm proposal for the homeless, shifting instead to an approach drafted by Hongisto advisors that called for assistance vouchers in exchange for public work, tax credits for businesses that employed the homeless, board and care homes and residential hotels as alternative shelters, and a rent deposit fund.[51] To refute Agnos's charges made late in the campaign that he was fostering a reactionary politics of hate, Jordan opened his arms wide to embrace all San Franciscans and promised to build bridges: "We must guard against a troublesome old myth that resurfaces each election in San Francisco. It's a myth of us versus them, west versus east, left versus right, liberal versus conservative, straight versus gay. A mayor must unite . . . make this city whole once again."[52] Dee Dee Myers put it more tartly to Agnos: "Frank Jordan isn't the one who has been pitting groups against each other, or the one who spent four years dividing the city into loyalists and traitors."[53] As if to demonstrate the spirit of inclusiveness on the Right, Hsieh endorsed Jordan, marking the occasion with a parade of dragons and drumbeating supporters.[54] Hsieh and Jordan, had exchanged some very harsh words during the primary campaign. It was not a given that they would bury the hatchet, but they did. The progressives still had a use for theirs.

Jordan also continued to say what business leaders wanted to hear. From the start he had declared himself a "pro-business mayor, someone who understands that you can't spend on social programs without having a stable economic base."[55] He promised repeatedly throughout his campaign to veto any sanctuary or foreign policy resolution passed by the Board of Supervisors unless it related directly to the management of city affairs. Jordan's pledge to review city department budgets line-by-line won kudos from business economists, including Kent Sims, who deplored Agnos's reluctance to discuss budgets or the projected 1992 deficit. Business columnist Thom Calandra opined that "the issue of City Hall fat will be the grease that burns one of the runoff candidates and lubes the other into office."[56] Jordan's promise of a more hospitable business climate figured heavily in the *Chronicle*'s endorsement of him as the kind of mayor who would put a stop to the "negative, small-minded, restrictive attitude that drives business out of the city and that is inexorably draining the vigor from what should be a glowing headquarters city."[57]

The Agnos campaign moved in fits and starts during the last few weeks, pausing now and then to surrender a contrite Agnos to the progressives for ritual flagellation. Now more than ever, Agnos needed progressive votes. As Jordan's campaign gained momentum, Agnos's seemed slowly to sink. A preelection poll of five hundred registered voters showed Agnos beating Jordan 45 percent to 40 percent, the rest undecided or committed to minor candidates. Among those most likely to turn out to vote, however, sample respondents favored Jordan over Agnos 48 percent to 43 percent.[58] Even more disturbing to Agnos supporters, voters had requested a record number of absentee ballots, which are traditionally cast in favor of conservative candidates and issues in San Francisco elections. With days still to go in the campaign, there was a good chance that Agnos's fate was being decided right then at kitchen tables west of Twin Peaks. Things looked grim. As Supervisor Terence Hallinan, an Agnos backer, put it, "In this election we are not fighting for the liberal agenda, we're fighting for our lives."[59]

Endorsements from Hongisto and Alioto might have lifted the Agnos campaign, but they never came. Alioto confessed an honest fear of Agnos: "Art doesn't forget. Even if I endorse [him], he'll make my life difficult on the board."[60] Some of her supporters even urged her to back Jordan. "If you stab the king," they advised, "you better kill the king."[61] She stopped short of that. As Dick Pabich, her campaign manager, commented, "I don't think very many of [Alioto's supporters] will vote for Frank Jordan, but they can do Art in by not voting at all. . . . There's an awful lot of progressives who aren't going to bother to vote."[62] As Agnos's crisis deepened, he became more receptive to pushy demands for quid pro quo. Supervisor Carole Migden, an Alioto backer, demanded that Agnos make concessions to the lesbian and gay community to win its votes. "Art needs more than names on paper," she said. "A lot of people are going to have to fall on their swords if he expects the enthusiastic support of the gay and lesbian community." At the top of Migden's hit list was Larry Bush, an Agnos advisor and speech writer. Bush had been nicknamed "Cobra Woman" for his alleged overzealous attacks on the gay and lesbian community in defending Agnos against accusations that the mayor cared more about ballparks than AIDS.[63] "The humbling of Agnos—that's what's required here," insisted Migden.[64]

The *Bay Guardian*, instigators and patrons of Hongisto's failed campaign, submitted a much longer list of grievances and demands. "If Agnos has any hope of winning on December 10," wrote the *Guardian* editors, "he must persuade progressive activists to work for him, and he must give progressive voters a reason to go to the polls."[65] To earn the progressive vote, Agnos had to make "substantive, lasting changes" over the next four weeks—changes such as firing Dean Macris; firing his Sacramento advisors; being more accessible to people like Britt, Welch, Hestor, Alioto, and Hongisto; installing a FAX line for public input; creating a more open government; asking the Board of Supervisors to authorize funding of a feasibility study of public power; appointing two public-power advocates to the Public Utilities Commission; restructuring city government using Hongisto's plans for eliminating four thousand jobs; pushing for district elections; abolishing the small business tax; and cleaning the streets.[66] Agnos actually responded to some of these demands. He immediately installed the requested FAX line, for example, and he appointed public-power advocate Nancy Walker to the Public Utilities Commission,[67] opened communications with Calvin Welch and Sue Hestor, and reassigned Larry Bush from city hall to the Friends of Art Agnos Committee.[68] In return for these concessions, the *Bay Guardian* endorsed the incumbent mayor "with little enthusiasm, and plenty of reservations," noting that "Agnos may not keep his promises after winning re-election. But during four years in office he has shown that even if he doesn't advance the progressive agenda, he will not go about dismantling it."[69] As the text of this half-hearted endorsement makes clear, *Guardian* editors were assuming that Agnos would win reelection, oblivious to the possibility that they were helping to prevent that from happening.

In the midst of this retributive frenzy the *SF Weekly* editors called once again for consensus seeking and pragmatism on the Left: "It's not surprising that politicians are trying to extract everything they can from the mayor in his moment of crisis. But in the situation we now face, it's almost suicidal for any liberal not to support Art Agnos." They concluded that "dialogue can help restore a working liberal-progressive coalition, but blackmail can only pave the way for a Frank Jordan victory."[70]

One last incident must be noted here because it was symptomatic of Agnos's tendency to behave in ways that hurt his own political cause. Warren Hinckle, a self-declared Agnos enemy, wrote a slashing attack on Agnos that was serialized in the *San Francisco Independent* under the title "The Agnos Years." Ted Fang, publisher of the *Independent*, distributed the series in book form throughout the city. The real problem for Agnos was not the publication's influence on voters but rather developed when his campaign staff requested that the city Tax Collector's Office investigate the Fang family's financial records and holdings. Agnos's press secretary, Scott Shafer, defended the action on grounds that Hinckle's book was political material promoting the Jordan campaign. "When a major Republican family spends between $100,000 and $150,000 on a book to get Frank Jordan elected," argued Shafer, "we think the public has a right to know about the family.

And we're trying to shed a little light on the Fang family and their holdings."[71] Presumably the "we" in this quote included Shafer's boss, Art Agnos. Shafer's claim that the book was campaign material requiring public disclosure eventually held up in court.[72] But the decision to pressure the Tax Collector's Office to pry into the Fang family's finances was unethical and politically stupid, especially so near the end of the run-off campaign. A *Bay Guardian* editorial articulated the reactions of many observers: "Ironically, the Fang incident comes just as the Agnos camp is trying to play down Agnos' image for vindictiveness against his political enemies."[73] Against the background of episodes like this, one can at least understand why Angela Alioto and other progressives might abandon all thoughts of peace with Agnos or might not mourn his political demise.

When the 197,442 total votes were counted on 10 December, Jordan had beaten Agnos 51.7 percent to 48.3 percent. Agnos actually won the election-day vote by around 5,000 votes. But Jordan won 61 percent of the record 66,000 absentee ballots cast.[74] Frank Jordan would be the next mayor of San Francisco.

AFTERMATH

Reactions to Agnos's defeat in the progressive community were varied. The *Guardian*'s Craig McLaughlin wrote a piece called "The Wicked Witch Is Dead" in which he tried to explain why Hongisto and Alioto were celebrating Agnos's loss. He applauded them for running against Agnos because "they taught all hypocritical moderates who run as progressives an important lesson: If they ever abandon their base they will suffer the same embarrassment as Art Agnos."[75] Buck Bagot, Redevelopment Commission president, commented, "I fear that the message nationally will be that the most progressive city in America rejected the most progressive mayor in America in the death rattle of liberalism. That definitely was not the message, but you have to be close to the scene to understand what really happened."[76] The editors of the *SF Weekly* wrote that "the true legacy of the 1991 elections won't be the person who occupies City Hall in January, but the vindictive and highly destructive divisions the campaign has exposed within San Francisco's liberal-progressive majority." They concluded that "many on the left have a priorities problem. The fact is, if we can't leave our infantile ideological battles behind and move forward together, we don't deserve the chance to run this city."[77] Art Agnos offered his own opinion: "I don't think the City has lost its liberalness, not in any wholesale way. San Francisco will always be a progressive city."[78]

CONCLUSION

Frank Jordan's victory over Art Agnos in the 1991 mayoral election closed a chapter on San Francisco's progressive movement, but it did not close the book.

It had been Agnos's election to lose, and the primary reason he lost was that many of his former supporters lost confidence in him. Jordan's well-organized campaign squeezed the maximum number of votes from a smaller conservative base, but even so he still won mainly by default. He slipped in through the door left open at city hall while the progressives wrestled Agnos out. The only real mandate Jordan can claim to have received from voters is to be friendly and accessible, to do something about the homeless, and to clean the streets. Some of Jordan's downtown business allies will push him to retrench on social reforms and to dismantle the slow-growth machinery—especially the hated Proposition M. But in a mirror-image reflection of George Moscone's situation in 1976, Jordan must cope with a liberal-progressive majority on the Board of Supervisors and with a bifurcated bureaucracy designed to frustrate central control. With limited formal authority, Mayor Jordan can do little in the short run to undo what the progressives have wrought over two decades. If Jordan knows the score, he knows that he is mayor by historical accident, that his powers are small, and that what the progressives did to make Agnos's life miserable they can also do to him. By sheer force of cultural and institutional inertia, San Francisco remains a progressive city.

What progressive leaders need to worry about most is the long run. The divisive 1991 mayoral campaign was merely an outcropping of deeper conflicts and contradictions within the city's progressive movement. It would be a mistake to dismiss Art Agnos as the "wicked witch" who cursed the progressives and to pretend that he alone was to blame for four years of wasted opportunities. While serving as mayor, Agnos attempted in his own flawed way to address certain political and economic realities that many progressives seem unwilling to face.

One reality is that the progressive movement has given lowest priority to the needs and concerns of working-class people and ethnic minorities. Since the passage of Proposition M in 1986, the movement's middle-class preservationists and environmentalists have become preoccupied with their own agendas and increasingly less sensitive to the plight of the poor, unemployed, and homeless. Agnos's progrowth approach to providing jobs and housing was unacceptable to progressives because it violated the new constraints on land use and development. Unfortunately, in a time of fiscal stress and federal neglect, imposition of those contraints drastically restricted the feasible set of alternative local solutions. The progressives were firm and clear in telling Agnos what he could not do, but they offered little more than sophisticated variants of "soak the rich" and "support small business" in telling him what he should do to solve these real problems. It came as no surprise that most African Americans, Latinos, and low-income renters voted for Agnos in the 1991 election and that a large fraction of the city's white working-class home owners voted for Jordan.

A second reality progressives must face is that a small business economy by itself is inadequate to support a progressive regime. For the reasons discussed in the last chapter, the city's small businesses are not always beautiful, and its petty bourgeoisie will never be the economic vanguard of radicalism. Leftist arguments that romanticize small business and demonize big business fail to capture the diversity and complexity of San Francisco's business community. In the city's service economy, what most small service firms serve are big businesses. To discount the economic importance of large corporations or to view them simply as objects of expropriation is to validate claims that progressives are unable to think strategically about the city as a whole. Mayor Agnos, at the other extreme, took big business too seriously. Burdened by a heavy agenda and strapped for funds, he saw the power and resources controlled by large corporations and rushed to embrace the downtown business elites. Progressive critics rightly condemned Agnos for his lack of principle: He came to the dance with the neighborhood mom-and-pop operations and then eloped with Bob Lurie and Catellus. But it is important to understand Agnos's compulsive attraction to big business and the conditions that fostered it. As long as the progressives fear big business, they will not take any steps to harness its power and will be inclined to punish those who do.

Yet the progressives are onto something in their love affair with small business. Their emphasis on preserving and promoting small firms and neighborhood shops follows logically from a slow-growth perspective on land use and physical development. The political organization of small businesses seems quite advanced in San Francisco, and the productivity of this sector in terms of jobs, income, and tax revenues is substantial enough to make progressive growth management economically viable. The China Basin stadium controversy, for example, was a conflict not only between progrowth and slow-growth perspectives on land use but also between big business and small business approaches to economic development. The progressives won that battle partly because slow-growth planning and small business entrepreneurship were so mutually supportive in the greater China Basin. If progressive leaders can replicate that political-economic experiment in other parts of the city, the case for "small is beautiful" will be strengthened.

A third reality progressives must confront is that San Francisco is not an autonomous city-state. There are two facets to this that activists often ignore. First, the city as a governing entity is a creature of the state. If it misbehaves in the eyes of those on high, its legal wings can be clipped and its home-rule powers restricted. Even now scissors are being sharpened in Sacramento on the issues of local growth management, rent control, and regional government. Second, the city's fiscal health still depends on federal and state assistance, and its ability to cope with many problems requires regional cooperation with other Bay Area cities. The point of these observations is that governing the city requires knowledge about intergovernmental relations and the outside political world. The isolationist mentality of some progressives does not serve their broader goals. San Francisco can survive as a progressive city despite its lack of a foreign policy, but it cannot survive for long without leaders at the top who know their way around Sacramento and Washington, D.C. A disturbing aspect of the 1991 mayoral campaign was how Agnos's political savvy was transformed in voters' minds from an asset into a liability. The progressives were only slightly less parochial than the conservatives in their criticism of Art Agnos as an outsider from Sacramento who spent too much time away from the city hustling grants and drumming up business. In some ways, it is charming that San Franciscans are able to create such a village politics atmosphere in their world-class city. But it is not the kind of atmosphere one associates with the nation's capital of progressivism; in fact, it can become a dangerous illusion if it blinds citizens and their leaders to the complexities of political life beyond the city limits.

A fourth reality that progressives must face is their tendency to overestimate the size of their core constituency and to underestimate the sacrifices they must make to build a durable coalition that can support a progressive regime. Madeline Landau's observations on this point are astute.

Obstacles to effective coalition building within government encourage political activists to pursue the politics of circumvention and short term interest. In turn, the severe polarization, instability, and *ad hoc* character of community politics fuels further public cynicism towards government which leads to voter apathy. Yet, the extent of apathy and cynicism leaves advocates and organizers without broad constituencies. They attempt to compensate for the lack of a strong popular base through additional series of "hard ball" tactics that continue to reinforce existing cynicism on the part of political moderates—the political "center."[79]

The progressives have tried to take the easy way out of this vicious circle by seeking an inspirational leader to lay the foundations for a broader coalition—a leader who would forge new solidarities across the divisions of race, class, and turf and resolve disharmonies among competing values within a singular vision of progressive reform. Such great expectations are bound to be disappointed. What the progressives wanted in 1987 was a latter-day T. E. Lawrence to pull them together; what they got instead was Art Agnos, who betrayed their cause and divided them further into factions of loyalists and traitors. Agnos has now been excommunicated, but the restless waiting for an enchanted and enchanting leader continues. As illustrated in the 1991 mayoral campaign, this kind of Bonapartist thinking encourages the scapegoating of leaders when they inevitably fail to perform miracles. The negative aspect of San Francisco's celebrated social diversity is that it makes governance almost impossible and undermines the capacity to get anything done. The progressives must do more of the necessary coalition building by themselves. They especially need to give leaders bigger building blocks of power with which to construct a stable progressive regime. Promising moves in this direction include the formation of the Small Business Network, the birth of the Coalition for San Francisco Neighborhoods, and the increased militancy of labor unions in organizing service workers and participating in city politics.

A final reality progressives must consider is that their ideological and programmatic thinking about progressivism has become muddled, contradictory, and shallow. The incoherence of local progressive thought became evident in the 1991 mayoral campaign when Agnos's critics and rivals bombarded him from all directions with single-interest group demands and idiosyncratic litmus tests but offered no comprehensive assessment of the city's problems or new ideas to advance the progressive agenda. During his tenure as mayor, the ideological guidance Agnos received from progressives was limited mainly to proscriptions and prescriptions: a long list of "don'ts," a short list of "dos," and very little strategic analysis of the city itself and its future. However, before progressives can become as proficient at strategic analysis as downtown business elites are, they must first formulate a point of view. A place to start is with Proposition M and especially its statement of policy priorities. It is only an outline and is full of holes, but it is the closest thing to a progressive manifesto that exists. All of the assumptions, principles, and ideas compressed in that text should be fully exposed, rigorously critiqued, and possibly amended to illuminate the path that progressives must walk if they wish to move San Francisco beyond the antiregime.

APPENDIX A

Data Sources

Geographic Units

San Francisco's 710 election precincts (1982 boundaries) provide the main geo-graphic unit of analysis used in the text. For some purposes, precinct election data have been averaged and then reported for 38 larger neighborhoods. The neighbor-hood boundaries are shown in maps 2.1 and 2.2, and a list of neighborhood names is provided in Table 2.3. Sociodemographic data for the city's 105 census tracts (1980 census boundaries) were used in precinct-level analysis but are not reported separately in the text.

Sociodemographic Data

Census tract data for 105 San Francisco census tracts were taken from the 1980 Census of the Population and Housing, San Francisco–Oakland Standard Metro-politan Statistical Area (SMSA), Census Tracts, Two Parts, PHC 80-2-321. The same tract statistics were assigned to all precincts falling entirely or mainly within a tract, using the 1980 census tract map and the 1982 precinct map for San Francisco. The following census tract data were used in the analysis.

1. Percentage Asian, Hispanic, Black: Tables P2–P6.
2. Percentage living in same house 1975: Table P-9.
3. Percentage high school graduates of those twenty-five years of age or older: Table P-9.
4. Percentage below 125 percent of the official poverty line: Table P-11.
5. Percentage unemployed of civilian labor force, sixteen years of age or older: Table P-10.
6. Percentage managerial or professional occupations: Table P-15.
7. Income per capita: Table P-15.
8. Percentage owner occupied: Table H-1.

9. Percentage individuals over age of eighteen: Table P-1.
10. Gay dummy variable: Tract classifications were made by David Binder, San Francisco political consultant. Precincts were classsified as "gay" and assigned a value of one if located in a census tract with at least 30 percent single males, where the number of males also exceeds the number of females by at least 15 percent within the 25–44 age category. All other precincts were scored zero. This indicator of "gay" precincts is commonly used by local political campaign consultants for polling and targeting purposes.
11. SES Index: Precinct scores on this index were computed using factor scores derived from a principal components analysis of 1980 census tract data. These scores have been metrically converted to a zero-to-one-hundred scale. High-scoring precincts on the SES Index are those with high percentages of professional-managerial workers and high school graduates, high median rents and home values, high income per capita, and low levels of poverty and unemployment.

Precinct Electoral Data

Precinct voting data were collected for various elections, 1979–90, from computer tapes and statements of votes obtained from the San Francisco Registrar of Voters. Descriptions of ballot propositions were taken from various voter handbooks distributed by the registrar over this period. Data collected for elections that occurred before and after 1982 were adjusted for reapportionments to fit the 1982 precinct boundaries. These data were collated with census tract data and compiled in a single file, the San Francisco Election File (SFEF), maintained and updated by the Public Research Institute, San Francisco State University. Principal creators of the SFEF are Prof. Richard DeLeon, Prof. Sandra Powell, Jeffrey Sutter, Derek Hackett, and Walter Maguire.

San Francisco Neighborhood Data

These are 1980 census tract and precinct electoral data mapped to thirty-eight San Francisco neighborhoods. The source of neighborhood boundary lines is *Coro Handbook, 1979* (San Francisco: Coro Foundation, 1979).

APPENDIX B

Empirical Evidence of the
Three Lefts and Progressivism
in San Francisco Voting Patterns

To understand the leftist as the person who values equality over freedom and fraternity
is to miss the main point of the leftist undertaking, though leftists have often laid
themselves open to this misrepresentation, particularly when accused of not facing up
to the insoluble disharmonies among competing values.
—Roberto Mangabeira Unger

The argument is that San Francisco's ideological space is essentially three-dimensional, each dimension corresponding to one of the three Left-Right axes discussed in the text: liberalism, environmentalism, and populism. One body of evidence that such a three-dimensional space exists comes from a detailed factor analysis of precinct voting patterns in San Francisco elections. The analysis focuses on voter responses to thirty-four city and statewide ballot propositions (bond measures, initiatives, referenda) over the 1979–90 period. The selected propositions represent a very wide range of substantive policy issues.

The Data

The ballot measures analyzed include four growth-control initiatives (O-1979, M-1983, F-1985, M-1986); an initiative to ban construction of buildings that cast shadows on public parks (K-1984); an initiative to exempt the proposed Mission Bay development project from growth-control restrictions (I-1990); an initiative barring hotel construction on waterfront property pending city approval of a strategic development plan for the port (H-1990); an initiative to establish residential rent controls (R-1979); an initiative to set up an affordable housing fund (J-1990); three initiatives to increase taxes on local corporations (P-1979, M-1980, V-1980); an initiative requiring a feasibility study of municipalization of public utilities (K-1982); two initiatives to construct a new downtown baseball stadium (W-1987, P-1989); an initiative to improve the existing Candlestick Park facilities (V-1989, presented as an alternative to P-1989); an initiative to allow city employees to transfer vacation credits (I-1989, presented as a way to benefit people with AIDS); two ballot measures creating domestic partners legislation, the first a referendum on an ordinance passed by the Board of Supervisors (S-1989), the second an initiative proposing similar legislation with fewer implied health benefits attached (K-1990); two ballot measures calling for the repeal of bilingual ballots in elections (38-1982, O-1983); statewide ballot measures proposing bonds for improving public schools (1-1982), beverage container deposits to promote recycling (11-1982), handgun registration controls (15-1982), establishment of a statewide lottery (37-1982), creation of a nonpartisan reapportionment commission (39-1982), limitations on political campaign contributions (40-1982), and establishment of a commission to limit spending on public assistance and medical benefits (41-1982); a referendum on a city ordinance to prohibit smoking in work places (P-1983); an initiative to establish district elections for the Board of Supervisors to replace the at-large system (P-1987); and resolutions calling for the federal government to end military assistance to El Salvador (N-1983), restrict the city's pension fund investments in South African business firms (J-1984), and declare the city a nuclear-free zone (U-1987). (Lettered propositions are city-level, numbered ones are statewide. See appendix A for data sources.)

Most of these ballot measures, particularly the city-level ones, were selected for study precisely because they aroused significant political controversy in election campaigns. The list includes several measures (e.g., Proposition M in 1986, Proposition K in 1990) that produced legislation considered to be pioneering not only locally but nationally. There is a selection bias, therefore, favoring inclusion of significant, controversial measures and exclusion of more mundane ones, such as technical amendments to the city charter requiring voter approval. Further, the list is confined to voting results for ballot propositions, not for candidate races. The tilt here, especially in the case of citizen-initiated measures, is in the direction of policy issues typically excluded from the city hall agenda and brought to the voters via these instruments of direct democracy. These biases in data selection should be taken into account when interpreting the results of the analysis. Still, the biases are offset to some extent by the sheer number and variety of ballot measures analyzed and also by the fact that a fair amount of the legislation produced in city hall during this period was designed either to preempt the success of anticipated citizen initiatives (e.g., rent-control legislation to preempt passage of Proposition R in 1979, the Downtown Plan to preempt passage of Proposition M in 1983) or to originate vanguard policies that actually were a few steps ahead of the voters (e.g., the domestic partners ordinance in 1989, subjected later that year by conservative opponents to referendum vote as Proposition S). All in all, the thirty-four ballot measures analyzed here do provide a fairly representative cross section of significant and controversial policy issues arising in San Francisco politics over the last decade.

A Note on Factor Analysis

Factor analysis is a multivariate statistical method used to reduce a large amount of information to a smaller set of "factors," which, if they exist, can be interpreted as theoretically significant source variables (sometimes called "latent variables") accounting for observed relationships in the data. Medical analogies are always hazardous, but here is one anyway. A patient complains of coughing, chest pains, shortness of breath, and fatigue. Each of these complaints could have its own unique set of causes unrelated to the others, or each could be a symptom of the same underlying cause (disease). The physician decides that the four types of complaints are in fact multiple symptoms of the same disease, which is diagnosed to be pneumonia. By analogy with factor analysis, the separate complaints in this case are interpreted (diagnosed) as merely four different indicators (symptoms) of a single underlying factor (disease) that gave rise to the data (complaints). The physician's analysis has reduced the data in a way that simplifies understanding of something that seemed more complex. Using factor analysis, can the precinct voting data on the thirty-four ballot measures be so reduced?

It is possible that the thirty-four sets of election results merely reflect slightly different facets of a single, underlying ideological conflict—e.g., liberals versus conservatives. If so, the election results would provide (and factor analysis would reveal) thirty-four different measures (indicators) of the same underlying thing (factor). (Visualize thirty-four arrows radiating outward like spokes from a single hub.) In this case, the conclusion might be drawn that San Francisco politics is essentially "one-dimensional." A single number for each precinct (called a factor score) could predict thirty-four others (the voting results), although the accuracy of prediction might vary according to the unique circumstances (campaign tactics, personalities, and so on) surrounding each election. It is also possible, however, that the thirty-four sets of election results have no common pattern, no single underlying cause. (Visualize each of the thirty-four arrows set on its own pivot.) In this case, the conclusion might be drawn that San Francisco politics is at least "thirty-four-dimensional"—a conclusion some local observers would embrace no matter what the statistics might say.

The Results

An empirical question: Is San Francisco's political universe less complicated than it appears? Specifically, is the electoral corner of that universe structured in the three-dimensional way argued in this book? The answer is yes, based on an interpretation of the results obtained from a factor analysis of precinct voting on the thirty-four ballot propositions. The factor analysis results reported in Table B.1 identify three, and only three, distinct factors giving rise to the voting patterns observed for the thirty-four ballot propositions. Based on how well each ballot measure "indicates" each of the three factors, the first factor is interpreted as

Table B.1. Rotated Factor Loadings (Promax Oblique Rotation) on Three Principal Factors Extracted from Analysis of Precinct Voting on Thirty-four City and State-wide Ballot Propositions, 1979–90 (San Francisco Precincts)

Ballot Proposition	Liberalism	Environ-mentalism	Populism	Uniqueness
J-1990 (Affordable Housing)	0.98439	-0.13663	0.00149	.08
1-1982 (School Bonds)	0.98102	-0.16393	-0.11170	.13
J-1984 (Anti-Apartheid)	0.94567	0.03925	-0.00234	.09
N-1983 (Out of El Salvador)	0.94414	-0.02588	0.00410	.12
R-1979 (Residential Rent Control)	0.82473	0.13473	-0.00464	.25
K-1990 (Domestic Partners)	0.81914	0.32923	-0.06131	.11
M-1980 (Tax Corporations)	0.80924	-0.10914	0.26293	.22
P-1979 (Tax Corporations)	0.80516	-0.13563	0.29154	.19
M-1986 (High-rise Growth Controls)	0.74563	0.34887	-0.00835	.19
U-1987 (City Nuclear-Free Zone)	0.74557	0.33281	0.09591	.15
K-1984 (Shadow Ban)	0.73091	0.38426	-0.03317	.19
M-1983 (High-rise Growth Controls)	0.71634	0.44790	-0.02017	.13
V-1980 (Tax Corporations)	0.71664	0.10459	0.28868	.24
P-1987 (District Elections)	0.71553	0.25910	0.24567	.15
S-1989 (Domestic Partners)	0.71531	0.45792	-0.05611	.14
I-1989 (Vacation Credit Transfer)	0.71033	0.37774	-0.03442	.23
K-1982 (PG&E Municipalization Study)	0.67257	0.48726	0.05868	.11
I-1990 (Mission Bay Exemption)	0.54641	-0.43215	-0.50056	.46
O-1979 (High-rise Growth Controls)	0.53034	0.58707	-0.03069	.23
F-1985 (High-rise Growth Controls)	0.52456	0.35563	0.17513	.40
V-1989 (Candlestick Park Improvements)	0.40000	-0.27306	0.59436	.40
37-1982(Statewide Lottery)	0.20463	-0.31585	0.17114	.86
H-1990 (City Plan for Port)	0.19926	0.75975	0.15969	.22
W-1987 (Build New Ballpark)	0.10756	-0.49597	-0.50115	.47
15-1982 (Handgun Controls)	0.06683	0.85883	-0.40161	.19
11-1982 (Beverage Container Refund)	0.03175	0.93496	-0.16276	.13
P-1989 (Build New Ballpark)	-0.13871	0.31322	-0.74282	.37
P-1983 (Prohibit Work-place Smoking)	-0.18988	0.78280	0.05884	.42
40-1982 (Limit Campaign Contributions	-0.70995	0.38062	0.01955	.49
41-1982 (Limit Public Assistance)	-0.79766	0.03170	-0.03067	.36
O-1983 (Repeal Bilingual Ballots)	-0.85359	-0.11637	0.04896	.23
36-1982 (Limit Taxes-Save Prop. 13)	-0.92822	-0.14814	0.24937	.12
39-1982 (Reapportionment Commission)	-0.93516	0.18826	-0.15849	.09
38-1982 (Repeal Bilingual Ballots)	-0.96244	0.07996	0.04738	.13
Eigenvalues	19.39	4.49	1.84	

Source: San Francisco Registrar of Voters, statements of vote, 1979–90. Number of precincts ranges from 1,500 (1979) to 621 (1990); data mapped to 1982 precinct boundaries (n = 710) in longitudinal San Francisco Election File (SFEF). Lettered propositions are city-level, numbered ones are statewide. "Uniqueness" indicates the proportion of variance unexplained by three principal factors. Stata Version 2.1 was used to perform principal factor analysis with promax oblique rotation on the precinct voting data. Summary descriptions of ballot measures are available from the author on request.

"liberalism," the second as "environmentalism," and the third as "populism." As shown in Table B.1, the first and main factor, "liberalism," is strongly and positively correlated with voter support for affordable housing, public-school spending, anti-apartheid investment policies, nonintervention in El Salvador, rent control, domestic partners legislation, and higher taxes on local corporations. This factor is also positively linked to voter support for all of the high-rise growth-control measures, the shadows ban, district elections, municipalization of public utilities, and declaration of the city as a nuclear-free zone. The factor results also indicate strong voter opposition to the repeal of bilingual ballots, a Republican-sponsored reapportionment commission, limits on public aid and medical assistance, and reduction of property taxes. The underlying political cleavage reflected in this voting pattern is congruent with national partisan divisions on social welfare and foreign policy issues and with traditional liberal-conservative conflicts on matters involving racial discrimination and distributive justice.

The second factor is "environmentalism." Table B.1 shows that this factor is strongly and positively correlated with voter support for an environmentalist-sponsored waterfront development plan, a conservationist-sponsored beverage container deposit recycling measure, more restrictive handgun controls, and prohibition on smoking in work places. This factor is also positively linked to all of the high-rise growth-control measures, particularly Proposition O in 1979, which was motivated almost entirely by aesthetic and environmental concerns. The factor results also indicate strong voter opposition to building a new downtown baseball stadium, along with weaker opposition to an exemption for Mission Bay from growth restrictions, improvements in Candlestick Park, and the statewide lottery. The underlying political cleavage reflected in this voting pattern is consistent with the new value-based postmaterialism Inglehart sees emerging in advanced postindustrial societies. A Left position on this cleavage favors government regulation of individual behavior to enhance the quality of life in the areas of public health, public safety, and the environment.

The third factor is "populism." Compared with the liberalism and environmentalism factors, the populism factor is a relatively weak predictor of the overall pattern of voting results. But statistically it does explain a residual "extra something" that cannot be explained by the other two factors. Table B.1 shows that the populism factor is strongly and positively correlated with voter support for improvements in Candlestick Park (proposed in the 1989 election as an alternative to building a new ballpark), neighborhood-based district elections, limitations on property taxes, and new taxes on downtown corporations. The factor results also indicate voter opposition to building a new baseball stadium in the China Basin district, exemptions for the Mission Bay development project from growth-control restrictions, and stricter handgun controls. The underlying political cleavage reflected in this voting pattern is consistent with conflicts involving neighborhoods versus downtown, small property versus big government, and neighborhood popular control versus political leadership by citywide elites.

Discussion

The overall conclusion of this analysis is that liberalism, environmentalism, and populism are distinct Left-Right axes of conflict that lie beneath the surface complexity of city elections and that simplify voter decisions within a three-dimensional ideological space. The Left polarities on these three axes correspond to the "three Lefts" in San Francisco politics that are discussed in chapter 2.

Voting outcomes on each of the ballot issues analyzed here can be viewed as the composite net effect produced by activating one or some combination of these three latent political cleavages. (The only major exception is voting on the state-wide lottery, which has a unique pattern unrelated to the other three.) A useful analogy is that of music produced by strings plucked on a guitar. The three political cleavages are the strings, the election campaigns do the plucking and strumming, and the election outcomes register the single notes or chords produced. As shown in Table B.1, some of the political "chords" are simple. The vote on the affordable housing fund (Proposition J, 1990), for example, was almost entirely a liberal-conservative vote involving little or no activation of the other two cleavages. Other chords struck were more subtle and complex. The Mission Bay vote (Proposition I, 1990), for example, activated all three Left-Right cleavages to produce a composite electoral outcome, with a lot of political noise (measured by the vote's "uniqueness" in Table B.1) mixed in. The voting patterns on *development policy* issues in particular exhibit much of what statisticians call "factorial complexity." These kinds of issues activate multiple political cleavages and produce true composite net effects in shaping the vote. The structural origins of conflicts on such issues cannot be traced to a single primordial base in class, race, or turf.

At the risk of overextending a good analogy, one might argue that San Francisco is a particularly interesting city to study precisely because it has more political strings to play than other U.S. cities do. Cities that lack a large professional middle class, for example, are unlikely to give much scope to environmentalism. It is simply not in their structural repertoire of political possibilities. In other cities, the latent political cleavages might exist but are somehow suppressed or lack the means of expression through local political institutions. In this regard, San Francisco's tools of direct democracy—the initiative, referendum, and recall—have revelatory significance to the extent that they activate and expose latent cleavages and give them political form. One broader implication of this line of reasoning is that social diversity itself can be a political resource for (and not merely an obstacle to) regime transformation. To some observers, "hyperpluralistic" San Francisco is a scene of cacophonous political bedlam crying out for disciplined orchestration and directed social change. But only a false necessity dictates that change must occur solely along one line of cleavage, or that political protest must express itself in a single chord of discontent.

APPENDIX C
Regression Analyses

Liberalism, Environmentalism, Populism, and Overall Progressivis in San Francisco Precincts as a Function of Race/Ethnicity, Sexual Orientation Home Ownership, and Socioeconomic Status (SES)

Predictors	Liberalism	Environmentalism	Populism	Overall Progressivism
Percent Black	.614**	-.302**	-.252**	.020
Percent Hispanic	.749**	.335**	.114	.399**
Percent Asian	.047	-.105*	-.446**	-.168**
Gay (Dummy)	14.914**	8.150**	9.802**	10.956**
Percent Home Owners	-.461**	-.360**	.172**	-.216**
SES	1.129**	1.470**	.510**	1.036**
SES²	-.011**	-.011**	-.011**	-.011**
Constant	31.427**	32.473**	58.909**	40.936**
Standard Error of Estimate	12.031	10.952	12.548	8.788
Adjusted R²	.71	.64	.49	.58
(Adjusted R² without SES²)	(.65)	(.55)	(.41)	(.44)
Number of Precincts	710	710	710	710

Sources: See appendix A. Index scores for liberalism, environmentalism, populism, and overall progressivism are precinct factor scores computed from principal factor analysis (see appendix B) and standardized to a 0–100 scale.

* p < .05
** p < .01

Notes

CHAPTER ONE. THE CAPITAL OF PROGRESSIVISM

1. Corrie M. Anders, "Cross-Cultural Marketplace," *San Francisco Examiner* (hereafter *SFE*), 16 June 1991. Also see Derek Walters, *The Feng Shui Handbook: A Practical Guide to Chinese Geomancy and Environmental Harmony* (London: Aquarian Press, 1991).

2. Quoted in Kevin Starr, "Art Agnos and the Paradoxes of Power," *San Francisco Magazine*, January/February 1988, 157.

3. Ibid., 44. This is a plausible claim in view of the fact that San Franciscans gave Michael Dukakis 74 percent of the vote in the 1988 presidential election, a larger percentage than voted for him in Boston. See Carol Pogash, "The Education of Art Agnos," *Image* (the weekly Sunday magazine of the *San Francisco Chronicle/Examiner*), 16 April 1987, 10–11.

4. See Todd Swanstrom, "Semisovereign Cities: The Politics of Urban Development," *Polity* 21 (Fall 1988): 83–110. Also see Timothy Barnekov, Robin Boyle, and Daniel Rich, *Privatism and Urban Policy in Britain and the United States* (Oxford: Oxford University Press, 1989), and Paul Kantor, *The Dependent City* (Glenview, Ill: Scott, Foresman and Co., 1988).

5. John H. Mollenkopf invented the concept of the "progrowth coalition" in 1975 to explain the postwar politics of urban development in large U.S. cities. Mollenkopf's early work established a foundation for later theoretical contributions by Molotch ("growth machine"), Stone ("urban regime"), and other urban scholars. See John H. Mollenkopf, "The Post-War Politics of Urban Development, *Politics and Society* 5 (1975): 247–95. Also see Mollenkopf's *The Contested City* (Princeton, N.J.: Princeton University Press, 1983); Harvey Molotch, "The City as a Growth Machine," *American Journal of Sociology* 82 (1976): 309–30; and Clarence N. Stone, *Regime Politics: Governing Atlanta, 1946–1988* (Lawrence: University Press of Kansas, 1989).

6. See Howard S. Becker and Irving Louis Horowitz, "The Culture of Civility: San Francisco," *Transaction* 6 (April 1970): 46–55. Also see William Issel, "Politics, Culture, and Ideology: Three Episodes in the Evolution of San Francisco's 'Culture of Civility'" (Paper presented at the annual meeting of the California American Studies Association, Long Beach, 26 April 1986), and William Issel, "Business Power and Political Culture in San Francisco, 1900–1940," *Journal of Urban History* 16 (November 1989): 52–77.

7. Quoted in Lonny Shavelson and Loralie Froman, "Why the Prayer Warrior Came," *This World* (a *San Francisco Chronicle/Examiner* publication), 18 November 1990, 11.

8. Ibid.

9. *San Francisco Chronicle* (hereafter *SFC*), 27 February 1991.

10. Quoted in ibid., 28 January 1991.

11. Examples include Berkeley, California; Santa Monica, California; and Burlington, Vermont. See studies by Pierre Clavel, *The Progressive City* (New Brunswick, N.J.: Rutgers University Press, 1986), and W. J. Conroy, *Challenging the Boundaries of Reform: Socialism in Burlington* (Philadelphia, Pa.: Temple University Press, 1990).

12. Paul Peterson, *City Limits* (Chicago: University of Chicago Press, 1981).

13. Douglas Yates, *The Ungovernable City* (Cambridge: MIT Press, 1977).

14. See Peterson, *City Limits*, 40–44ff.

15. Yates, *The Ungovernable City*, 34.

16. John R. Logan and Todd Swanstrom, eds., *Beyond the City Limits: Urban Policy and Economic Restructuring in Comparative Perspective* (Philadelphia, Pa.: Temple University Press, 1990).

17. Barbara Ferman, *Governing the Ungovernable City: Political Skill, Leadership, and the Modern Mayor* (Philadelphia, Pa.: Temple University Press, 1985).

18. H. V. Savitch, *Post-Industrial Cities: Politics and Planning in New York, Paris, and London* (Princeton, N.J.: Princeton University Press, 1988), 9.

19. Stone, *Regime Politics*, 6.

20. Ibid., 9.

21. Ibid., 206.

22. Ibid., 235.

23. Ibid., 8.

24. See Clarence N. Stone, "Preemptive Power: Floyd Hunter's 'Community Power Structure' Reconsidered," *American Journal of Political Science* 32 (1988): 82–104.

25. Stephen Elkin, *City and Regime in the American Republic* (Chicago: University of Chicago Press, 1987), 32.

26. Stone, *Regime Politics*, 228.

27. Manuel Castells, *The City and the Grassroots* (Berkeley and Los Angeles: University of California Press, 1983), 326.

28. Manuel Castells, *The Urban Question: A Marxist Approach* (Cambridge: MIT Press, 1977), 272.

29. Castells, *City and the Grassroots*, 331.

30. Ibid., 327.

31. Charles C. Ragin, *The Comparative Method: Moving beyond Qualitative and Quantitative Strategies* (Berkeley and Los Angeles: University of California Press, 1987), 27.

32. See Juan J. Linz, *The Breakdown of Democratic Regimes: Crisis, Breakdown, and Reequilibration* (Baltimore, Md.: Johns Hopkins University Press, 1978), 10–11.

33. On the concept of "political carrying capacity," see Adam Przeworski and John Sprague, *Paper Stones: A History of Electoral Socialism* (Chicago: University of Chicago Press, 1986), 69–70.

34. Chester Hartman, *The Transformation of San Francisco* (Totowa, N.J.: Rowman and Allanheld, 1984).

35. See Rufus P. Browning, Dale Rogers Marshall, and David H. Tabb, *Protest Is Not Enough: The Struggle of Blacks and Hispanics for Equality in Urban Politics* (Berkeley and Los Angeles: University of California Press, 1984).

CHAPTER TWO. ECONOMIC CHANGE AND SOCIAL DIVERSITY: THE LOCAL CULTURE OF PROGRESSIVISM

Major portions of this chapter are drawn from Richard DeLeon, "The Progressive Urban Regime: Ethnic Coalitions in San Francisco," in *Racial and Ethnic Politics in California,* ed. Bryan O. Jackson and Michael B. Preston (Berkeley, Calif.: Institute of Governmental Studies, 1991), and Richard DeLeon, "San Francisco: Postmaterialist Populism in a Global City," in *Big City Politics in Transition,* ed. H. V. Savitch and John Clayton Thomas (Beverly Hills, Calif.: Sage, 1991).

1. This description was invented by Herb Caen. As the city's leading newspaper columnist, Caen opposed the Manhattanization of San Francisco from the beginning and continues to articulate in his writings the spirit of the "old" San Francisco.

2. Dennis J. Coyle, "The Balkans by the Bay," *Public Interest* 11 (Spring 1983): 67-78.

3. The 1990 population statistics reported here and later in the text are taken from San Francisco Planning Department summaries of 1990 U.S. Bureau of the Census data for the city. Except where noted, other population statistics are taken from U.S. Bureau of the Census, *County and City Data Book, 1988* (Washington, D.C.: Government Printing Office, 1988), and U.S. Bureau of the Census, *County and City Data Book,* 1967 (Washington, D.C.: Government Printing Office, 1967).

4. Bay Area Council, *Making Sense of the Region's Growth* (San Francisco: Bay Area Council, 1988).

5. Richard LeGates, Stephen Barton, Victoria Randlett, and Steven Scott, *BAYFAX: The 1989 San Francisco Bay Area Land Use and Housing Data Book* (San Francisco: San Francisco State University Public Research Institute, 1989).

6. James P. Allen and Eugene Turner, "The Most Ethnically Diverse Places in the United States" (Paper presented at the meeting of the Association of American Geographers, Phoenix, Ariz., 1988).

7. See Kevin McCarthy, "San Francisco's Demographic Future," in *The City We Share: A Conference on the Future of San Francisco* (San Francisco: San Francisco Forward, 1984), 15-18, and Brian J. Godfrey, *Neighborhoods in Transition: The Making of San Francisco's Ethnic and Nonconformist Communities* (Berkeley and Los Angeles: University of California Press, 1988).

8. See note 2. Also see Bruce Cain and Roderick Kiewiet, "California's Coming Minority Majority," *Public Opinion* (February/March 1986): 50-52.

9. Frederick Wirt, *Power in the City: Decision Making in San Francisco* (Berkeley and Los Angeles: University of California Press, 1974), 240-71.

10. Ibid., 245.

11. U.S. Bureau of the Census, Census of Population and Housing, 1980: *Public-Use Microdata Sample (PUMS): San Francisco, 5 Percent Sample* (Washington, D.C.: Government Printing Office, 1983). The PUMS data for San Francisco were made available to me for analysis as a machine-readable data file prepared by the Office of Computing and Communications Resources, Chancellor's Office, California State University. It is assumed that the overall pattern of group comparisons has remained fairly stable since 1980. Sample surveys of registered voters in 1985 and 1989 (see discussion in chapters 4 and 9) revealed similar socioeconomic disparities among the city's ethnic groups.

12. Based on my analysis of the PUMS data. Byran O. Jackson has reported a similar profile of ethnic group differences in Los Angeles. See Byran O. Jackson, "Racial and Ethnic Cleavages in Los Angeles Politics," in *Racial and Ethnic Politics in California,* eds. Byran O. Jackson and Michael B. Preston (Berkeley, Calif.: Institute of Governmental Studies, 1991).

13. Based on my analysis of the PUMS data. For a more detailed discussion, see DeLeon, "The Progressive Urban Regime."

14. See Carlos Córdova, "Undocumented El Salvadoreans in the San Francisco Bay Area: Migration and Adaptation Dynamics," *Journal of La Raza Studies* 1 (1987): 9–37. Also see Frank Viviano, "Bay Area in the 1990s—Preview of Big Changes," *SFC*, 5 December 1988.

15. See Saskia Sassen-Koob, "The New Labor Demand in Global Cities," in *Cities in Transformation: Class, Capital, and the State*, ed. Michael Peter Smith (Beverly Hills, Calif.: Sage, 1984). Also see John H. Mollenkopf, *The Contested City* (Princeton, N.J.: Princeton University Press, 1983).

16. Sassen-Koob, "The New Labor Demand," 157–63.

17. This is the highest per capita death rate from AIDS in the country. With the case load of AIDS patients still rising in June 1990, San Francisco spent nearly $25 million in city revenue on AIDS, much more than federal and state contributions combined ($15.6 million). Local foundations, nonprofit organizations, businesses, and community groups have worked together to create and fund what many consider to be the nation's model program for dealing with AIDS. But these local private- and nonprofit-sector efforts have nearly reached their limit. Despite frequent pleas by Mayor Art Agnos, New York City's Mayor David Dinkins, and others, the Reagan and Bush administrations have consistently avoided treating the *national* problem of AIDS as a *federal* government problem. President Reagan was six years into his presidency before he even mentioned AIDS publicly, much less attempted to exercise national leadership to deal with the epidemic. Severely impacted cities like San Francisco and New York have been forced to cope with the problem locally by draining their own resources—resources that could have been earmarked for genuinely local problems and projects under the privatization model. See Judith Randal and William Hines, "Local Communities Take the Lead in Coping with AIDS," *Governing*, November 1987, 34–40; Elizabeth Fernandez, "A City Responds," *SFE*, 17 June 1990; Art Agnos and David Dinkins, "Mayors Plea for Help in War on AIDS," *SFC*, 12 September 1990. On the growth of the gay and lesbian community in San Francisco, see Godfrey, *Neighborhoods in Transition*; Randy Shilts, *The Mayor of Castro Street: The Life and Times of Harvey Milk* (New York: St. Martin's Press, 1982); and Manuel Castells, *The City and the Grassroots* (Berkeley and Los Angeles: University of California Press, 1983).

18. Michael Barone and Grant Ujifusa, *Almanac of American Politics 1990* (Washington, D.C.: National Journal, 1989), 94. Also see James W. Haas, "The New San Francisco: World's First 'Gaysian' City," *Golden State Report* 2 (July 1986): 32–33.

19. Castells, *City and the Grassroots*, 156.

20. For a detailed discussion of these spatial patterns, see Godfrey, *Neighborhoods in Transition*.

21. Mollenkopf, *Contested City*, 204.

22. See E. O. Wright, "What Is Middle about the Middle Class?" in *Analytical Marxism*, ed. J. Roemer (Cambridge: Cambridge University Press, 1986), 127, 130–31.

23. Ronald Inglehart, *Culture Shift in Advanced Industrial Society* (Princeton, N.J.: Princeton University Press, 1990), 337–40.

24. Ben Goddard, "The Rise of Grass-Roots Populism: Quality-of-Life Issues Spur a Fast-Growing Movement," *Campaigns and Elections* 8 (January 1988): 83.

25. For an overview of the research literature, see Bennett Harrison and Barry Bluestone, *The Great U-Turn: Corporate Restructuring and the Polarizing of America* (New York: Basic Books, 1988).

26. Association of Bay Area Governments (ABAG), *Projections—87: Forecasts for the San Francisco Bay Area to the Year 2005* (Oakland, Calif.: ABAG, 1987).

27. ABAG, *Trends in Income: An Analysis of Income Tax Returns for San Francisco Bay Area Counties, 1978–1987*, Working paper 88-3 (Oakland, Calif.: ABAG, 1991), 32.

28. Ibid., 33.

29. San Francisco Planning and Urban Research Association (SPUR), "Vitality or Stagnation? Shaping San Francisco's Economic Destiny," *SPUR Report* no. 234 (1987).

30. Bay Area Council, *Making Sense of the Region's Growth*, 13.

31. Paul Lord, *The San Francisco Arts Economy: 1987* (San Francisco: San Francisco Planning Department and San Francisco State University Public Research Institute, 1990).

32. Louis Trager, "Trouble in Touristland," *SFE*, 30 July 1989.

33. See Niels Erch, "Tangled Priorities at Fisherman's Wharf: What's the Catch?" *San Francisco Business*, August 1987, 5–15.

34. The first approach has been proposed by Kent Sims, president of the San Francisco Economic Development Corporation (EDC). See Kent Sims, *Competition in a Changing World: White Paper on the Economy of San Francisco* (San Francisco: EDC, 1989).

35. Wirt, *Power in the City*, 11. Much of the discussion that follows draws heavily upon Wirt's excellent treatment of these topics.

36. For a useful analysis of the failed charter reform effort in 1980, see Stephanie Mischak, "Why Charter Reform Has Failed in San Francisco" (Unpublished graduate seminar paper, Department of Political Science, San Francisco State University, 1987).

37. Wirt, *Power in the City*, 11.

38. Ibid., 13.

39. For a discussion of California's weak county party organizations and the anticipated effects of court decisions, see Richard DeLeon and Roy Christman, "The Party's Not Over," *Golden State Report* 4 (November 1988): 38–40. In 1989, the U.S. Supreme Court ruled that California's political parties had a protected First Amendment right to endorse candidates in partisan primary races. At this writing, however, the entire issue of partisan endorsements of candidates in local nonpartisan races has been clouded by a recent U.S. Supreme Court decision, *Renne v. Geary*, which overturned a decision by the U.S. Court of Appeals for the Ninth Circuit that had found a ban on such endorsements to be in violation of the freedom of speech. See Harriet Chang, "State's Law on Nonpartisan Races Revived," *SFC*, 18 June 1991. Also see Jim Fay, "Geary v. Renne," *Party Times* (a publication of the Northern California Committee for Party Renewal), January 1991, 1–2.

40. For an analysis of this power vacuum and how it was created, see Jerry Roberts, "Why S.F. Politics Became a Free-for-All," *SFC*, 27 March 1987.

41. For a detailed account, see Chester Hartman, *The Transformation of San Francisco* (Totowa, N.J.: Rowman and Allanheld, 1984), 157–65.

42. For a general discussion of the origins and uses of citizen initiatives, see David B. Magleby, "Taking the Initiative: Direct Legislation and Direct Democracy in the 1980's," *PS* 21 (1988): 600–601.

43. For a discussion of the distinction between "elite directing" and "elite directed," see Inglehart, *Culture Shift in Advanced Industrial Society*, 335–38.

44. Daniel J. Curtin, Jr., and M. Thomas Jacobson, "Growth Management by the Initiative in California: Legal and Practical Issues," *Urban Lawyer* 21 (1989): 508. Curtin and others have called on the American Planning Association to condemn this spreading practice. See David L. Callies and Daniel J. Curtin, Jr., "On the Making of Land Use Decisions through Citizen Initiative and Referendum," *APA Journal* 56 (Spring 1990), 222–23, and the rebuttal by Bruce W. McClendon, "An Alternative Proposal," ibid., 223–25.

45. Quoted in Paul DeMeester and Evangeline Tolleson, "Putting It on the Ballot," *San*

Francisco Business, May 1988, 25. The incredible barrage of citizen tax reform and growth-control initiatives in recent years has prompted conservative state legislators to propose laws that would undercut the initiative process by doubling the number of signatures required on petitions. See, for example, Greg Lucas, "An Initiative to Protect Initiatives," *SFC*, 26 June 1990.

46. See the account of this episode by Hartman, *Transformation of San Francisco*, 173–82.

47. Frederick Wirt, "Alioto and the Politics of Hyperpluralism," *Transaction* 7 (April 1971): 46–55.

48. Tony Kilroy, *Kilroy's Directory of San Francisco's Politically Active Groups*, 1985 and 1990 editions.

49. For an array of statistics showing these trends and their regional impacts, see Gordon L. Clark, *Unions and Communities under Siege: American Communities and the Crisis of Organized Labor* (Cambridge: Cambridge University Press, 1989), 4–15.

50. Ibid., 69.

51. Ibid., 27. Also see Robert A. Beauregard, "Space, Time, and Economic Restructuring," in *Economic Restructuring and Political Response*, ed. Robert A. Beauregard (Beverly Hills, Calif.: Sage, 1989), 209–40.

52. See "Bay Area Business Report 1991," *San Francisco Business*, December 1990, A-21. Original data source was the State of California Economic Development Department.

53. Clark, *Unions and Communities under Siege*, 70.

54. Ibid, 241.

55. William Issel and Robert W. Cherny, *San Francisco 1865–1932: Politics, Power, and Urban Development* (Berkeley and Los Angeles: University of California Press, 1986), 213.

56. Ibid., 203.

57. Ibid., 206.

58. Ibid., 214.

59. Ibid.

60. Quoted in Carl T. Hall, "S.F. Has Changed since Harry's Day," *SFC*, 31 March 1990. (The "Harry" referred to is Harry Bridges, San Francisco's famous labor organizer and leader of the city's general strike in 1934. He died in March 1990.)

61. Issel and Cherny, *San Francisco 1865–1932*, 215.

62. Hall, "S.F. Has Changed."

63. Clifford Carlsen, "Union Officials Claim a Victory over Marriott," *San Francisco Business Times* (hereafter *SFBT*), 11 September 1989. Only two of Marriott's five hundred hotels are unionized, reflecting its strong anti-union stance.

64. Quoted in "Unions Chalk Up New Victories in Recent Elections," *SFBT*, 27 September 1991.

65. *SFBT*, 30 November 1990; *SFC*, 28 December 1990.

66. "Union Delegates Debate Global Strategy," *SFC*, 23 August 1991.

67. See "Disputed ILWU Election Goes to a Second Ballot," *SFC*, 2 October 1991, and "Longshoremen Install Maverick Leader Today," *SFC*, 8 October 1991.

68. See Carl T. Hall, "Historic Union Relocates to San Francisco," *SFC*, 24 July 1991. Only sixty Bay Area workers carry the IWW's red membership card, and it is doubtful that many unorganized workers will respond to the union's continuing attacks on the "wage slave system" or to its vision of a "world without bosses." Yet the IWW presence might add some definition to the city's mushy, complex progressivism. Nostalgic and quixotic the Wobblies might be, but at least their leftist views are clear and consistent.

69. Tim Redmond, "Behind the Bitter Lobbying of Declining Power," *SFBG*, 14 May 1986.

70. Ibid.

71. Quoted in ibid.

72. Grant Din, "An Analysis of Asian/Pacific American Registration and Voting Patterns in San Francisco" (Unpublished master's thesis, Claremont Graduate School, 1984), 52.

73. Louis Freedberg, "Latinos: Building Power from the Ground Up," *California Journal* (January 1987): 15.

74. Rufus P. Browning, Dale Rogers Marshall, and David H. Tabb, *Protest Is Not Enough: The Struggle of Blacks and Hispanics for Equality in Urban Politics* (Berkeley and Los Angeles: University of California Press, 1984). 58.

75. Din, "An Analysis of Asian/Pacific American Registration and Voting Patterns in San Francisco," 80.

76. Frank Viviano, "In Politics, A Giant Is Awakening," *SFC*, 7 December 1988.

77. Quoted in Frank Viviano and Sharon Silva, "The New San Francisco," *San Francisco Focus*, September 1986, 74.

78. *SFC*, 1 July 1991.

79. See Castells, *City and the Grassroots*, 357-59.

80. Indeed, political organizers of the Asian American community are using the gay and lesbian community as a model of how to mobilize. As James Fang comments, "What we're trying to do is model our political experience after them [gays and lesbians]. They do politics every single day of the year. Rain or shine, they're out on the street registering people to vote and educating people on the issues." Quoted in Chin, "S.F. Asian American Vote Could Tilt Mayoral Election."

81. Quoted in Jerry Roberts, "Crossing the Bridge to the New San Francisco," *Golden State Report* (May 1987): 29.

82. Quoted in Michele DeRanleau, "Hitchens' Victory for Diversity," *SF Weekly*, 13 June 1990.

83. These results are based on a telephone sample survey of 406 registered San Francisco voters conducted between 20 April-2 May 1989 by San Francisco State University's Public Research Institute (*State of the City Poll: 1989*). The Pearson chi-square for the cross-tabulated responses to the first question was 11.48 (3 df), p < .05; the chi-square for responses to the second question was 8.14 (3 df), p < .05. Logistic regressions were run to control for the possible confounding effects of other factors such as race, income, age, and gender. Responses to the first question ("influence") were dichotomized and coded as a dummy variable (1 = "a lot" or "a moderate amount," 0 = "a little" or "none at all"). Responses to the second question ("help from Board") also were coded as a dummy variable (1 = "a lot" or "some," 0 = "very little" or "none at all"). In both cases the model tested on the survey data was Prob $\{Y = 1\}$ = $1/(1 + \exp(-(XB)))$, where X is a vector of independent variables and B is a vector of logistic regression coefficients estimated using maximum likelihood techniques. The set of independent variables included dummies for the following: home ownership, middle income group, high income group, middle age group, oldest age group, female gender, black race/ethnicity, Hispanic race/ethnicity, Asian race/ethnicity, labor union membership, landlord status, and gay/lesbian sexual orientation. The reference group was young white nongay low-income male nonunion nonlandlord renters. Gay/lesbian sexual orientation was the *only* statistically significant positive predictor of perceived influence on local government decisions (p < .07, odds ratio = 2.00, 95% CI = .96 to 4.18) and of perceived board attention to complaints (p < .02, odds ratio = 2.46, 95% CI = 1.18 to 5.13). The odds ratios imply that, even controlling for the other specified factors, gay and lesbian voters are two to two-and-one-half times as likely as nongay voters to view themselves as politically influential in local government decision making. The only other statistically significant predictors in this analysis were age and gender. Respondents in the oldest age group were much less likely

than those in the younger age groups to claim having influence over local government decisions. Women were less likely than men to expect the Board of Supervisors to pay attention to their complaints. (Detailed logistic regression results are available from the author on request.)

84. Clarence N. Stone, *Regime Politics: Governing Atlanta, 1946-1988* (Lawrence: University Press of Kansas, 1989), 232.

85. Stone uses the gravitation metaphor similarly in ibid., 235.

86. Pierre Clavel, *The Progressive City* (New Brunswick, N.J.: Rutgers University Press, 1986), 230.

87. Inglehart, *Culture Shift in Advanced Industrial Society*, 293.

88. Ibid., 298.

89. Ibid., 66-103.

90. For discussions of contemporary forms of American populism, see Harry C. Boyte and Frank Riessman, eds., *The New Populism: The Politics of Empowerment* (Philadelphia, Pa.: Temple University Press, 1986); Clarence Y. H. Lo, *Small Property versus Big Government: Social Origins of the Property Tax Revolt* (Berkeley and Los Angeles: University of California Press, 1990); and Joseph M. Kling and Prudence S. Posner, eds., *Dilemmas of Activism: Class, Community, and the Politics of Local Mobilization* (Philadelphia, Pa.: Temple University Press, 1990).

91. Cf. David S. Daykin, "The Limits to Neighborhood Power: Progressive Politics and Local Control in Santa Monica," in *Business Elites and Urban Development*, ed. S. Cummings (Albany: State University of New York Press, 1988), 357-87.

92. These estimated maxima were computed from the model fits reported in appendix C by taking the partial derivatives of Left voting with respect to SES, setting the derivatives equal to zero, and solving for SES.

93. These results are based on analysis of aggregate precinct and census tract data; therefore, it is unsafe to generalize any conclusions to the level of individual voters. (The logical error of making such inferences from aggregate data is sometimes known as the "ecological fallacy.") The claim can be made that these findings do hold for precinct electorates as units of analysis, however, and the plausibility of individual-level inferences is strengthened somewhat by the presence of statistical controls in the multivariate analyses reported in appendix C. Regarding the parabolic relationship between Left voting and SES, chapter 4 reports corroborative sample survey data indicating that such a relationship exists with respect to voter attitudes toward growth controls.

94. The source of neighborhood boundary lines is the *Coro Handbook*, 1979 (San Francisco: Coro Foundation, 1979).

CHAPTER THREE. THE INVENTION AND COLLAPSE OF THE PROGROWTH REGIME

1. On the concept of "growth machine," see John R. Logan and Harvey L. Molotch, *Urban Fortunes: The Political Economy of Place* (Berkeley and Los Angeles: University of California Press, 1987), chapter 3.

2. Castells defines urban meaning as "the structural performance assigned as a goal to cities in general (and to a particular city in the inter-urban division of labor) by the conflictive process between historical actors in a given society." Urban meaning shapes urban function—"the articulated system of organizational means aimed at performing the goals assigned to each city." And urban meaning and urban function jointly determine urban form—"the symbolic expression of urban meaning" in the spatial arrangement and architecture of the city. See Manuel Castells, *The City and the Grassroots* (Berkeley and Los Angeles: University of California Press, 1983), 303. For another treatment of the

"meaning" of cities, see Anthony M. Orum, "Apprehending the City: The View from Above, Below, and Behind," *Urban Affairs Quarterly* 26 (June 1991): 589-609.

3. John H. Mollenkopf, *The Contested City* (Princeton, N.J.: Princeton University Press, 1983), 160.

4. Chester Hartman, *The Transformation of San Francisco* (Totowa, N.J.: Rowman and Allanheld, 1984), 61.

5. See Stephen E. Barton, "The Neighborhood Movement in San Francisco," *Berkeley Planning Journal* 2 (Spring/Fall 1985): 85-105.

6. See Frederick Wirt, *Power in the City: Decision Making in San Francisco* (Berkeley and Los Angeles: University of California Press, 1974); Mollenkopf, *Contested City*; Hartman, *Transformation of San Francisco*.

7. Hartman, *Transformation of San Francisco*, 19.

8.See Mollenkopf, *Contested City*.

9. Paul Cohen, "San Francisco's Commercial Real Estate Industry," *San Francisco Business*, April 1985, 16.

10. Wirt, *Power in the City*, 212-13.

11. Barton, "The Neighborhood Movement in San Francisco," 93.

12. Bruce B. Brugmann, ed., *The Ultimate Highrise*, (San Francisco: San Francisco Bay Guardian Book, 1971).

13. Quoted in Wirt, *Power in the City*, 205.

14. Ibid., 206.

15. Ibid. According to Wirt's interpretation of an *Examiner* analysis of the election results (ibid.), majority support for Duskin's second initiative came from "wealthy liberal areas (Pacific Heights) and sites of recent highrise controversy (Russian, Telegraph, and Nob Hills)." It is worth noting that all four of these areas are classified as conservative and antipopulist by my own analysis in chapter 2, yet three of them (Pacific Heights, Nob Hill, and Telegraph Hill) scored high on what I have called environmentalism. Majority opposition to the initiative, according to Wirt, came from "conservatives, middle-class, working-class, and minority neighborhoods." Precincts in Bayview-Hunters Point and Chinatown are cited as examples. In my own analysis, however, Bayview-Hunters Point is liberal and populist but votes Right on environmentalist issues, while Chinatown votes Right on all three. Wirt's interpretation shows the limitations of a one-dimensional "liberal-conservative" vocabulary in analyzing the vote on complex issues such as growth control. The class and racial descriptors clarify his meaning, but the ideological analysis confuses rather than illuminates understanding. The three-dimensional scheme of analysis proposed in this book suggests that environmentalism was the dominant cleavage determining the vote and that this cleavage crosscut traditional liberal-conservative categories.

16. Ibid., 203.

17. Ibid.

18. Mollenkopf, *Contested City*, 173.

19. Hartman, *Transformation of San Francisco*, 73-74.

20. Quoted in Mollenkopf, *Contested City*, 193.

21. Ibid., 194.

22. See Barbara Ferman, *Governing the Ungovernable City: Political Skill, Leadership, and the Modern Mayor* (Philadelphia, Pa.: Temple University Press, 1985), 100.

23. Ibid., 187.

24. Ibid., 189.

25. *SFC*, 4 July 1990.

26. See, for example, Camille Peri, "The Buying and Selling of North Beach," *Image*, 26 April 1987, 18-25. 38; Michael McCall, "The Clement Street Shuffle—Neighborhood Evolution or Exploitation," *San Francisco Business*, March 1984, 16-20; Stephanie Salter, "Fight to Save Character of Neighborhoods," *SFE*, 5 May 1985. Former planning

director Allan B. Jacobs (1966-75) is reported to have "blamed himself for not trying harder to stop the Transamerica Building, which he has long regarded as a planning mistake because it extends the high-density office tower district into low-density North Beach and Jackson Square." See Gerald D. Adams, "Planners' Tales of the City," *SFE*, 16 April 1989.

27. For discussions of Moscone's reform agenda and the character of his campaign, see Hartman, *Transformation of San Francisco*, 135-36; Randy Shilts, *The Mayor of Castro Street: The Life and Times of Harvey Milk* (New York: St. Martin's Press, 1982), 100-110; Castells, *City and the Grassroots*, 104-5; and Rufus P. Browning, Dale Rogers Marshall, and David H. Tabb, *Protest Is Not Enough: The Struggle of Blacks and Hispanics for Equality in Urban Politics* (Berkeley and Los Angeles: University of California Press, 1984), 57-58.

28. Ferman, *Governing the Ungovernable City*, 110-11.

29. Hartman, *Transformation of San Francisco*, 148.

30. Ferman, *Governing the Ungovernable City*, 65.

31. See Hartman, *Transformation of San Francisco*, 157-66.

32. Quoted in Shilts, *The Mayor of Castro Street*, 162. Also see Hartman's account, *Transformation of San Francisco*, 165ff.

33. Hartman, *Transformation of San Francisco*, 167-68.

34. See, for example, Ferman's analysis in *Governing the Ungovernable City*.

35. Ibid., 105-6.

36. Quoted in John Jacobs and Phillip Matier, "Feinstein Years Reshape the City," *SFE*, 30 March 1987.

37. Ibid.

38. Sheldon S. Wolin, *Politics and Vision* (Boston: Little, Brown and Company, 1960), 65.

39. Ibid.

40. Quoted in *SFC*, 9 December 1987.

41. See chapter 1.

42. See Richard Rapaport, "While the City Slept," *San Francisco Magazine*, April 1987, 40-45, 86-88. On the broader impact of corporate takeovers and mergers in the Bay Area, see Bay Area Council, *Corporate Restructuring: Profiling the Impacts on the Bay Area Economy* (San Francisco: Bay Area Council, 1987).

43. Rapaport, "While the City Slept," 43.

44. Bay Area Council, *Corporate Restructuring*, 11.

45. Ibid.

46. Randall K. Rowe, "Capital Excess in '80s Leads to Shortage in '90s," *National Real Estate Investor* 32 (October 1990): 210.

47. Anthony Downs saw all this irrational handwriting on the wall and warned about it in his prophetic book, *The Revolution in Real Estate Finance* (Washington, D.C.: Brookings Institution, 1985).

48. For a much deeper and more sophisticated exposition of such reasoning, see David Harvey, *The Limits to Capital* (Chicago: University of Chicago Press, 1982), especially chapters 10 and 13.

director Allan B. Jacobs (1966-75) is reported to have "blamed himself for not trying harder to stop the Transamerica Building, which he has long regarded as a planning mistake because it extends the high-density office tower district into low-density North Beach and Jackson Square." See Gerald D. Adams, "Planners' Tales of the City," *SFE*, 16 April 1989.

49. Rowe, "Capital Excess," 210.

50. Jürgen Habermas, *Legitimation Crisis* (Boston: Beacon Press, 1973), 36.

51. Ibid.

52. See David Weber, "Who Owns San Francisco?" *San Francisco Magazine*, January/February 1988, 57–63.

CHAPTER FOUR. THE BIRTH OF THE SLOW-GROWTH MOVEMENT
AND THE BATTLE FOR PROPOSITION M

1. For a general discussion, see David Harvey, *The Limits to Capital* (Chicago: University of Chicago Press, 1982), chapters 12–13.

2. Manuel Castells and J. Henderson, "Techno-Economic Restructuring, Socio-Political Processes, and Spatial Transformation: A Global Perspective," in *Global Restructuring and Territorial Development*, ed. M. Castells and J. Henderson (London: Sage, 1987), 7. Also see Joe R. Feagin and Michael Peter Smith, "Cities and the New International Division of Labor: An Overview," in *The Capitalist City: Global Restructuring and Community Politics*, ed. Michael Peter Smith and Joe R. Feagin (London: Basil Blackwell, 1987), 3–34.

3. Karl Marx, *Grundrisse* (Harmondsworth, Middlesex: Penguin, 1973), 740.

4. Harvey, *Limits to Capital*, 428.

5. David Harvey, *Consciousness and the Urban Experience: Studies in the History and Theory of Capitalist Urbanization* (Baltimore, Md.: Johns Hopkins University Press, 1985), 273. Also see Henri Lefebvre, *The Survival of Capitalism* (London: Allison & Busby, 1976), and M. Gottdiener, *The Social Production of Urban Space* (Austin: University of Texas Press, 1985).

6. M. Gottdiener, *The Decline of Urban Politics: Political Theory and the Crisis of the Local State* (Beverly Hills, Calif.: Sage, 1987), 253. Also see Sidney Plotkin, *Keep Out: The Struggle for Land Use Control* (Berkeley: University of California Press, 1987).

7. Chester Hartman, *The Transformation of San Francisco* (Totowa, N.J.: Rowman and Allanheld, 1984), 288.

8. See Arthur C. Nelson, "Development Impact Fees: Introduction," *Journal of the American Planning Association* 54 (Winter 1988): 3–6. Also see Douglas Porter, ed., *Downtown Linkages* (Washington, D.C.: Urban Land Institute, 1985).

9. Hartman, *Transformation of San Francisco*, 288.

10. Michael Peter Smith, "The Uses of Linked Development Policies in U.S. Cities," in *Regenerating the Cities: The UK Crisis and the US Experience*, ed. Michael Parkinson, Bernard Foley, and Dennis Judd (Manchester: Manchester University Press, 1988), 107.

11. Hartman, *Transformation of San Francisco*, 272.

12. Tim Redmond, "Darkness at Noon," *San Francisco Bay Guardian* (hereafter *SFBG*), 9 May 1984.

13. For a Marxian critique of this view of the built environment as a "geographically ordered, complex, composite commodity," see Harvey, *The Limits to Capital*, 233 and especially chapter 8.

14. For details on campaign spending, see Richard DeLeon and Sandra Powell, "Growth Control and Electoral Politics: The Triumph of Urban Populism in San Francisco," *Western Political Quarterly* 42 (June 1989): 316ff.

15. Hartman, *Transformation of San Francisco*, 276.

16. For a summary, see Jayne Garrison, "Downtown Plan Given Final OK by Supervisors," *SFE*, 11 September 1985.

17. Quoted in Hartman, *Transformation of San Francisco*, 273. For a more recent discussion of San Francisco's Downtown Plan and of how it compares with downtown plans in Cleveland, Denver, Philadelphia, Portland, and Seattle, see W. Dennis Keating

and Norman Krumholz, "Downtown Plans of the 1980s: The Case for More Equity in the 1990s," *APA Journal* 57 (Spring 1991): 136-52.

18. Other analysts of New York City's problems were not so sanguine, however, including George Sternlieb of Rutgers University, who observed that New York City "will spend $200 million just to house the homeless this year [1985]. It needs a tax base. San Francisco can pull on the development reins, but New York's [spending] needs make San Francisco look small-town." The Messinger and Sternlieb quotes are from Joseph Ferullo, "S.F.'s Downtown Plan May Help Mold Manhattan's Skyline," *SFE*, 22 December 1985.

19. *SFE*, 11 September 1985. Although Boston modeled its comprehensive linked development policies on San Francisco's earlier pioneering efforts, growth-control measures such as San Francisco's Downtown Plan (to say nothing of the more radical Proposition M) continue to be perceived by Bostonians as politically dangerous and economically unnecessary. See Gerald Adams, "Boston Says No to the City's Downtown Plan," *SFE*, 12 April 1987.

20. *SFE*, 11 September 1985.

21. *SFBG*, 5 December 1984.

22. Allan Temko, "Downtown Plan Space Swap May Mean Bigger Buildings," *SFC*, 1 November 1985.

23. *SFE*, 11 September 1985.

24. Hartman, *Transformation of San Francisco*, 290.

25. Kirstin Downey, "Payment Avalanche May Grow," *SFBT*, 11 February 1985.

26. Ibid.

27. Ibid.

28. Ibid.

29. Quoted in Hartman, *Transformation of San Francisco*, 267.

30. Terry Jill Lassar, "Shadow Ban Shapes San Francisco Buildings," *Urban Land* 47 (October 1988): 36-37.

31. Quoted in *SFC*, 1 November 1985.

32. Ibid.

33. *SFBG*, 30 October 1985.

34. *SFC*, 3 November 1985.

35. Quoted in *SFBT*, 14 October 1985.

36. *SFC*, 1 November 1985.

37. Reported in *SFBG*, 30 October 1985.

38. The correlation between the Proposition M vote in 1983 and the Proposition F vote in 1985 is r = .74.

39. At the invitation of Regina Sneed, then president of San Francisco Tomorrow, I was invited to sit in on an early meeting of the IOC which took place 10 February 1986. The discussion in the text of the IOC's decisions and activities is based largely on extensive notes I took at that meeting and on draft memoranda, membership lists, and other materials that were circulated to IOC participants.

40. Jeffrey Henig makes this same general point when he distinguishes today's urban crisis from that of the 1960s, when issues were framed in the language of "justice," "equality," and "civil rights." These concepts had "complicated intellectual referents" yet still conveyed a "strong prescription for action" and an emotional message that was "direct, simple, and intense." Today's urban crisis, in contrast, "is debated in more technical terms. Its dimensions are discussed in terms of bond ratings, investment tax credits, infrastructure, business climate, and efficiency. The message they carry is that these are complicated matters, that decisions should be deferred to those with expertise." Jeffrey R. Henig, "Collective Responses to the Urban Crisis: Ideology and Mobilization," in *Cities in Stress*, ed. M. Gottdiener (Beverly Hills, Calif.: Sage, 1986), 221-45.

41. From the 4 November 1986 voter's handbook, San Francisco Registrar of Voters.

42. *SFC*, 8 August 1986.

43. Public Research Institute, *Poll of San Francisco Voters* (San Francisco: San Francisco State University, 1985).

44. Adolph Reed, Jr., "The Black Urban Regime: Structural Origins and Constraints," in *Power, Community, and the City*, ed. M. Smith (New Brunswick, N.J.: Transaction Books, 1988), 168.

45. Interview conducted by Prof. Sandra S. Powell, quoted in DeLeon and Powell, "Growth Control and Electoral Politics," 325.

46. San Francisco Mayor's Housing Advisory Committee, *An Affordable Housing Action Plan for San Francisco: Draft Report, 12 May 1989*, 29.

47. Darryl Cox, in an informal conversation with me in early 1986, told of an encounter he had with black leaders in Bayview–Hunters Point. Some of them complained that the black population was dwindling while Asians seemed to be taking over the neighborhood. Cox remembered telling them that there was no takeover conspiracy involved. Some black home owners were simply exercising their property rights by selling their houses at terrific prices to those who were willing and able to buy. The pool of willing and able buyers included quite a few Asians but not many black people. He urged them to think about what originally caused the accelerated appreciation in home values, which in turn gave many low-income black home owners irresistible incentive to sell their homes, collect windfall profits, then leave the neighborhood for a more comfortable life. In similar circumstances, wouldn't they do the same? The original cause, he believed, was uncontrolled downtown development.

48. Quoted in Alice Z. Cuneo, "Crowley Worries as Union Strength Ebbs in the City," *SFBT*, 27 August 1984.

49. *SFE*, 2 November 1986.

50. Quoted in Richard Halstead, "The Initiative That Refuses to Die Returns from the Coffin," *SFBT*, 23 June 1986.

51. Quoted in *SFC*, 18 September 1986.

52. Quoted in *SFC*, 17 July 1986.

53. Ibid.

54. Ibid.

55. Ibid.

56. Gerald Adams and John Jacobs, "Inner Circles," *SFE*, 15–18 June 1986.

57. Quoted in Tim Redmond and Jim Balderston, "The Mayor vs. the Growth Initiative," *SFBG*, 10 September 1986.

58. These insights into the "No on M" campaign strategy were obtained from a post-election interview with "No on M" campaign manager Jack Davis, conducted by Prof. Sandra S. Powell. Also see DeLeon and Powell, "Growth Control and Urban Politics," 316–18.

59. Quoted in *SFBG*, 24 September 1986.

60. Quoted in *SFE*, 16 September 1986.

61. Quoted in Gerald Adams, "Black Ministers Meet to Defeat Anti-Growth Plan," *SFE*, 28 August 1986.

62. Ibid.

63. Ibid.

64. Ibid.

65. Ibid.

66. Alvin Rabushka and Kenneth A. Shepsle, *Politics in Plural Societies: A Theory of Democratic Stability* (Columbus, Ohio: Charles E. Merrill Publishing Co., 1972), 60.

67. Technically, it is an error to compare regression models with different dependent variables. For example, the R^2s for the two models cannot meaningfully be compared.

(For a discussion, see Gary King, *Unifying Political Methodology: The Likelihood Theory of Statistical Inference* [Cambridge: Cambridge University Press, 1989], 23–24.) The cross-model comparisons made in the text, therefore, should be evaluated with this caution in mind. Lacking better data, however, the regression analyses do allow the conclusion that variable X is a better predictor of the vote in election A than it is in election B. Further, precinct-level analyses and neighborhood-level tracking of the growth-control vote over time corroborate the evidence shown in the text on all major points.

68. The correlation between the 1983 vote and the 1986 vote is .84.

69. Mike Davis, *City of Quartz: Excavating the Future in Los Angeles* (New York: Verso, 1990), 159.

70. See DeLeon and Powell, "Growth Control and Electoral Politics," 322–24.

71. H. V. Savitch, *Post-Industrial Cities: Politics and Planning in New York, Paris, and London* (Princeton, N.J.: Princeton University Press, 1988), 9.

72. Ibid., 7.

73. "Seattle Voters Slap California-Style Limits on Downtown Growth," *California Planning Development Report*, (Torf Fullton Associates) June 1989, 10.

74. Bernard Frieden and Lynne B. Sagalyn, *Downtown, Inc.: How America Rebuilds Cities* (Boston: MIT Press, 1989), 311.

CHAPTER FIVE. FROM SOCIAL MOVEMENT TO POLITICAL POWER: THE ELECTION OF MAYOR ART AGNOS

1. Arthur L. Stinchcombe, *Constructing Social Theories* (New York: Harcourt, Brace & World, 1968), 182.

2. Ibid.

3. For a detailed analysis of this "power vacuum," see Jerry Roberts, "Crossing the Bridge to the New San Francisco," *Golden State Report* 3 (May 1987): 24–30.

4. Quoted in *SFC*, 9 December 1987.

5. *SFC*, 27 October 1987. For deeper background on the political careers of Agnos and Molinari, see Jeff Gillenkirk, "Molinari vs. Agnos," *San Francisco Magazine*, May 1987, 31–38, 85–88.

6. For excellent accounts of the campaign and the strategies and tactics employed, see John Jacobs, "The Miracle of Market Street," *Golden State Report* 4 (January 1988): 7–13; Jerry Roberts, "How Agnos Turned the Tide against Molinari," *SFC*, 9 December 1987; and Arlene Stein, "Agnos Did It the Grass-Roots Way," *Nation*, 6 February 1988, 156–58.

7. *SFC*, 3 June 1987.

8. See Tim Redmond, "The Battle for Alice," *SFBG*, 15 July 1987.

9. *SFBG*, 28 October 1987.

10. *SFE*, 1 November 1987.

11. *SFBT*, 2 November 1987.

12. For a discussion of this "secret weapon" in the Agnos campaign, see Roberts, "How Agnos Turned the Tide."

13. *SFE*, 4 November 1987.

14. *SFC*, 6 November 1987.

15. *SFC*, 16 November 1987.

16. *SFC*, 24 November 1987.

17. *SFBT*, 7 December 1987.

18. Roberto M. Unger, *False Necessity: Anti-Necessitarian Social Theory in the Service of Radical Democracy* (Cambridge: Cambridge University Press, 1987), 402.

19. Quoted in *SFE*, 22 November 1987.

20. The concept of the "political carrying capacity" of electoral coalitions is brilliantly developed and applied by Adam Przeworski and John Sprague in *Paper Stones: A History of Electoral Socialism* (Chicago: University of Chicago Press, 1986).

21. It is a sad commentary on the times that such a strategy seemed foolhardy and daring to many local political consultants. It is likely that Agnos's success convinced at least some of them to stop underestimating the sophistication of San Francisco voters.

22. Art Agnos, *Getting Things Done: Visions and Goals for San Francisco*, campaign book, October 1987, 44.

23. Ibid., 36.

24. Ibid., 33.

25. Ibid., 61.

26. Ibid., 44.

27. Ibid.

28. For a discussion, see Juan J. Linz, *The Breakdown of Democratic Regimes: Crisis, Breakdown, and Reequilibration* (Baltimore, Md.: Johns Hopkins University Press, 1978), 40–42.

29. Stinchcombe, *Constructing Social Theories*, 183.

30. Based on a multiple regression analysis of precinct voting data and 1980 census statistics, the model fit for the percent Agnos vote (of total votes cast) is

$$\% \text{ Agnos Vote} = 23.042 + .619*SES - .007*SES^2 + .217*RENTERS + 4.487*GAY$$
$$+ .191*BLACK + .285*HISPANIC - .185*ASIAN$$

(Adjusted R^2 = .59. All coefficients are significant at p < .05.)

(Adjusted R^2 = .52 in the model fit without SES^2.)

31. The regression results reported in note 30 are of some theoretical interest because they seem to challenge the claims made by some radical scholars that racial solidarities suppress the formation of class consciousness and distort the natural Left-voting tendencies of working-class poor. Ira Katznelson, for example, brilliantly analyzes the "trenches" in American cities that establish "boundaries and rules that stress ethnicity, race and territoriality, rather than class, and that emphasize the distribution of goods and services, while excluding questions of production and workplace relations" (*City Trenches: Urban Politics and the Patterning of Class in the United States* [New York: Pantheon Books, 1981], 6). Among the consequences, according to Norman Fainstein, are "racially and ethnically segmented communities and a local politics of particularistic exchange and ethnic symbolism. The urban politics that Americans take for granted simultaneously insulates capital from popular demands within cities and reproduces ethnic and racial, rather than class, solidarities" ("Class and Community in Urban Social Movements," *Urban Affairs Quarterly* 20 [1985]: 561–62). If racial solidarities do in fact suppress working-class consciousness and Left-voting tendencies, and if we accept the vote for Agnos as a defensible measure of Left voting, then we would expect to find (1) a large negative coefficient for SES, (2) a statistically insignificant coefficient for SES^2 (i.e., around zero), and (3) large negative coefficients for BLACK and HISPANIC reflecting the suppressive and distorting effects of race unmasked by the statistical controls. To the contrary, what the actual results in note 30 suggest is that Agnos got more support from low-SES voters than he "should" have received (given this model) because of their black and Hispanic race, not despite it. Class conflict can be said to exist in San Francisco: the very rich and the very poor against the middle class. This generalization holds strongest for environmental issues, weakest for liberal issues. It holds moderately well for the Agnos vote, qualified by the fact that blacks and Hispanics (typically low SES) were strong Agnos supporters and voted for him against the grain of what appear to be work-

ing-class conservative tendencies. One further qualification to note is that these results are based on aggregate precinct data and thus are vulnerable to ecologically fallacious deductions. The generalization holds for precincts as units of analysis, however, and inferences to the level of individual voters are made more plausible by the presence of statistical controls. One last methodological comment that has theoretical relevance: As shown in note 30, inclusion of the SES^2 term adds 7 percent additional variance explained over the model fit without it. This is not a trivial improvement. It is typical of results I have obtained in analyses using other indicators of Left voting (available on request). In many of those analyses, the SES variable (a measure of class) proved to be statistically insignificant when the SES^2 term was omitted. It would be easy to conclude, based on such results, that class is irrelevant in shaping the vote and that race, etc., are the only factors that count. In fact, class (as measured here) is a very powerful predictor of the vote—at least in San Francisco. The same might hold true for other cities.

32. For profiles of those whose names went into the Agnos rolodex and those whose names were tossed out, see Dawn Garcia, "Who Holds the Keys to Power in S.F. under Agnos," *SFC*, 11 July 1988.

33. Quoted in Dawn Garcia and Susan Sward, "The Agnos Record a Year after Election," *SFC*, 16 December 1988.

34. H. V. Savitch and John Clayton Thomas report figures on the decline in federal aid to San Francisco and other large U.S. cities between 1960 and 1988. As a percentage of city revenue, federal aid to San Francisco declined from a high of 17.57 percent in 1976 to 4.66 percent in 1988. See H. V. Savitch and John Clayton Thomas, "Conclusion: End of the Millennium Big City Politics," in *Big City Politics in Transition*, ed. H. V. Savitch and John Clayton Thomas (Beverly Hills, Calif.: Sage, 1991), 237.

35. Barbara Ferman, *Governing the Ungovernable City: Political Skill, Leadership, and the Modern Mayor* (Philadelphia, Pa.: Temple University Press, 1985), 52–53.

36. Ibid., 105–8, 200–203.

37. *San Francisco Independent*, 29 May 1990.

38. *Citireport* (weekly political newsletter, formerly *Pettit Report*), 15 February 1988.

39. *SFE*, 9 December 1987.

40. *San Francisco Independent*, 29 May 1990.

41. Ibid.

42. For details, see Garcia, "Who Holds the Keys."

43. Quoted in ibid.

44. For examples, see ibid.

45. Quoted in *SFE*, 15 November 1987.

46. See Andrew Ross, "Agnos Troops Hit the Street," *SFE*, 24 July 1988.

CHAPTER SIX. PROTECTING COMMUNITY FROM CAPITAL: THE URBAN ANTIREGIME

Major portions of this chapter are taken from Richard DeLeon, "The Urban Anti-regime: Progressive Politics in San Francisco," *Urban Affairs Quarterly* (1992), forthcoming.

1. Victor A. Thompson, *The Regulatory Process in OPA Rationing* (New York: Columbia University Press, 1950), 27–30.

2. L. Evanson, "S.F.'s Planning Department under Fire," *SFC*, 17 December 1990.

3. Terry Jill Lassar, "Shadow Ban Shapes San Francisco Buildings," *Urban Land* 47 (October 1988): 36–37.

4. Thom Calandra, "Money Talks," *SFE*, 2 September 1990.

5. Scott Hidula, "Difficulties in Financing Slow Towers," *SFBT*, 13 August 1990.

6. See Lisa Breim, "City Punches Raise Chevron Executive's Ire," *SFBT*, 13 September 1991.

7. Quoted in Evanson, "S.F.'s Planning Department under Fire."

8. Public Research Institute, *State of the City Poll: 1989* (San Francisco: San Francisco State University, 1989). The figures reported are based on my analysis of these telephone sample survey results.

9. Quoted in Patrick Danner, "San Francisco, Oakland Battle for Transit Agency," *SFBT*, 20 March 1989.

10. Quoted in Steve Massey, "Highrise Developer Sweetens the Pot," *SFC*, 30 May 1990.

11. For a discussion of this episode, see Thom Calandra, "Wells Fargo: Adios to S.F.," *SFE*, 13 October 1991.

12. The following account draws heavily on a participant-observation study by Diana Bik: "The Haight-Ashbury Preservation Society [HAPS] versus Thrifty Jr. Corporation: An Analysis of the Problems Involved in Preserving the Haight-Ashbury and Other San Francisco Neighborhoods" (Unpublished master's project report, Department of Political Science, San Francisco State University, 1987).

13. *SFBT*, 15 June 1987. The quoted remarks are those of Calvin Welch. For historical background on the Haight-Ashbury, see Charles Perry, *The Haight-Ashbury: A History* (New York: Vintage, 1985).

14. San Francisco Planning Department, *Report on Neighborhood Commercial Rezoning*, December 1986, 7.

15. Ibid.

16. Ibid.

17. Quoted in Bik, "HAPS versus Thrifty," 17.

18. Ibid.

19. Gerald Adams, "Critics Protest Approval of Thrifty in Haight," *SFE*, 20 August 1987.

20. Quoted in Bik, "HAPS versus Thrifty," 18. Henry would be shocked by the eventual fiery outcome of this story, but there is no question that he embarked on the project with his eyes wide open. Even as early as June he had said, "We tackled a community that was strong in its political leadership. If we were doing it again, our efforts would not be to make Haight our first entry" (quoted in *SFBT*, 15 June 1987).

21. *SFC*, 25 October 1988.

22. Ibid.

23. Ibid.

24. *SFC*, 28 July 1990.

25. Quoted in ibid.

26. *SFC*, 25 June 1990.

CHAPTER SEVEN. SAVE OUR GIANTS:
POLITICAL HARDBALL IN CHINA BASIN

1. Translation: "From his claw one can tell a lion."

2. See S. A. Riess, *City Games: The Evolution of American Urban Society and the Rise of Sports* (Urbana: University of Illinois Press, 1989). Also see John Pelissero, Beth Henschen, and Edward Sidlow, "Urban Policy Agendas and Sports Franchises: The Case of Chicago" (paper presented to the annual meeting of the American Political Science Association, 30 August–2 September 1990, San Francisco).

3. These results are based on a telephone sample survey of 416 registered voters conducted between 19 and 23 June 1986 by David Binder, a local political consultant.

(1) Question: "It has been proposed that the city build a new baseball stadium for the Giants to replace Candlestick Park. Some people say that we need a new ballpark because Candlestick is cold and windy and San Francisco can't afford to lose its professional baseball team. Other people say building a new ballpark will end up being costly to the taxpayers and will make traffic congestion worse. Which view comes closer to your own—should a new baseball stadium be built, or should it not?" Results: 26 percent yes, 65 percent no, 9 percent undecided. (2) Question: "Building a new baseball stadium would be a good idea if the taxpayers didn't have to pay for it." Results: 55 percent agreed, 40 percent disagreed, 5 percent undecided. For a full report, see David Binder, "Downtown Stadium May Depend on Who Pays," *Pettit Report*, 9 July 1986.

4. Lease revenue bonds are issued by a public agency payable from earmarked revenues obtained from leasing fees—as distinguished from general obligation bonds in which the general credit of the city is pledged. This type of "off-budget financing" has become increasingly popular in U.S. cities as a way to promote large-scale development projects under conditions of fiscal stress. See Charles Abrams, *The Language of Cities: A Glossary of Terms* (New York: Avon Books, 1971), 27–28, for a general discussion of public bonds. Also see Bernard J. Frieden and Lynne B. Sagalyn, *Downtown, Inc.: How America Rebuilds Cities* (Boston: MIT Press, 1989), chapters 8 and 12, for a discussion of specific off-budget financing techniques, including lease revenue bonds.

5. Quoted in *Pettit Report*, 19 August 1987.

6. Statement against Proposition W published in the San Francisco voter information pamphlet for the 3 November 1987 consolidated municipal election.

7. The correlation between the 3 November 1987 precinct vote for Agnos and the vote for Proposition W was -.30.

8. Quoted in Thomas G. Keane, "City Pact with Developer Helped Swing the Deal," *SFC*, 29 July 1989.

9. Quoted in ibid.

10. These details on the city's pact with Spectacor were drawn from ibid. and from Thomas G. Keane, "Mayor to Answer Stadium Questions," *SFC*, 4 February 1989.

11. Keane, "City Pact with Developer Helped Swing the Deal."

12. Quoted in Ray Tessler and Thomas G. Keane, "The Politics of the Stadium Decision," *SFC*, 1 July 1989.

13. Quoted in Keane, "City Pact with Developer Helped Swing the Deal."

14. Quoted in *SFC*, 14 August 1989.

15. Tessler and Keane, "The Politics of the Stadium Decision."

16. Quoted in ibid.

17. Quoted in *SFC*, 15 April 1989.

18. Quoted in ibid.

19. Quoted in *SFC*, 18 July 1989. On the rise of "fiscal populism" (the combination of economic conservatism and social liberalism) in San Francisco and other U.S. cities, see Terry Nichols Clark, "A New Breed of Cost-Conscious Mayors," *Wall Street Journal*, 10 June 1985, and Terry Nichols Clark and Lorna Ferguson, *City Money: Political Processes, Fiscal Strain, and Retrenchment* (New York: Columbia University Press, 1983).

20. Quoted in Thomas G. Keane, "Why Agnos Is Gambling on Stadium," *SFC*, 10 July 1989.

21. Quoted in ibid. Evidence of a shift in constituency began to appear early in Agnos's second year of office. For example, in his first "State of the City" address, he declared that "City Hall's passive attitude toward business planning is gone, replaced with an aggressive agenda that can benefit all San Franciscans." One item on that agenda was a proposed study of China Basin as a possible site for a new Giants baseball stadium. Another was a planned trip to the Far East that would allow Agnos to explore business

opportunities and trade agreements with Pacific Rim countries. On hearing Agnos's speech, John Jacobs, executive director of the Chamber of Commerce, commented that he was "really surprised and pleased with [Agnos's] emphasis on business needs. I must admit, we've had our categorical differences, but he's been available to promote business at every turn." (See Thomas G. Keane, "Agnos Talks Business and Baseball," *SFC*, 4 October 1988.) Agnos actually made the Far East trip accompanied by an entourage of San Francisco business leaders. By several accounts, that trip heightened Agnos's receptivity to downtown business perspectives on economic development issues. For example, Gerald Newfarmer, Jacobs's successor as the chamber's executive director, observed that "businessmen have gone from animosity to schizophrenia [in their feelings toward Agnos]. There have been some things we've been able to cooperate on lately. The Asian trip was very important. It was a real bonding experience for those involved" (quoted in Glenn Dickey, "Stadium Is a 'Good Issue,'" *SFC*, 17 July 1989).

22. Quoted in Dickey, "Stadium Is a 'Good Issue.'"

23. These and other details of the deal are reported in Thomas G. Keane, "Giants and Agnos Show Off Stadium Plan," *SFC*, 28 July 1989.

24. *San Jose Mercury-News*, 27 July 1989.

25. *SFE*, 30 July 1989.

26. Quoted in *SFC*, 28 July 1989.

27. Attempts by Supervisor Bill Maher and others to persuade the board to rescind the lease amendment ended in deadlock. See Jim Castleberry, "Prop. V Brings City Back to 'Stick," *San Francisco Independent*, 15 November 1989. The perception of attempted blackmail by Lurie and Agnos was widely shared among slow-growth opponents of the China Basin stadium. In a recent analysis of the Proposition P campaign, for example, San Francisco Tomorrow leader Peter Moylan writes, "Prop. P was viewed as being 'forced down the voters' throats,' ... It didn't help that the deal included releasing the Giants from their Candlestick Park lease. That move, which probably backfired, created the impression of 'blackmail,' that the Giants were going to move immediately if voters did not approve Prop. P." See "A Proposal to Save the Giants for the City of San Francisco. From San Francisco Tomorrow," unpublished paper, 14 October 1991.

28. *SFC*, 16 August 1989.

29. Financial disclosure figures quoted in *SFC*, 1 February 1990.

30. Estimates from a Department of Recreation and Parks study, quoted in *San Francisco Independent*, 15 November 1989.

31. Figures are taken from estimates prepared by Harvey Rose, budget analyst for the Board of Supervisors, quoted in *SFE*, 5 November 1989.

32. Interestingly, former mayor Dianne Feinstein refrained from taking a position on the China Basin stadium proposal, as did Mayor Agnos's foe, State Senator Quentin Kopp. Lack of an endorsement from these two key political figures probably cost the "Yes on P" campaign a number of votes, especially among upper-scale Pacific Heights liberals and among conservative home owners in West of Peaks.

33. On opposing views on the transit and parking effects of the proposed stadium, see Kathy Bodovitz, "Plan Would Rely Heavily on Public Transportation," *SFC*, 29 July 1989.

34. Warren Hinckle, "Mayor Art's Baseball Figures," *SFE*, 2 November 1989.

35. See Glenn Dickey, "Agnos' Homey Campaign for a New Ballpark," *SFC*, 14 August 1989.

36. Quoted in Bodovitz, "Plan Would Rely Heavily on Public Transportation."

37. Quoted in Keane, "Why Agnos Is Gambling on Stadium."

38. James Haas, "Voters Opted for Housing over Baseball Stadium," *SFBT*, 20 November 1989.

39. See ibid. for a thoughtful and informative discussion of these and other develop-

ments in the greater China Basin area. Also see Jack Morrison, "Downtown Stadium Plan No Better than Prior Ones," *SFBT*, 22 May 1989.

40. Haas, "Voters Opted for Housing over Baseball Stadium."

41. Letter to the editor, *SFBT*, 17 July 1989.

42. Logrolling is a form of vote trading in which A agrees to vote B's way on issue X (of greatest concern to B) if B agrees to vote A's way on issue Y (of greatest concern to A). Logrolling is widely practiced in legislative bodies, such as the California State Assembly.

43. See Geoffrey Minter, "Stonewall Reverses Ballpark Endorsement," *San Francisco Sentinel*, 5 October 1989.

44. One additional indicator of the failure of this tactic came from a poll conducted by Teichner Associates one week before the election. Gay and lesbian voters supported Proposition P at the citywide rate (41 percent) but overwhelmingly supported Proposition S (92 percent). See "Poll Finds Ballpark a Victim of Quake," *SFE*, 1 November 1989.

45. Detailed estimates of earthquake damages and repair costs are reported in "Earthquake Aftermath: One Year Later," *SFBT*, 15 October 1990.

46. See Phillip Matier, "Election Momentum Crippled by Temblor," *SFE*, 29 October 1989. Also see Tim Schreiner, "Quake Shook Views on S.F. Ballot Issues," *SFC*, 27 October 1989.

47. Thomas G. Keane, "Stadium Campaign Begins a Last Quiet Drive for Voters," *SFC*, 1 November 1989.

48. For example, see Art Agnos, "Reject Pessimism," *SFE*, 6 November 1989.

49. *SFE*, 29 October 1989.

50. Quoted in Keane, "Stadium Campaign Begins a Last Quiet Drive."

51. These are Williams's words, quoted in Kathy Bodovitz, "Social Services Leaders Back New S.F. Ballpark," *SFC*, 3 November 1989. "No on P" leader Jim Firth asked rhetorically, "Why are these [social services] people spending time going to press events to support a baseball park and not doing their jobs?" (quoted in ibid.).

52. See "Prop. P: A Yes for San Francisco," *SFE*, 29 October 1989.

53. See Andrew Nash, "We Don't Need It," *SFE*, 6 November 1989.

54. "Prop. P and Limits to Growth," *SFBG*, 1 November 1989.

55. Quoted in Eric Brazil, "New Mailer Angers Backers of Ballpark," *SFE*, 5 November 1989.

56. Quoted in ibid.

57. A detailed account of this episode and its ugly aftermath is found in Richard Rapaport, "Hard Ball: How the Political Power Brokers Shut Out the Best Little Ballpark in America," *San Francisco Focus*, June 1991, 68-71, 90-108.

58. *SFE*, 7 November 1989.

59. Quoted in ibid.

60. Brazil, "Defeated Lurie Wonders: What Next?" *SFE*, 8 November 1989.

61. Voter turnout was 44 percent, much higher than the more typical 27 percent turnout recorded in 1985 in the most recent off-year nonmayoral election. Thus, one familiar explanation of progressive defeats—the preponderance of conservatives in low-turnout elections—did not apply in this case. (See Bruce Pettit, "Responsibility and Prop. S," *San Francisco Independent*, 15 November 1989.) A more significant influence on the outcome was the fact that approximately one out of six votes was cast as an absentee ballot just after the earthquake but before the Proposition S and Proposition P campaigns shifted back into gear. Indeed, both propositions won the election-day vote. Yet Proposition S lost the absentee vote by more than eight thousand votes, Proposition P by more than six thousand votes. See Kathy Bodovitz, "Absentee Vote Decided Key S.F. Measures," *SFC*, 9 November 1989.

62. David Binder, a local political analyst, suggested that the constituencies mobilized

to support Proposition P and Proposition S actually cancelled rather than reinforced each other in the manner intended by Mayor Agnos. (Binder's views are reported in *SFE*, 8 November 1989.) Analysis of the election-day precinct vote provides evidence to support this view. The correlation between the Proposition P "yes" vote and the Proposition S "yes" vote was a statistically insignificant r = -.07. In multiple regression analyses, percent home owners was the strongest negative predictor of both the Proposition P "yes" vote and the Proposition S "yes" vote, suggesting that antiballpark appeals to the fiscal conservatism of that constituency also activated a potent social conservatism in voting on domestic partners. Voters in precincts with large Asian populations supported Proposition P but opposed Proposition S—a pattern consistent with that community's overall economic boosterism and social conservatism. Gay precinct electorates overwhelmingly supported Proposition S and tended slightly to oppose Proposition P. Percent black and percent Hispanic were positive predictors of the Proposition S vote but had no significant correlation with the Proposition P vote. Statistically controlling for other factors, voters in middle-class precincts were much more likely to support Proposition S than were those in low-SES and high-SES precincts. This parabolic pattern was reversed but also substantially muted in the case of voting on Proposition P. If these results show nothing else, they illustrate the formidable obstacles facing leaders of social movements in forging multiple-issue progressive alliances that are capable of electoral success. Many progressive leaders were quick to blame Mayor Agnos for what they perceived to be his desultory performance in allowing the defeat of Proposition S. But if blame is to be assigned, progressive antiballpark leaders might also consider blaming themselves for yielding to political opportunism and tactical expediency. They were playing with fire when they welcomed conservative home owner associations and taxpayer unions into their camp. To a considerable degree, votes that were gained from such quarters in stopping Proposition P were also votes lost in the fight for Proposition S.

The equation predicting the Proposition P "yes" vote is

$$\% \text{ Yes P} = 46.29 - .033*\text{SES} + .002*\text{SES}^2 - .047*\text{OWNER} - 1.152*\text{GAY} - .005*\text{BLACK} + .048*\text{HISPANIC} + .122*\text{ASIAN}.$$

(Adjusted R^2 = .32. All coefficients [except SES, BLACK, and HISPANIC] are significant at $p < .05$.)

The equation predicting the Proposition S "yes" vote is

$$\% \text{ Yes S} = 34.09 + 1.076*\text{SES} - .009*\text{SES}^2 - .445*\text{OWNER} + 17.683*\text{GAY} + .172*\text{BLACK} + .513*\text{HISPANIC} - .163*\text{ASIAN}.$$

(Adjusted R^2 = .65. All coefficients are significant at $p < .05$.)

63. Quoted in *SFE*, 8 November 1989.
64. Quoted in Brazil, "Defeated Lurie Wonders: What Next?"
65. Quoted in *San Francisco Independent*, 15 November 1989.
66. Quoted in ibid.
67. Quoted in *SFE*, 3 April 90.
68. Reported in *SFE*, 23 June 1990.
69. Quoted in ibid.
70. For more details on the Ballpark Five case, see especially Rapaport, "Hard Ball: How the Political Power Brokers Shut Out the Best Little Ballpark in America." Also see "Agnos Calls Developer 'A Liar,' " *SFC*, 5 February 1990; "Five Foes of S.F. Ballpark Indicted," *SFE*, 3 April 1990; "The Intrigue behind Ballpark Indictments," *SFC*, 6 April 1990; "Ballpark Fight a 'Sleazy' Affair," *SFE*, 27 May 1990; and "Judge Dismisses All Charges in Ballpark Case: Political Embarrassment for Agnos, Arlo Smith," *SFC*, 23 June 1990.
71. Quoted in *SFE*, 6 February 1991.

72. For reports on these more recent ballpark proposals, see "Hopes in S.F. to Keep Giants," *SFC*, 13 September 1990; "Agnos Vows to Keep Giants in Bay Area," *SFE*, 8 November 1990; "Ballpark Boosters Won't Ditch Battle after Third Strike," *SFBT*, 9 November 1990; "Agnos 'Exploring' Site for New Giants Stadium," *SFC*, 6 February 1991; "New S.F. Plan to Consider Giants Ballpark," *SFC*, 10 April 1991; and "Agnos Pushing Airport Site for New Giants Ballpark," *SFC*, 19 July 1991.

73. Precinct voting analyses support this interpretation of Agnos's political backsliding on land-use and development issues. The correlation is r = -.30 between the November 1987 precinct vote for Agnos and the Proposition P vote, r = .48 between the 1987 Agnos vote and the Proposition V vote, and r = .77 between the Agnos vote and the Proposition S vote. Despite the much higher priority Agnos gave in his campaigning to Proposition P over Proposition S, if Proposition S had won, he might have received some of the credit. Since it lost by a close margin, however, Agnos's priorities were called into question, and his lukewarm support for Proposition S was blamed for its defeat.

CHAPTER EIGHT. THE POLITICS OF URBAN DEALS: THE MISSION BAY PROJECT AND THE WATERFRONT

1. Harvey Molotch, "Urban Deals in Comparative Perspective," in *Beyond the City Limits: Urban Policy and Economic Restructuring in Comparative Perspective*, ed. John R. Logan and Todd Swanstrom (Philadelphia, Pa.: Temple University Press, 1990), 184.

2. For a summary and critique of this early proposal, see Tim Redmond and Alan Kay, "Mission Bay: Will the Deal Hold?" *SFBG*, 8 August 1984.

3. Ibid.

4. "Mission Bay Project: Citizens Push Plan to Enrich City, Not Developers," *San Francisco Tomorrow Newsletter*, August 1989.

5. San Francisco Department of City Planning, *Mission Bay: Draft Environmental Impact Report*, vol. 1, *Highlights and Conclusions*, 1988. Volumes 2 and 3 contain technical analyses and appendixes. For a useful summary, see Dan Borsuk, "Mission Bay EIR Offers Some Startling Facts," *San Francisco Progress*, 17 August 1988.

6. Mission Bay draft EIR, vol. 1, part 2.2.

7. For a summary of citizen critiques of the Mission Bay plan, see the *SFBG*, entire issue, 31 August 1988. Also see "Citizens' Alternative Plan vs. Santa Fe Plan," *San Francisco Tomorrow Newsletter*, August 1989.

8. By one calculation, "4,800 cars fill 4 lanes, five miles long, *bumper to bumper!*" See *San Francisco Tomorrow Newsletter*, April 1991.

9. See "Lurking in the Background—Toxics," *San Francisco Tomorrow Newsletter*, August 1989.

10. See Thom Calandra, "Man on a Mission," *SFE*, 21 October 1990.

11. Indeed, many of them suspected that "development" of the Mission Bay site was not the true aim of the project at all. The real motivation behind the Mission Bay plan, some argued, was Catellus's intention to secure a voter-approved development agreement with the city, thus appreciating the value of the land, which could then be sold off in chunks to the highest bidder. That would allow Catellus and its corporate partners, Olympia and York and Itel Corporation, to pocket a tidy profit without turning a shovel. Fueling such suspicions was the fact that Catellus insisted on including a clause in the development agreement giving it the right to sell all or part of the project at any time "whether or not Catellus Corp. is the surviving entity." Further, Olympia and York, Itel, and Catellus's parent corporation, Santa Fe Pacific Corporation, were all trying to bail out from the collapsing commercial real estate market by cashing in their properties rather

than developing them. Shorenstein's own suspicions darkened even further when Catellus officials approached his son Doug, asking "if we would be interested in buying any pieces of Mission Bay once it was approved. I said, 'Wow! I thought they were going to develop this, not sell it off.' " See Warren Hinckle, "Developer Is Bullish on Prop. I," *SFE*, 28 October 1990. Also see Danny Pearl, "Catellus Contends Prop. I Rout Won't Kill Mission Bay," *SFBT*, 2 November 1990, and Warren Hinckle, "The 2 Biggest Lies in the '90 Campaign," *SFE*, 4 November 1990.

12. Pearl, "Catellus Contends Rout Won't Kill Mission Bay."

13. Donald Doyle, "Neighborhoods, Business Can Meet on Mission Bay," *SFBT*, 2 November 1990.

14. For details, see Calandra, "Man on a Mission." In a pro-Mission Bay editorial, the *San Francisco Chronicle* claimed that Shorenstein contributed "about $85,000" to the "No on I" campaign, commenting, "A downtown mogul is not going to be happy about a new and vibrant development rising to one flank—which will be highly competitive with his own real estate interests." See "A Sour Note," *SFC*, 26 October 1990.

15. Nor did it help matters that, one week before the election, the Board of Supervisors rejected Mayor Agnos's proposed increase of the transfer tax on home sales. The tax proposal was intended in part to provide the funds needed to subsidize construction of affordable housing in Mission Bay. If the tax had passed, a key uncertainty regarding financing of the project would have been removed. This did not happen.

16. Calvin Welch, "Mission Bay Would Make Office Market Uncertain," *SFBT*, 17 September 1990.

17. Ibid.

18. Ibid.

19. "Mission Bay Project—Still a Long Way to Go," *San Francisco Tomorrow Newsletter*, October 1990.

20. Quoted in *SFC*, 11 November 1990.

21. For a summary of the revisions and concessions, see Donna Moody, "Developer Sweetens Pot with Mission Bay Plan Amendments," *San Francisco Independent*, 8 December 1990, and L. A. Chung, "S.F. Supervisors OK New Deal for Mission Bay," *SFC*, 20 February 1991.

22. "Mission Bay," *San Francisco Tomorrow Newsletter*, April 1991.

23. Quoted in Jim Doyle, "Rebuilding the S.F. Waterfront a Mandate for Port Director," *SFC*, 17 February 1990.

24. *SFC*, 11 March 1991.

25. See Jeff Polline, "A Conflict between Shipping, Shopping," *SFC*, 19 December 1988.

26. Thom Calandra, "On the Waterfront," *Image*, 18 February 1990, 6.

27. Ibid.

28. Ibid.

29. Doyle, "Rebuilding the S.F. Waterfront."

30. In 1980, for example, three national hotel chains pushed to build luxury hotels in the Tenderloin, a neighborhood district then viewed by many civic leaders as a "sleazy" cesspool of crime and drug abuse fit for bulldozing "to make way for tourism or higher and better uses, gentrified or condominiumized or highrised." The hotels went up, but only after Tenderloin residents fought the developers and exacted millions of dollars for community services and housing rehabilitation. See Rob Waters, "The Tenderloin Transformed," *Image*, 1 November 1987, 12.

31. This particular story has wheels within wheels within wheels. Here is a sample. Chronicle Ventures is a subsidiary of the Chronicle Publishing Company, owner of the *San Francisco Chronicle*, whose editors heartily endorsed the project as being in the best

economic interests of the city. Assembly Speaker Willie Brown, a San Francisco Democrat, served as paid lobbyist for the project. He sponsored state legislation allocating $1 million to the California Academy of Sciences, keeper of Steinhart Aquarium, for academy refurbishing and rebuilding. Brown also persuaded Underwater World to agree to pay Steinhart Aquarium $200,000 a year for eight years to compensate for any loss of patronage. The academy then reversed its opposition to the Pier 39 aquarium, smoothing the way for approval. See Steve Massey, "Aquarium Plans for Pier 39 Get Key OK," *SFC*, 7 September 1990; Donna Moody, "Port Panel OKs Pier 39 Aquarium," *San Francisco Independent*, 18 September 1990.

32. Calandra, "On the Waterfront," 16.

33. Ibid.

34. What some critics consider to be Mayor Agnos's "secretive" deal-making style was apparent in his behind-the-scenes negotiations with Giants owner Bob Lurie in formulating the China Basin baseball stadium proposal in 1989 and also in his collaboration with Catellus executives in hammering out a development agreement for the Mission Bay project. Another example that shows Agnos and his planners juggling two deals at once was a land-swap agreement between the port and Santa Fe Pacific Realty. The port agreed to give Santa Fe some property near China Basin to be used for apartments and a shoreline park in Mission Bay. In exchange, Santa Fe gave the port some land that would allow expansion of the Pier 80 container terminal. Although Agnos and Huerta defended the swap as a good deal for the city because it would bring the port an estimated $2 million a year in additional revenues, SFT's Jack Morrison called it a "tragedy that they traded away that land [in China Basin]," land that could have been used to preserve open space and create a new wetlands. The issue here was not only the substantive one of economic versus environmental trade-offs but, more important, one of process and public consultation. Agnos and Huerta clearly believed that "good deals," no matter how they were made, should command the support of citizens. In San Francisco, however, it matters very much how deals are made and who it is that makes them. (For details on the land swap, see Doyle, "Rebuilding the S.F. Waterfront.")

35. Agnos, *Getting Things Done: Visions and Goals for San Francisco*, campaign book, October 1987, 69.

36. Donna Moody, "Port Says Ban Will Hurt Business," *San Francisco Independent*, 23 October 1990.

37. Quoted in Steve Massey, "S.F. Port Tenants Assail Anti-Hotel Initiative," *SFC*, 15 August 1990.

38. Ibid.

39. *SFBG*, 24 October 1990.

40. Registrar of Voters, voter information pamphlet, 6 November 1990 election, 116.

41. Ibid.

42. *San Francisco Independent*, 23 October 1990.

43. Danny Pearl, "Port Pursues Plans for Hotels in Spite of H," *SFBT*, 26 October 1990.

44. Registrar of Voters, voter information pamphlet, 6 November 1990 election, 125.

45. Quoted in Eric Nelson, "Cruise Terminal Even Draws Praise from Hotel Critics," *SFBT*, 1 February 91.

46. Quoted in *SFE*, 8 November 1990.

CHAPTER NINE. CREATING A PROGRESSIVE URBAN REGIME:
THE ARCHITECTURE OF COMPLEXITY

1. Herbert A. Simon, "The Architecture of Complexity," in *The Sciences of the Artificial*, 2d ed. (Cambridge: MIT Press, 1981), 200.

2. Ibid., 209.

3. H. V. Savitch and John Clayton Thomas, "Conclusion: End of the Millennium Big City Politics," in *Big City Politics in Transition*, ed. H. V. Savitch and John Clayton Thomas (Beverly Hills, Calif.: Sage, 1991).

4. Ibid., 249.

5. Ibid., 249–50.

6. Kent Sims, *Competition in a Changing World: White Paper on the Economy of San Francisco* (San Francisco: Economic Development Corporation, 1989), V-2, V-6.

7. See Kevin Starr, "San Francisco Is Losing Its Identity as a World-Class City," *Image*, 1 May 1988, 19–31.

8. Ibid., 22.

9. One can go even further and state that the first assumption underlies the very definition of political disorder as a problem. A multiplicity of tongues was a problem for the biblical men of Shinar, for example, because it confounded their efforts to build the Tower of Babel. But what if they had shown no interest in building such a tower? What if tower building had not been on the Shinarian agenda? Would the "Babel of tongues" then have been so crippling? From a slow-growth perspective, the major problem with political disorder is that it undermines collective efforts to prevent tower building by well-organized capitalist elites.

10. Stephen E. Barton, "The Neighborhood Movement in San Francisco," *Berkeley Planning Journal* 2 (Spring/Fall 1985): 100–101.

11. Manuel Castells, *The City and the Grassroots* (Berkeley and Los Angeles: University of California Press, 1983), 331.

12. The following discussion is based on accounts reported in *SFBG*, 28 March 1990; *SFC*, 17 December 1990; *SFC*, 12 April 1991.

13. Quoted in *SFBG*, 28 March 1990.

14. Quoted in *SFC*, 17 December 1990.

15. In political discourse, NIMBY has come to be used solely in a pejorative sense. But Kraft and Clary have recently published an interesting empirical study of the NIMBY "syndrome" that views the phenomenon in a more sympathetic light. In analyzing testimony of community residents opposed to local siting of radioactive waste disposal, they found that opponents were moderately well-informed on the technical issues, were not excessively emotional in their responses, and showed concern about environmental and economic impacts outside the local area. See Michael E. Kraft and Bruce B. Clary, "Citizen Participation and the Nimby Syndrome: Public Response to Radioactive Waste Disposal," *Western Political Quarterly* 44 (June 1991): 299–328.

16. Sidney Plotkin, "Enclave Consciousness and Neighborhood Activism," in *Dilemmas of Activism: Class, Community, and the Politics of Local Mobilization*, ed. Joseph M. Kling and Prudence S. Posner (Philadelphia, Pa.: Temple University Press, 1990).

17. A number of the city's leading progressives, particularly those who have a broader view of the progressive agenda, are painfully aware of these trade-offs and of the need to make them. In a postmortem analysis of the Potrero Hill case, for example, the *Bay Guardian*'s Tim Redmond supports the Planning Commission's decision to approve the project, but he does so begrudgingly in the context of what he calls a "loop of doom." He writes, "If San Francisco is going to have any significant new affordable housing and keep the artists, writers, musicians, rebels, and outcasts who have always made this such a wonderful city, then we're going to have to give up a few things. We'll have to accept higher-density (that is, more crowded) neighborhoods, and uglier buildings, and less open space." (See "A Loop of Doom," *SFBG*, 17 April 1991.) San Francisco Tomorrow's directors also were willing to "choose between competing SFT priorities—housing and open space," giving a "qualified" endorsement to the Potrero Hill project by an eleven to five vote. See *San Francisco Tomorrow Newsletter*, September 1990.

18. For synopses of only the more recent examples of NIMBYism in San Francisco, see Ingfei Chen, "Neighborhoods Rise to Halt New Housing," *SFC*, 14 March 1991.

19. Michael Robertson and Evelyn White, "Activism That Hits Home," *SFC*, 8 April 1987.

20. For a fascinating study of the informal planning powers wielded by these neighborhood-level boards, see Karl F. Heisler, "Neighborhood Planning in Bernal Heights," *Urban Action* (Journal of the Urban Studies Program at San Francisco State University) (1989): 72–79.

21. Susan Herbert, "Bernal Leaders Face Challenge over Housing Plan," *San Francisco Independent*, 5 February 1991.

22. Susan Herbert, "Farmers Market Housing Gets a Go-Ahead," *San Francisco Independent*, 2 April 1991. (If old-fashioned politics cannot resolve contradictions within the progressive agenda, perhaps this mandated San Francisco-style group therapy will do so.)

23. Chen, "Neighborhoods Rise to Halt New Housing."

24. In 1990, San Francisco builders constructed 2,065 housing units. Of that total, more than half the units were built by the Redevelopment Agency. Nonprofit housing sponsors built 278 units, all for lower-income residents, representing 61 percent of all such units produced that year. Source: City Planning Department statistics, reported in *SFC*, 7 June 1991.

25. See Tim Schreiner and Mark Z. Barabak, "How S.F. May Turn into a City Without Any Poor," *SFC*, 18 September 1985.

26. See Michael Peter Smith and Dennis Judd, "American Cities: The Production of Ideology," in *Cities in Transformation: Class, Capital, and the State*, ed. Michael Peter Smith (Beverly Hills, Calif.: Sage, 1984), 190.

27. Plotkin, "Enclave Consciousness," 231–32.

28. Sheldon S. Wolin, *The Presence of the Past: Essays on the State and the Constitution* (Baltimore, Md.: Johns Hopkins University Press, 1989), 131. For what might be described as a neo-Federalist, anti-Montesquieuian critique of San Francisco politics, see Dennis J. Coyle, "The Balkans by the Bay," *Public Interest* 11 (Spring 1983): 67–78. The last sentence of Coyle's article is: "Anti-Federalism is running amok in the neighborhoods of San Francisco."

29. See Frank Viviano, "New Regional Spirit Springs Up in Bay Area," *SFC*, 8 February 1989, and Bay Area Council, *Making Sense of the Region's Growth* (San Francisco: Bay Area Council, 1988).

30. See Bay Vision 2020, *The Commission Report*, May 1991.

31. Ibid., 38.

32. Ibid., 44.

33. Quoted in *SFC*, 23 October 1990.

34. Quoted in Frank Viviano, "Bay Area 'Turf Wars' Stymie Regional Planning," *SFC*, 9 February 1989.

35. Quoted in Frank Viviano, "Key Issues Taking Shape in Regional Debate," *SFC*, 4 March 1991.

36. Dan Smith, Joan Radovich, and Raymond Smith, "Crusade against Growth," *Golden State Report* 4 (January 1988): 31.

37. Quoted in ibid.

38. See, for example, Bernard Frieden, *The Environmental Protection Hustle* (Cambridge: MIT Press, 1979); Mike Davis, *City of Quartz: Excavating the Future in Los Angeles* (New York: Verso, 1990), chapter 3.

39. Bradley Inman, "Brown Proposes Restructuring of Developmental Regulation," *SFE*, 8 July 1990.

40. Michael Peter Smith, *The City and Social Theory* (New York: St. Martin's Press,

1979), 273. Also see K. R. Cox and A. Mair, "Urban Growth Machines and the Politics of Local Economic Development," *International Journal of Urban and Regional Research* 13 (1989): 137–46.

41. Leaders of the city's ethnic minority and immigrant communities also have expressed wariness regarding regional government proposals. Asian American and Hispanic community organizers, for example, have registered their concern that the Bay Vision 2020 proposal's "talk of population limits takes aim at the thousands of immigrant newcomers among their constituents" (Viviano, "Key Issues Taking Shape in Regional Debate"). Bay Area black leaders have expressed worry that black political power, "which arises from their large numbers in the central cities, will be diluted by regional approaches" (quoted in Michael Taylor, "Minority Role Urged in Regional Planning," *SFC*, 24 July 1990). Jess Payne, executive director of the Bay Area Urban League, commented, "Our people are a bit suspicious of this concept. Historically, regional development has worked against the interests of African Americans" (quoted in Frank Viviano, "Bay Minorities Suspicious of Regionalism," *SFC*, 16 April 1991).

42. Robert Dahl and Edward Tufte, *Size and Democracy* (Stanford, Calif.: Stanford University Press, 1973), 135.

43. David Harvey, *Consciousness and the Urban Experience: Studies in the History and Theory of Capitalist Urbanization* (Baltimore, Md.: Johns Hopkins University Press, 1985), 218.

44. For a discussion of materialist and postmaterialist ideologies, see Ronald Inglehart, *Culture Shift in Advanced Industrial Society* (Princeton, N.J.: Princeton University Press, 1990). Also see James Savage, "Postmaterialism of the Left and Right: Political Conflict in Postindustrial Society," *Comparative Political Studies* 17 (January 1985): 431–51. For discussions of possible "red-green" fusions of social movements, see Carl Boggs, *Social Movements and Political Power: Emerging Forms of Radicalism in the West* (Philadelphia, Pa.: Temple University Press, 1986), especially 247–49ff. Also see Ferenc Feher and Agnes Heller, "From Red to Green," *Telos* 59 (Spring 1984): 35–44.

45. See chapter 3 for a brief discussion of these categories of comparison, most of which are drawn from Inglehart, *Culture Shift in Advanced Industrial Society.*

46. Quoted in *SFC*, 12 February 1990.

47. *SFC*, 13 September 1990.

48. Ibid.

49. *SFC*, 12 July 1991.

50. Ibid.

51. Ibid.

52. See "Black Leaders Push for Role in Redevelopment," *SFBG*, 3 July 1991.

53. Ibid. The assumption underlying such decisions appears to be that the black community would be better served on net by investments that expanded existing (mainly white-owned) businesses rather than those that capitalized black entrepreneurs starting riskier, small business enterprises. Tim Redmond quotes a memo from Buck Bagot, the Redevelopment Agency president, to the agency's executive director Ed Helfeld: "I don't think we can have much success in starting new non-white businesses" (quoted in Tim Redmond, "They Just Don't Get It," *SFBG*, 22 May 1991). Also see Dan Levy, "Blacks Angry ove Use of Agency's Funds," *SFC*, 15 May 1991. For an earlier, contrary view that most Bayview-Hunters Point residents regard gentrification of their neighborhood with "unabashed hope, even anticipation," see Mark Z. Barabak and Tim Schreiner, "Along Third Street, Residents Would Welcome Gentrification," *SFC*, 19 September 1985.

54. Good summaries of the conflict and the issues involved are found in L. A. Chung, "Behind S.F.'s Neighborhood Building Wars," *SFC*, 21 July 1987; Robert Reinhold, "San

Francisco Passes Sweeping Limit on Growth," *New York Times*, 8 December 1987; and Danny Pearl, "Blocky Additions Stir Neighborhoods," *SFBT*, 24 September 1990.

55. Pearl, "Blocky Additions Stir Neighborhoods."

56. "City's Plan Leaves All Sides Unhappy," *SFBG*, 22 May 1991.

57. On the concept of "essentially contested concepts," see William Connolly, *The Terms of Political Discourse*, 2d ed. (Princeton, N.J.: Princeton University Press, 1983), chapter 1.

58. C. B. Macpherson, "A Political Theory of Property," in *Property, Profits, and Economic Justice*, ed. Virginia Held (Belmont, Calif.: Wadsworth Publishing Co., 1980), 218, 220.

59. Quoted in Ingfei Chen, "Fight for Victorian-Style Homes," *SFC*, 23 April 1991.

60. Alan Ryan, *Property* (Minneapolis: University of Minnesota Press, 1987), 36.

61. Multiple regression analyses of precinct voting on propositions H and I support these conclusions. The estimated equation for the "yes" vote on Proposition H is

$$\% \text{ Yes H} = 41.38 + .633*SES - .006*SES^2 + .147*RENT + 5.286*GAY$$
$$- .096*BLACK + .140*HISPANIC - .113*ASIAN$$

(Adjusted R^2 = .47. All coefficients are significant at p < .05.)

The estimated equation for the "yes" vote on Proposition I is:

$$\% \text{ Yes I} = 48.27 - .209*SES + .003*SES^2 + .057*RENT + 3.223*GAY$$
$$+ .234*BLACK + .008*HISPANIC + .098*ASIAN.$$

(Adjusted R^2 = .44. All coefficients [except HISPANIC] are significant at p < .05.

See chapter 3 for a discussion of methods and appendix A for data sources.

62. Abraham Maslow, *The Farther Reaches of Human Nature* (New York: Penguin Books, 1977), 232–33.

63. Inglehart, *Culture Shift in Advanced Industrial Society*, 334.

64. This distinction is discussed in Barbara Ferman, *Governing the Ungovernable City: Political Skill, Leadership, and the Modern Mayor* (Philadelphia, Pa.: Temple University Press, 1985), 13ff.

65. "Why Won't Agnos Tax the Rich?" *SFBG*, 22 May 1991.

66. The last two paragraphs are a highly condensed reconstruction of arguments advanced by Tim Redmond in essays published over the years in the *San Francisco Bay Guardian*. No claim is made here that this exposition captures the full depth, sophistication and lively style of Redmond's writings. For a sample of Redmond's thinking on these topics, see especially "Of God and Adam Smith," *SFBG*, 18 July 1990; "Budget Crunch: A Crash Course," *SFBG*, 24 April 1991; and "Budget Crunch: Playing Chicken," *SFBG*, 8 May 1991.

67. Cf. A. O. Hirschman's *Exit, Voice, and Loyalty* (Cambridge: Harvard University Press, 1970).

68. Michael Pitre, "San Francisco Has Regional Flash for Specialized Firms," *SFBT*, 28 June 1991.

69. David S. Daykin, "The Limits to Neighborhood Power: Progressive Politics and Local Control in Santa Monica," in *Business Elites and Urban Development*, ed. S. Cummings (Albany: State University of New York Press, 1988), 383. Also see Harvey Molotch, "Urban Deals in Comparative Perspective," in *Beyond the City Limits: Urban Policy and Economic Restructuring in Comparative Perspective*, ed. John R. Logan and Todd Swanstrom (Philadelphia, Pa.: Temple University Press, 1990).

70. Tim Turner, "Survey Reveals Many City Firms Expect to Move," *SFBT*, 21 March 1988.

71. *SFC*, 24 March 1989.

72. See Hirschman, *Exit, Voice, and Loyalty*; also T. Bledsoe, "Those Left Behind: Exit, Voice, and Loyalty in Detroit, 1954-1990" (Paper presented at the annual meeting of the American Political Science Association, San Francisco, 30 August-2 September 1990).

73. C. Rauber, "Chamber Finds Its Public Image Tarnished over Newfarmer Flap," *SFBT*, 22 January 1990.

74. Quoted in *SFBT*, 18 July 1988.

75. Quoted in Thomas G. Keane, "Chamber of Commerce OKs Rise in Payroll Tax," *SFC*, 12 July 1988.

76. Pacific Telesis Chairman Sam Ginn organized the Chamber of Commerce and thirteen of the city's biggest employers (AT&T, BankAmerica, Bechtel Group, Charles Schwab, Chevron, Levi Strauss, McKesson, Pacific Gas & Electric, Potlatch, Shaklee, Shorenstein & Co., Transamerica, and Wells Fargo Bank) in mounting this image-rehabilitation effort. This group, known as the "Big Thirteen," contracted with Solem & Associates, a well-known local public relations firm, to design a campaign to strengthen ties between big and small businesses, to reach out to the neighborhoods to build alliances organized around economic development issues, and to articulate ways to improve the city's deteriorating business climate. Noting that this initiative is "long overdue," the *San Francisco Business Times* warned that "business here tends to talk solely to itself" and that the new campaign "needs quickly to include all elements of the business community. It will be difficult enough to open dialogue with the neighborhoods to improve San Francisco's business climate." See "Effort to Revitalize Economy Needs to Broaden Its Base," *SFBT*, 15 March 1991.

77. See Carol Migden, "The Chamber Promotes a Wrong Image for S.F.," *SFC*, 30 April 1991.

78. See Richard DeLeon and Sandra Powell, "Growth Control and Electoral Politics: The Triumph of Urban Populism in San Francisco," *Western Political Quarterly* 42 (June 1989): 315ff.

79. See "Bay Area Business Report 1991," *San Francisco Business*, December 1990, A2-A25.

80. See Peter Navarro and Richard Carson, "Growth Controls: Policy Analysis for the Second Generation," *Policy Sciences* 24 (1991): 127-52.

81. William Witte, "San Francisco's Slow Growth Educates Developers," *SFBT*, 2 January 1990.

82. Norman Gilroy, panel presentation on "The Pacific Rim Confronts NIMBY (No Growth)," 1990 Pacific Rim Real Estate Conference, San Francisco, 7 February 1990 (my transcription of audiotaped remarks).

83. Jeffrey Heller, panel presentation on "The Pacific Rim Confronts NIMBY (No Growth)," 1990 Pacific Rim Real Estate Conference, San Francisco, 7 February 1990 (my transcription of audiotaped remarks).

84. Quoted in Lloyd Watson, "Cutting through the Regulatory Labyrinth," *SFC*, 4 April 1990.

85. See Reynolds Holding, "Attorneys Find New Specialty," *SFC*, 8 April 1991. Also see John Case and Elizabeth Conlin, "Second Thoughts on Growth," *Inc.*, March 1991, 46-57.

86. Donald Keough, "Business Must Reassess Strategy," *SFBT*, 9 May 1988.

87. Ibid.

88. Stephen Elkin, *City and Regime in the American Republic* (Chicago: University of Chicago Press, 1987), 124-25.

89. Tim Redmond, "The Chamber's Anti-Business Jobs Study," *SFBG*, 16 March 1988.

90. Jane Jacobs, *The Economy of Cities* (New York: Random House, 1969).

91. For a brief summary of current economic research that provides empirical support for some of Jacobs's theories, see Elizabeth Corcoran and Paul Wallich, "The Rise and Fall of Cities," *Scientific American*, August 1991, 103.

92. Roberto M. Unger, *False Necessity: Anti-Necessitarian Social Theory in the Service of Radical Democracy* (Cambridge: Cambridge University Press, 1987), 28–31.

93. Ibid., 28.

94. Ibid., 182.

95. J. Kotkin, "The Upside," *Image*, 12 April 1989, 19.

96. Quoted in Stephen Maita, "Small Business Tackles Big Role," *SFC*, 12 May 1986.

97. C. Lucas, "City Dependent on Small Business," *SFE*, 29 July 1990.

98. Reported in Kotkin, "The Upside," 20. Also see David L. Birch, *The Job Generation Process* (Cambridge: MIT Program on Neighborhood and Regional Change, 1979).

99. Buell's statistics are quoted in Maita, "Small Business Tackles Big Role."

100. See Clifford Carlsen, "A Vision with a Business: Abacus Inc. Melds Social Slant with Techie Smarts," *SFBT*, 19 July 1991. Abacus Inc. ranked forty-third in *Inc.* magazine's 1991 survey of the country's fastest-growing firms. Three other San Francisco firms ranked in the top two hundred. A total of seven ranked in the top five hundred—as compared with only four in Los Angeles and two in San Jose. (Survey statistics are reported in Don Clark, "Small Firms Doing Very Well in S.F.," *SFC*, 23 November 1991.)

101. Quoted in Carlsen, "A Vision with a Business."

102. Quoted in Tim Clark, "Stitch of Green Joins Small Firms," *SFBT*, 5 July 1991.

103. For a general discussion of immigrant enterprises in the United States and the conditions that support them, see Roger Waldinger, "Immigrant Enterprise in the United States," in *Structures of Capital: The Social Organization of the Economy*, ed. Sharon Zukin and Paul DiMaggio (Cambridge: Cambridge University Press, 1990), 395–424. Also see Ellen Auster and Howard Aldrich, "Small Business Vulnerability, Ethnic Enclaves and Ethnic Enterprises," in *Ethnic Communities in Business: Strategies for Survival*, ed. Robin Ward and Richard Jenkins (Cambridge: Cambridge University Press, 1984).

104. See Rachel Gordon, "Hope to Create a 'Little Saigon' in Tenderloin," *San Francisco Independent*, 12 March 1991.

105. See Bernard Ohanian, "The Misunderstood Minority," *San Francisco Focus*, June 1986, 40–50.

106. Public Research Institute, *State of the City Poll: 1989* (San Francisco: San Francisco State University, 1989).

107. In the summer of 1991, the Board of Supervisors passed and Mayor Agnos signed an ordinance proposed by Supervisor Hallinan banning the demolition or conversion of any neighborhood gas station that made a "fair return"—a profit of 9 percent or more—over the previous two years of business. In just the last two decades, the major oil companies had closed 300 neighborhood service stations, in many cases selling the sites or converting them to more profitable uses. By 1991, only 150 stations remained to serve the needs of neighborhood residents. The effort to halt the demolition or conversion (but not the sale) of neighborhood gas stations began in 1988 with a mobilization by Haight-Ashbury residents to prevent Chevron from evicting Tom Higa from his station in the neighborhood. This particular fight (which Higa and his supporters won) merged with the broader progressive movement to preserve neighborhood-serving businesses, and soon the neighborhood gas station issue acquired considerable symbolic importance. In a rare moment of swimming politically with the progressive tide rather than against it, Mayor Agnos signed the ordinance on 22 July at Tom Higa's thriving Chevron station. For an account, see Maitland Zane, "New Law to Save Gas Stations," *SFC*, 23 July 1991.

108. See John Bunzel, *The American Small Businessman* (New York: Arno Press, 1979), 113.

109. In his cross-national comparison of local economic development practices, Preteceille comments that small- and medium-sized businesses "do not seem to be eager to take part in any common elaboration with left-wing local authorities." Edmond Preteceille, "Political Paradoxes of Urban Restructuring: Globalization of the Economy and Localization of Politics?" in *Beyond the City Limits: Urban Policy and Economic Restructuring in Comparative Perspective*, ed. John R. Logan and Todd Swanstrom (Philadelphia, Pa.: Temple University Press, 1990), 44.

110. For accounts of Britt's proposal and reactions to it, see *SFC*, 1 July 1991, and *SFC*, 22 July 1991. Among the more prominent small business leaders seeking a better relationship with downtown business elites were Scott Hauge (Small Business Network), Steve Cornell (Council of District Merchants), Robert Wong (Asian Business League), and Elliot Hoffman (owner of Just Desserts, member of the Small Business Advisory Commission, and a major figure in the city's small business community). See "Business Leaders Cross Line between Large, Small Firms," *SFBT*, 19 July 1991. A 1987 profile of Elliot Hoffman offers insight into the emergence of San Francisco's small business community as a political force. See Paul Farhi, "Sugar Daddy," *Image*, 28 June 1987, 23–26, 34.

111. The suggestion here of an antiprogressive drift in the small business community is not meant to imply uniform hostility toward the progressive agenda. Members of the Small Business Network, for example, recently voted unanimously to support passage of Assembly Bill 101, which would have banned job discrimination based on sexual preference, and objected to Governor Pete Wilson's veto of that bill and to his argument that it would place an unfair burden on the state's small businesses. See Robert J. Casetta, "Small Businesses Back Gay Rights," *SFBT*, 11 October 1991.

112. Quoted in Chris Rauber, "Small Business Demands Input," *SFBT*, 14 May 1990.

113. Lucas, "City Dependent on Small Business." This is a particularly telling criticism (or at least reservation) in the case of San Francisco's garment industry, which represents about 20 percent of the city's entire manufacturing sector. The state labor commission regularly conducts raids on the city's estimated 350 sewing sweatshops. The most recent raid was in March 1991, when 60 shops were cited for violations. See *SFC*, 30 March 1991. For a more in-depth study of the local sewing industry and sweatshop practices, see Robert Collier, "Sewing for a Living: Unregulated Exploitation," *SF Weekly*, 24 July 1991. For a broader critique of the small business strategy of economic development, see Preteceille, "Political Paradoxes of Urban Restructuring," especially 43–44.

114. Lina Avidan, *Employment and Hiring Practices under the Immigration Reform and Control Act of 1986: A Survey of San Francisco Businesses* (San Francisco: Public Research Institute and Coalition for Immigrant and Refugee Rights and Services, 1989). San Francisco's Human Rights Commission reported a similar finding regarding business compliance with city antidiscrimination ordinances. Staff member Larry Brinkin stated, "We find that we have a lot more trouble with small businesses than with large businesses, because a surprising number don't know that the city laws exist." Quoted in David Tuller, "S.F. Rights Panel Reports on Bias Cases," *SFC*, 20 June 1991.

115. To illustrate these contradictions, most progressives (as defined in this book) would support increased health benefits for workers, liberalized leave without pay policies for family emergencies, and stress claims by new employees under workers' compensation. Yet these and related initiatives during the 1991 session of the California legislature were opposed by small business organizations. Martyn Hopper, director of the National Federation of Independent Businesses/California, boasted of her organization's lobbying efforts against these measures as a major political accomplishment serving small business needs. See Hopper, "Small Business Held Its Own," *SFBT*, 6 November 1991.

116. Quoted in *SFC*, 11 July 1988.

117. *SFBG*, 21 February 1990.

118. Clarence Stone, M. Orr, and D. Imbroscio, "The Reshaping of Urban Leadership in U.S. Cities: A Regime Analysis," in *Urban Life in Transition,* ed. M. Gottdiener and Chris G. Pickvance (Beverly Hills, Calif.: Sage, 1991): 224. Also see Frederick Wirt, *Power in the City: Decision Making in San Francisco* (Berkeley and Los Angeles: University of California Press, 1974), 213; and Todd Swanstrom, "Semisovereign Cities: The Politics of Urban Development," *Polity* 21 (Fall 1988): 100.

CHAPTER TEN. POSTSCRIPT:
THE 1991 MAYORAL ELECTION AND BEYOND

1. In the period immediately following the Loma Prieta earthquake, 50 percent rated Agnos as a good or excellent mayor, 11 percent as poor. *SFC*, 29 August 1991.

2. See Phillip Matier, "Can Agnos Be Beaten? Maybe," *SFE*, 17 February 1991.

3. Quoted in *SFC*, 12 August 1991.

4. See "Run, Dick, Run," *SFBG*, 16 January 1991.

5. Bill Mandel, "Know-Nothing Liberalism Is Agnos' Key," *SFE*, 3 February 1991.

6. Jerry Roberts, "Angela Alioto Considers Running for S.F. Mayor," *SFC*, 23 July 1991.

7. Quoted in *SFC*, 8 August 1991.

8. Kathleen Baca and Craig McLaughlin, "The Campaign's Regular-Season Kickoff," *SFBG*, 4 September 1991.

9. See Marc Sandalow, "Mayoral Candidates Often Agree but Differences Exist," *SFC*, 1 November 1991.

10. Quoted in *SFC*, 19 September 1991.

11. Quoted in *SFE*, 14 September 1991.

12. *SF Weekly*, 23 October 1991.

13. Quoted in ibid.

14. Quoted in *SFC*, 16 October 1991.

15. For detailed background on this flurry of street-cleaning pluralism, see Eric Brazil, "Candidates Sling Mud in Dirty-Streets Debate," *SFE*, 8 December 1991.

16. Rob Morse, "The Montagnoses and the Koppulets," *SFE*, 8 December 1991.

17. These are results of a poll of six hundred registered voters reported in *SFC*, 29 August 1991.

18. *SFC*, 16 September 1991.

19. Reported in *SFC*, 29 August 1991.

20. *SFC*, 26 September 1991.

21. Bill Mandel, "Goddess Politics in the City," *SFE*, 15 September 1991.

22. Quoted in Jerry Roberts, "Agnos Says He Has to Work on His Bedside Manner," *SFC*, 2 November 1991.

23. Quoted in *SFC*, 16 September 1991.

24. Quoted in Jerry Roberts, "Agnos Gets Humble, Jordan Gets Help," *SFC*, 14 September 1991.

25. Quoted in *SFC*, 6 November 1991.

26. Quoted in *SFC*, 4 November 1991.

27. Timothy Williams, "Open Season on Art Agnos," *California Journal* 22 (September 1991): 405–9. Also see Thom Calandra, "Agnos Gets the Business," *SFE*, 27 November 1991.

28. Quoted in *SFC*, 16 September 1991.

29. Susan Hestor, "Agnos Cut Too Many Secret Deals," *SFE*, 4 October 1991.

30. *SFBG*, 23 October 1991.

31. "PG&E: Still the Litmus-Test Issue," *SFBG*, 2 October 1991.

32. Tim Redmond, "No Success Like Failure," *SFBG*, 6 November 1991.

33. *SF Weekly*, 23 October 1991.

34. Quoted in *SFE*, 3 November 1991.

35. Election results are from the San Francisco Registrar of Voters, reported in *SFE*, 6 November 1991.

36. *SFE*, 6 November 1991.

37. Arthur Bruzzone, "Jordan, Hsieh Showing Underscores Tilt to Right," *SFE*, 18 November 1991.

38. Ibid. Hsieh exclaimed that, because of his candidacy, "politics will never be the same" in San Francisco. "In the past, 16,000 Asian Americans usually vote. This time, 25,000—that's my feeling." Quoted in Eric Brazil, "Festive Jordan Party Sparkles amid the Losers," *SFE*, 6 November 1991.

39. Quoted in *SFC*, 7 November 1991.

40. Quoted in Jerry Roberts, " 'Niceness' Issue May Be Theme of S.F. Mayoral Race," *SFC*, 9 November 1991.

41. Quoted in *SFE*, 6 November 1991.

42. Quoted in *SFC*, 7 November 1991.

43. Quoted in *SFE*, 25 November 1991.

44. Ibid.

45. Vince Bielski and George Cothran, "What Will a Jordan Win Cost S.F. Tenants?" *SF Weekly*, 27 November 1991.

46. Quoted in *SFC*, 7 November 1991.

47. Quoted in ibid.

48. Quoted in *SFC*, 13 November 1991.

49. Quoted in *SFE*, 27 November 1991.

50. *SFE*, 6 December 1991.

51. *SFC*, 6 December 1991.

52. Quoted in *SFC*, 21 November 1991.

53. Quoted in *SFC*, 19 November 1991.

54. *SFC*, 20 November 1991.

55. Quoted in *SFC*, 19 September 1991.

56. Thom Calandra, "Top Runoff Issue: Deficit," *SFE*, 6 November 1991.

57. *SFC*, 8 December 1991.

58. *SFE*, 5 December 1991.

59. Quoted in *SFC*, 26 November 1991.

60. Quoted in Kathleen Baca, "Time for the Art of Humility," *SFBG*, 13 November 1991.

61. Quoted in Roberts, " 'Niceness' Issue May Be Theme of S.F. Mayoral Race."

62. Quoted in *SFC*, 8 November 1991.

63. Quoted in Baca, "Time for the Art of Humility." In a later article, Baca quotes Michael Colbruno, political writer for *The Sentinel*, a gay and lesbian newspaper that withdrew its endorsement of Agnos: "Frank Jordan has to pander to the [gay and lesbian] community. If not, it will be the four most miserable years of his life, and he knows that. We're going to be watching his every step. And he doesn't want to become the next Pete Wilson [California's governor], with a trail of queers following him everywhere he goes. Basically, we're in a good situation with both Agnos and Jordan." Kathleen Baca, "Agnos Needs Gays, but Do They Need Him?" *SFBG*, 27 November 1991.

64. Quoted in George Cothran, "Will Liberals Stand behind Art Agnos?" *SF Weekly*, 13 November 1991.

65. "For Agnos, It's Time to Change," *SFBG*, 13 November 1991.

66. Ibid.

67. He appointed her only to a two-month term, as it turned out, a subtlety noticed later by *Guardian* editors and labeled a dirty trick.

68. Tim Redmond, "The Art of the Deal," *SFBG*, 20 November 1991, and Kathleen Baca, "Agnos Faces Penalty for Unnecessary Roughness," *SFBG*, 20 November 1991.

69. *SFBG*, 28 November 1991.

70. "For the Future: Time for Liberals to Close Ranks," *SF Weekly*, 13 November 1991.

71. Quoted in *SFBG*, 4 December 1991.

72. See *SFBG*, 11 December 1991.

73. *SFBG*, 4 December 1991.

74. Election results are from the San Francisco Registrar of Voters, reported in *SFE*, 11 December 1991. Also see Ramon G. McLeod, "How Absentee Voting Changed Mayor's Race," *SFC*, 13 December 1991. Voters also approved a ballot measure raising the San Francisco sales tax one-fourth of a penny to 8.5 percent to pay for the restoration of programs eliminated in public schools because of the budget crisis. One final note: Once again, the Asian American vote was important. Jordan won thirty-nine thousand votes in the eight predominately Asian districts as against twenty-eight thousand for Agnos. See Ramon G. McLeod, "Asians Crucial for Jordan," *SFC*, 12 December 1991.

75. Craig McLaughlin, "The Wicked Witch Is Dead," *SFBG*, 11 December 1991.

76. Quoted in Jerry Roberts, "A 'Personal Defeat' for Agnos, Not a Shift to the Right for S.F.," *SFC*, 12 December 1991.

77. "Get over It; S.F. Left Must Heal Wounds," *SF Weekly*, 6 November 1991.

78. Quoted in Jane Ganahl, "Agnos Takes Pride in Job He Did," *SFE*, 12 December 1991.

79. Madeline Landau, "Beyond the 'Politics of Negativity': SPUR as an Honest Broker," *SPUR* [San Francisco Planning and Urban Research Association] *Report* no. 264, 5.

Bibliography

Agnos, Art. 1987. *Getting Things Done: Visions and Goals for San Francisco*, campaign book (October).

Allen, James P., and Eugene Turner. 1988. "The Most Ethnically Diverse Places in the United States." Paper presented at the meeting of the Association of American Geographers, Phoenix, Ariz.

Association of Bay Area Governments (ABAG). 1987. *Projections—87: Forecasts for the San Francisco Bay Area to the Year 2005*. Oakland, Calif.: ABAG.

———. 1991. *Trends in Income: An Analysis of Income Tax Returns for San Francisco Bay Area Counties, 1978–1987*. Working paper 88-3. Oakland, Calif.: ABAG.

Auster, Ellen, and Howard Aldrich. 1984. "Small Business Vulnerability, Ethnic Enclaves and Ethnic Enterprises." In *Ethnic Communities in Business: Strategies for Survival*, ed. Robin Ward and Richard Jenkins. Cambridge: Cambridge University Press.

Avidan, Lina M. 1989. *Employment and Hiring Practices under the Immigration Reform and Control Act of 1986: A Survey of San Francisco Businesses*. San Francisco: Public Research Institute and Coalition for Immigrant and Refugee Rights and Services.

Barnekov, Timothy, Robin Boyle, and Daniel Rich. 1989. *Privatism and Urban Policy in Britain and the United States*. Oxford: Oxford University Press.

Barone, Michael, and Grant Ujifusa. 1989. *Almanac of American Politics 1990*. Washington, D.C.: National Journal.

Barton, Stephen E. 1985. "The Neighborhood Movement in San Francisco." *Berkeley Planning Journal* 2 (Spring/Fall): 85-105.

"Bay Area Business Report 1991." 1990. *San Francisco Business*, December, A1-A30.

Bay Area Council. 1987. *Corporate Restructuring: Profiling the Impacts on the Bay Area Economy*. San Francisco: Bay Area Council.

———. 1988. *Making Sense of the Region's Growth*. San Francisco: Bay Area Council.

Beauregard, Robert A. 1989. "Space, Time, and Economic Restructuring." In *Economic Restructuring and Political Response*, ed. Robert A. Beauregard, 209-40. Beverly Hills, Calif.: Sage.

Becker, Howard S., and Irving Louis Horowitz. 1970. "The Culture of Civility: San Francisco." *Transaction* 6 (April): 46-55.

Bik, Diana. 1987. "The Haight-Ashbury Preservation Society versus Thrifty Jr. Corporation: An Analysis of the Problems Involved in Preserving the Haight-Ashbury and Other San Francisco Neighborhoods." Unpublished master's project report, Department of Political Science, San Francisco State University.

Birch, David L. 1979. *The Job Generation Process*. Cambridge: MIT Program on Neighborhood and Regional Change.

Bledsoe, T. 1990. "Those Left Behind: Exit, Voice, and Loyalty in Detroit, 1954-1990." Paper presented at the annual meeting of the American Political Science Association, 30 August-2 September, San Francisco.

Boggs, Carl. 1986. *Social Movements and Political Power: Emerging Forms of Radicalism in the West*. Philadelphia, Pa.: Temple University Press.

Boyte, Harry C., and Frank Riessman, eds. 1986. *The New Populism: The Politics of Empowerment*. Philadelphia, Pa.: Temple University Press.

Browning, Rufus P., Dale Rogers Marshall, and David H. Tabb. 1984. *Protest Is Not Enough: The Struggle of Blacks and Hispanics for Equality in Urban Politics*. Berkeley and Los Angeles: University of California Press.

Brugmann, Bruce B., ed. 1971. *The Ultimate Highrise*. San Francisco: San Francisco Bay Guardian Book.

Bunzel, John. 1979. *The American Small Businessman*. New York: Arno Press.

Cain, Bruce, and Roderick Kiewiet. 1986. "California's Coming Minority Majority." *Public Opinion* (February/March): 50-52.

Calandra, Thom. 1990. "On the Waterfront." *Image*, 18 February.

Callies, David L., and Daniel J. Curtin, Jr. 1990. "On the Making of Land Use Decisions through Citizen Initiative and Referendum." *APA Journal* 56 (Spring): 222-23.

Case, John, and Elizabeth Conlin. 1991. "Second Thoughts on Growth." *Inc.*, March, 46-66.

Castells, Manuel. 1977. *The Urban Question: A Marxist Approach*. Cambridge: MIT Press.

————. 1983. *The City and the Grassroots*. Berkeley and Los Angeles: University of California Press.

Castells, Manuel, and J. Henderson. 1987. "Techno-Economic Restructuring, Socio-Political Processes, and Spatial Transformation: A Global Perspective." In *Global Restructuring and Territorial Development*, ed. M. Castells and J. Henderson, 1-17. London: Sage.

Clark, Gordon L. 1989. *Unions and Communities under Siege: American Communities and the Crisis of Organized Labor*. Cambridge: Cambridge University Press.

Clark, Terry Nichols. 1985. "A New Breed of Cost-Conscious Mayors." *Wall Street Journal*, 10 June.

Clark, Terry Nichols, and Lorna Ferguson. 1983. *City Money: Political Processes, Fiscal Strain, and Retrenchment*. New York: Columbia University Press.

Clavel, Pierre. 1986. *The Progressive City*. New Brunswick, N.J.: Rutgers University Press.

Cohen, Paul. 1985. "San Francisco's Commercial Real Estate Industry." *San Francisco Business*, April, 16-22.

Connolly, William. 1983. *The Terms of Political Discourse*. 2d ed. Princeton, N.J.: Princeton University Press.

Conroy, W. J. 1990. *Challenging the Boundaries of Reform: Socialism in Burlington*. Philadelphia, Pa.: Temple University Press.

Corcoran, Elizabeth, and Paul Wallich. 1991. "The Rise and Fall of Cities." *Scientific American*, August, 103.

Córdova, Carlos. 1987. "Undocumented El Salvadoreans in the San Francisco Bay Area: Migration and Adaptation Dynamics." *Journal of La Raza Studies* 1: 9-37.

Coro Handbook, 1979. 1979. San Francisco: Coro Foundation.

Cox, K. R., and A. Mair. 1989. "Urban Growth Machines and the Politics of Local Economic Development." *International Journal of Urban and Regional Research* 13: 137-46.

Coyle, Dennis J. 1983. "The Balkans by the Bay." *Public Interest* 11 (Spring): 67-78.
Curtin, Daniel J., Jr., and M. Thomas Jacobson. 1989. "Growth Management by the Initiative in California: Legal and Practical Issues." *Urban Lawyer* 21: 491-510.
Dahl, Robert, and Edward Tufte. 1973. *Size and Democracy.* Stanford, Calif.: Stanford University Press.
Davis, Mike. 1990. *City of Quartz: Excavating the Future in Los Angeles.* New York: Verso.
Daykin, David S. 1988. "The Limits to Neighborhood Power: Progressive Politics and Local Control in Santa Monica." In *Business Elites and Urban Development,* ed. S. Cummings, 357-87. Albany: State University of New York Press.
DeLeon, Richard. 1991. "The Progressive Urban Regime: Ethnic Coalitions in San Francisco." In *Racial and Ethnic Politics in California,* ed. Byran O. Jackson and Michael B. Preston. Berkeley, Calif.: Institute of Governmental Studies.
————. 1991. "San Francisco: Postmaterialist Populism in a Global City." In *Big City Politics in Transition,* ed. H. V. Savitch and John Clayton Thomas, 202-15. Beverly Hills, Calif.: Sage.
————. 1992. "The Urban Antiregime: Progressive Politics in San Francisco." *Urban Affairs Quarterly.* Forthcoming.
DeLeon, Richard, and Roy Christman. 1988. "The Party's Not Over." *Golden State Report* 4 (November): 38-40.
DeLeon, Richard, and Sandra Powell. 1989. "Growth Control and Electoral Politics: The Triumph of Urban Populism in San Francisco. "*Western Political Quarterly* 42 (June): 307-30.
DeMeester, Paul, and Evangeline Tolleson. 1988. "Putting It on the Ballot." *San Francisco Business,* May, 21-25.
Din, Grant. 1984. "An Analysis of Asian/Pacific American Registration and Voting Patterns in San Francisco." Unpublished master's thesis, Claremont Graduate School, Claremont, Calif.
Downs, Anthony. 1985. *The Revolution in Real Estate Finance.* Washington, D.C.: Brookings Institution.
Elkin, Stephen. 1987. *City and Regime in the American Republic.* Chicago: University of Chicago Press.
Erch, Niels. 1987. "Tangled Priorities at Fisherman's Wharf: What's the Catch?" *San Francisco Business,* August, 5-15.
Fainstein, Norman. 1985. "Class and Community in Urban Social Movements." *Urban Affairs Quarterly* 20: 557-63.
Farhi, Paul. 1987. "Sugar Daddy." *Image,* 28 June, 23-26, 34.
Feagin, Joe R., and Michael Peter Smith. 1987. "Cities and the New International Division of Labor: An Overview." In *The Capitalist City: Global Restructuring and Community Politics,* ed. Michael Peter Smith and Joe R. Feagin, 3-34. London: Basil Blackwell.
Feher, Ferenc, and Agnes Heller. 1984. "From Red to Green." *Telos* 59 (Spring): 35-44.
Ferman, Barbara. 1985. *Governing the Ungovernable City: Political Skill, Leadership, and the Modern Mayor.* Philadelphia, Pa.: Temple University Press.
Freedberg, Louis. 1987. "Latinos: Building Power from the Ground Up." *California Journal* (January): 12-17.
Frieden, Bernard. 1979. *The Environmental Protection Hustle.* Cambridge: MIT Press.
Frieden, Bernard, and Lynne B. Sagalyn. 1989. *Downtown, Inc.: How America Rebuilds Cities.* Boston: MIT Press.
Gillenkirk, Jeff. 1987. "Molinari vs. Agnos." *San Francisco Magazine,* May, 31-38, 85-88.

Goddard, Ben. 1988. "The Rise of Grass-Roots Populism: Quality-of-Life Issues Spur a Fast-Growing Movement." *Campaigns and Elections* 8 (January): 83-84.

Godfrey, Brian J. 1988. *Neighborhoods in Transition: The Making of San Francisco's Ethnic and Nonconformist Communities.* Berkeley and Los Angeles: University of California Press.

Gottdiener, M. 1985. *The Social Production of Urban Space.* Austin: University of Texas Press.

———. 1987. *The Decline of Urban Politics: Political Theory and the Crisis of the Local State.* Beverly Hills, Calif.: Sage.

Haas, James W. 1986. "The New San Francisco: World's First `Gaysian' City." *Golden State Report* 2 (July): 31-32.

Habermas, Jürgen. 1973. *Legitimation Crisis.* Boston: Beacon Press.

Harrison, Bennett, and Barry Bluestone. 1988. *The Great U-Turn: Corporate Restructuring and the Polarizing of America.* New York: Basic Books.

Hartman, Chester. 1984. *The Transformation of San Francisco.* Totowa, N.J.: Rowman and Allanheld.

Harvey, David. 1982. *The Limits to Capital.* Chicago: University of Chicago Press.

———. 1985. *Consciousness and the Urban Experience: Studies in the History and Theory of Capitalist Urbanization.* Baltimore, Md.: Johns Hopkins University Press.

Heisler, Karl F. 1989. "Neighborhood Planning in Bernal Heights." *Urban Action* (Journal of the Urban Studies Program at San Francisco State University): 72-79.

Henig, Jeffrey R. 1986. "Collective Responses to the Urban Crisis: Ideology and Mobilization." In *Cities in Stress*, ed. M. Gottdiener, 221-45. Beverly Hills, Calif.: Sage.

Hirschman, A. O. 1970. *Exit, Voice, and Loyalty.* Cambridge: Harvard University Press.

Inglehart, Ronald. 1990. *Culture Shift in Advanced Industrial Society.* Princeton, N.J.: Princeton University Press.

Issel, William. 1986. "Politics, Culture, and Ideology: Three Episodes in the Evolution of San Francisco's `Culture of Civility.'" Paper presented at the annual meeting of the California American Studies Association, Long Beach, 26 April.

———. 1989. "Business Power and Political Culture in San Francisco, 1900-1940." *Journal of Urban History* 16 (November): 52-77.

Issel, William, and Robert W. Cherny. 1986. *San Francisco 1865-1932: Politics, Power, and Urban Development.* Berkeley and Los Angeles: University of California Press.

Jackson, Byran O. 1991. "Racial and Ethnic Cleavages in Los Angeles Politics." In *Racial and Ethnic Politics in California*, ed. Byran O. Jackson and Michael B. Preston, 193-218. Berkeley, Calif.: Institute of Governmental Studies.

Jacobs, Jane. 1969. *The Economy of Cities.* New York: Random House.

Jacobs, John. 1988. "The Miracle of Market Street." *Golden State Report* 4 (January): 7-13.

Kantor, Paul. 1988. *The Dependent City.* Glenview, Ill.: Scott, Foresman and Co.

Katznelson, Ira. 1981. *City Trenches: Urban Politics and the Patterning of Class in the United States.* New York: Pantheon Books.

Keating, W. Dennis, and Norman Krumholz. 1991. "Downtown Plans of the 1980s: The Case for More Equity in the 1990s." *APA Journal* 57 (Spring): 136-52.

Kilroy, Tony. 1985. *Kilroy's Directory of San Francisco's Politically Active Groups* (June).

———. 1990. *Kilroy's Directory of San Francisco's Politically Active Groups* (August).

King, Gary. 1989. *Unifying Political Methodology: The Likelihood Theory of Statistical Inference.* Cambridge: Cambridge University Press.

Kling, Joseph M., and Prudence S. Posner, eds. 1990. *Dilemmas of Activism: Class,*

Community, and the Politics of Local Mobilization. Philadelphia, Pa.: Temple University Press.

Kotkin, J. 1989. "The Upside." *Image,* 12 April, 18–23.

Kraft, Michael E., and Bruce B. Clary. 1991. "Citizen Participation and the Nimby Syndrome: Public Response to Radioactive Waste Disposal." *Western Political Quarterly* 44 (June): 299–328.

Landau, Madeline. 1990. "Beyond the `Politics of Negativity': SPUR as an Honest Broker." *SPUR* [San Francisco Planning and Urban Research Association] *Report no.* 264.

Lassar, Terry Jill. 1988. "Shadow Ban Shapes San Francisco Buildings." *Urban Land* 47 (October): 36–37.

Lefebvre, Henri. 1976. *The Survival of Capitalism.* London: Allison & Busby.

LeGates, Richard, Stephen Barton, Victoria Randlett, and Steven Scott. 1989. *BAYFAX: The 1989 San Francisco Bay Area Land Use and Housing Data Book.* San Francisco: San Francisco State University Public Research Institute.

Linz, Juan J. 1978. *The Breakdown of Democratic Regimes: Crisis, Breakdown, and Reequilibration.* Baltimore, Md.: Johns Hopkins University Press.

Lo, Clarence Y. H. 1990. *Small Property versus Big Government: Social Origins of the Property Tax Revolt.* Berkeley and Los Angeles: University of California Press.

Logan, John R., and Harvey L. Molotch. 1987. *Urban Fortunes: The Political Economy of Place.* Berkeley and Los Angeles: University of California Press.

Logan, John R., and Todd Swanstrom, eds. 1990. *Beyond the City Limits: Urban Policy and Economic Restructuring in Comparative Perspective.* Philadelphia, Pa.: Temple University Press.

Lord, Paul. 1990. *The San Francisco Arts Economy: 1987.* San Francisco: San Francisco Planning Department and San Francisco State University Public Research Institute.

McCall, Michael. 1984. "The Clement Street Shuffle—Neighborhood Evolution or Exploitation?" *San Francisco Business,* March, 16–20.

McCarthy, Kevin. 1984. "San Francisco's Demographic Future." In *The City We Share: A Conference on the Future of San Francisco,* 15–18. San Francisco: San Francisco Forward.

McClendon, Bruce W. 1990. "An Alternative Proposal." *APA Journal* 56 (Spring): 223–25.

Macpherson, C. B. 1980. "A Political Theory of Property." In *Property, Profits, and Economic Justice,* ed. Virginia Held, 209–20. Belmont, Calif.: Wadsworth Publishing Co.

Magleby, David B. 1988. "Taking the Initiative: Direct Legislation and Direct Democracy in the 1980's." *PS* 21: 600–601.

Marx, Karl. 1973. *Grundrisse.* Harmondsworth, Middlesex: Penguin.

Maslow, Abraham. 1977. *The Farther Reaches of Human Nature.* New York: Penguin Books.

Mischak, Stephanie. 1987. "Why Charter Reform Has Failed in San Francisco." Unpublished graduate seminar paper, Department of Political Science, San Francisco State University.

Mollenkopf, John H. 1975. "The Post-War Politics of Urban Development." *Politics and Society* 5: 247–95.

———. 1983. *The Contested City.* Princeton, N.J.: Princeton University Press.

Molotch, Harvey. 1990. "Urban Deals in Comparative Perspective." In *Beyond the City Limits: Urban Policy and Economic Restructuring in Comparative Perspective,* ed. John R. Logan and Todd Swanstrom. Philadelphia, Pa.: Temple University Press.

Navarro, Peter, and Richard Carson. 1991. "Growth Controls: Policy Analysis for the Second Generation." *Policy Sciences* 24: 127–52.

Nelson, Arthur C. 1988. "Development Impact Fees: Introduction." *Journal of the American Planning Association* 54 (Winter): 3–6.

Ohanian, Bernard. 1986. "The Misunderstood Minority." *San Francisco Focus*, June, 40–50.

Orum, Anthony M. 1991. "Apprehending the City: The View from Above, Below, and Behind." *Urban Affairs Quarterly* 26 (June): 589–609.

Pelissero, John, Beth Henschen, and Edward Sidlow. 1990. "Urban Policy Agendas and Sports Franchises: The Case of Chicago." Paper presented at the annual meeting of the American Political Science Association, 30 August–2 September, San Francisco.

Peri, Camille. 1987. "The Buying and Selling of North Beach." *Image*, 26 April, 18–25, 38.

Perry, Charles. 1985. *The Haight-Ashbury: A History*. New York: Vintage.

Peterson, Paul. 1981. *City Limits*. Chicago: University of Chicago Press.

Plotkin, Sidney. 1987. *Keep Out: The Struggle for Land Use Control*. Berkeley and Los Angeles: University of California Press.

———. 1990. "Enclave Consciousness and Neighborhood Activism." In *Dilemmas of Activism: Class, Community, and the Politics of Local Mobilization*, ed. Joseph M. Kling and Prudence S. Posner. Philadelphia, Pa.: Temple University Press.

Pogash, Carol. 1987. "The Education of Art Agnos." *Image*, 16 April, 10–11.

Porter, Douglas, ed. 1985. *Downtown Linkages*. Washington D.C.: Urban Land Institute.

Preteceille, Edmond. 1990. "Political Paradoxes of Urban Restructuring: Globalization of the Economy and Localization of Politics?" In *Beyond the City Limits: Urban Policy and Economic Restructuring in Comparative Perspective*, ed. John R. Logan and Todd Swanstrom. Philadelphia, Pa.: Temple University Press.

Przeworski, Adam, and John Sprague. 1988. *Paper Stones: A History of Electoral Socialism*. Chicago: University of Chicago Press.

Public Research Institute. 1985. *Poll of San Francisco Voters*. San Francisco: San Francisco State University.

———. 1989. *State of the City Poll: 1989*. San Francisco: San Francisco State University.

Rabushka, Alvin, and Kenneth A. Shepsle. 1972. *Politics in Plural Societies: A Theory of Democratic Stability*. Columbus, Ohio: Charles E. Merrill Publishing Co.

Ragin, Charles C. 1987. *The Comparative Method: Moving beyond Qualitative and Quantitative Strategies*. Berkeley and Los Angeles: University of California Press.

Randal, Judith, and William Hines. 1987. "Local Communities Take the Lead in Coping with AIDS." *Governing*, November, 34–40.

Rapaport, Richard. 1987. "While the City Slept." *San Francisco Magazine*, April, 40–45, 85–87.

———. 1991. "Hard Ball: How the Political Power Brokers Shut Out the Best Little Ballpark in America." *San Francisco Focus*, June, 68–71, 90–108.

Reed, Adolf, Jr. 1988. "The Black Urban Regime: Structural Origins and Constraints." In *Power, Community, and the City*, ed. M. Smith. New Brunswick, N.J.: Transaction Books.

Riess, S. A. 1989. *City Games: The Evolution of American Urban Society and the Rise of Sports*. Urbana: University of Illinois Press.

Roberts, Jerry. 1987. "Crossing the Bridge to the New San Francisco." *Golden State Report* 3 (May): 24–30.

Rowe, Randall K. 1990. "Capital Excess in '80s Leads to Shortage in '90s." *National Real Estate Investor* 32 (October): 208–10.

Ryan, Alan. 1987. *Property*. Minneapolis: University of Minnesota Press.

San Francisco. Mayor's Housing Advisory Committee. 1989. *An Affordable Housing Action Plan for San Francisco: Draft Report, 12 May.*
San Francisco Planning Department. 1986. *Report on Neighborhood Commercial Rezoning* (December).
———. 1988. *Mission Bay: Draft Environmental Impact Report.* Vol. 1, *Highlights and Conclusions.*
San Francisco Planning and Urban Renewal (Research) Association (SPUR). 1987. "Vitality or Stagnation? Shaping San Francisco's Economic Destiny." *SPUR Report* no. 234.
Sassen-Koob, Saskia. 1984. "The New Labor Demand in Global Cities." In *Cities in Transformation: Class, Capital, and the State,* ed. Michael Peter Smith, 139-71. Beverly Hills, Calif.: Sage.
Savage, James. 1985. "Postmaterialism of the Left and Right: Political Conflict in Postindustrial Society." *Comparative Political Studies* 17 (January): 431-51.
Savitch, H. V. 1988. *Post-Industrial Cities: Politics and Planning in New York, Paris, and London.* Princeton, N.J.: Princeton University Press.
Savitch, H. V., and John Clayton Thomas. 1991. "Conclusion: End of the Millennium Big City Politics." In *Big City Politics in Transition,* ed. H. V. Savitch and John Clayton Thomas. Beverly Hills, Calif.: Sage.
Shavelson, Lonny, and Loralie Froman. 1990. "Why the Prayer Warriors Came." *This World,* 18 November.
Shilts, Randy. 1982. *The Mayor of Castro Street: The Life and Times of Harvey Milk.* New York: St. Martin's Press.
Simon, Herbert A. 1981. "The Architecture of Complexity." In *The Sciences of the Artificial,* 192-219. 2d ed. Cambridge: MIT Press.
Sims, Kent. 1989. *Competition in a Changing World: White Paper on the Economy of San Francisco.* San Francisco: Economic Development Corporation.
Smith, Dan, Joan Radovich, and Raymond Smith. 1988. "Crusade against Growth." *Golden State Report* 4 (January): 26-32.
Smith, Michael Peter. 1979. *The City and Social Theory.* New York: St. Martin's Press.
———. 1988. "The Uses of Linked Development Policies in U.S. Cities." In *Regenerating the Cities: The UK Crisis and the US Experience,* ed. Michael Parkinson, Bernard Foley, and Dennis Judd. Manchester: Manchester University Press.
Smith, Michael Peter, and Dennis Judd. 1984. "American Cities: The Production of Ideology." In *Cities in Transformation: Class, Capital, and the State,* ed. Michael Peter Smith. Beverly Hills, Calif.: Sage.
Starr, Kevin. 1988. "Art Agnos and the Paradoxes of Power." *San Francisco Magazine,* January/February, 157-62.
———. 1988. "San Francisco Is Losing Its Identity as a World-Class City." *Image,* 1 May, 19-31.
Stein, Arlene. 1988. "Agnos Did It the Grass-Roots Way." *Nation,* 6 February, 156-58.
Stinchcombe, Arthur L. 1968. *Constructing Social Theories.* New York: Harcourt, Brace & World.
Stone, Clarence N. 1988. "Preemptive Power: Floyd Hunter's 'Community Power Structure' Reconsidered." *American Journal of Political Science* 32: 82-104.
———. 1989. *Regime Politics: Governing Atlanta 1946-1988.* Lawrence: University Press of Kansas.
Stone, Clarence, Marion Orr, and David Imbroscio. 1991. "The Reshaping of Urban Leadership in U.S. Cities: A Regime Analysis." In *Urban Life in Transition,* ed. M. Gottdiener and Chris G. Pickvance, 222-39. Beverly Hills, Calif.: Sage.

Swanstrom, Todd. 1985. *The Crisis of Growth Politics: Cleveland, Kucinich, and the Promise of Urban Populism*. Philadelphia, Pa.: Temple University Press.

——. 1988. "Semisovereign Cities: The Politics of Urban Development." *Polity* 21 (Fall): 83-110.

Thompson, Victor A. 1950. *The Regulatory Process in OPA Rationing*. New York: Columbia University Press.

Unger, Roberto M. 1987. *False Necessity: Anti-Necessitarian Social Theory in the Service of Radical Democracy*. Cambridge: Cambridge University Press.

U.S. Bureau of the Census. 1967. *County and City Data Book, 1967*. Washington, D.C.: Government Printing Office.

——. 1988. *County and City Data Book, 1988*. Washington, D.C.: Government Printing Office.

——. 1983. Census of Population and Housing, 1980. *Public-Use Microdata Sample (PUMS): San Francisco, 5 Percent Sample*. Washington, D.C.: Government Printing Office.

Viviano, Frank, and Sharon Silva. 1986. "The New San Francisco." *San Francisco Focus*, September, 64-74.

Waldinger, Roger. 1990. "Immigrant Enterprise in the United States." In *Structures of Capital: The Social Organization of the Economy*, ed. Sharon Zukin and Paul DiMaggio, 395-424. Cambridge: Cambridge University Press.

Walters, Derek. 1991. *The Feng Shui Handbook: A Practical Guide to Chinese Geomancy and Environmental Harmony*. London: Aquarian Press.

Waters, Rob. 1987. "The Tenderloin Transformed." *Image*, 1 November, 10-14.

Weber, David. 1988. "Who Owns San Francisco?" *San Francisco Magazine*, January/February, 59-63.

Williams, Timothy. 1991. "Open Season on Art Agnos." *California Journal* 22 (September): 405-9.

Wirt, Frederick. 1971. "Alioto and the Politics of Hyperpluralism." *Transaction* 7 (April): 46-55.

——. 1974. *Power in the City: Decision Making in San Francisco*. Berkeley and Los Angeles: University of California Press.

Wolin, Sheldon S. 1960. *Politics and Vision*. Boston: Little, Brown and Company.

——. 1989. *The Presence of the Past: Essays on the State and the Constitution*. Baltimore, Md.: Johns Hopkins University Press.

Wright, E. O. 1986. "What Is Middle about the Middle Class?" In *Analytical Marxism*, ed. J. Roemer, 114-40. Cambridge: Cambridge University Press.

Yates, Douglas. 1977. *The Ungovernable City*. Cambridge: MIT Press.

Index